# A HISTORY OF GERMANY

# A History of Germany

H.E. MARSHALL

This edition published 2023
By Living Book Press
Copyright © Living Book Press, 2023

ISBN:   978-1-922950-89-5 (B&W Softcover Edition)
        978-1-922950-91-8 (B&W Hardcover Edition)
        978-1-922974-14-3 (Color Softcover Edition)
        978-1-922974-15-0 (Color Hardcover Edition)

First published in 1913.

All rights reserved. No part of this publication may be reproduced, stored in a retrieval system, or transmitted in any other form or means – electronic, mechanical, photocopying, recording or otherwise, without the prior permission of the copyright owner and the publisher or as provided by Australian law.

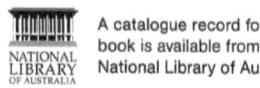

A catalogue record for this book is available from the National Library of Australia

# CONTENTS

| | | |
|---|---|---|
| 1. | ABOUT THE GOD TEW AND HIS CHILDREN | 1 |
| 2. | TEUTONS AND ROMANS | 4 |
| 3. | ARIOVISTUS, THE FIRST GREAT GERMAN | 8 |
| 4. | HERMANN, THE HERO OF GERMANY | 11 |
| 5. | THE HUNS AND GOTHS | 16 |
| 6. | WINFRID, THE APOSTLE OF THE GERMANS | 18 |
| 7. | CHARLEMAGNE | 22 |
| 8. | CHARLEMAGNE | 28 |
| 9. | CHARLEMAGNE | 31 |
| 10. | CHARLEMAGNE | 34 |
| 11. | LEWIS THE GERMAN | 38 |
| 12. | LEWIS I AND CHARLES THE FAT | 44 |
| 13. | ARNULF OF CARINTHIA | 51 |
| 14. | LEWIS THE CHILD | 55 |
| 15. | CONRAD I | 59 |
| 16. | HENRY I THE FOWLER | 64 |
| 17. | OTTO I THE GREAT | 71 |
| 18. | OTTO I THE GREAT | 79 |
| 19. | OTTO II THE RED | 85 |
| 20. | OTTO III | 92 |
| 21. | HENRY II THE HALT | 97 |
| 22. | CONRAD II | 102 |
| 23. | HENRY III THE BLACK | 109 |
| 24. | HENRY IV | 116 |
| 25. | HENRY IV | 121 |
| 26. | HENRY V | 128 |
| 27. | LOTHAR THE SAXON | 131 |
| 28. | CONRAD III | 134 |
| 29. | FREDERICK I, REDBEARD | 141 |
| 30. | FREDERICK I, REDBEARD | 148 |
| 31. | HENRY VI | 153 |
| 32. | PHILIP OF SWABIA | 156 |
| 33. | OTTO IV | 158 |
| 34. | FREDERICK II, THE WORLD'S WONDER | 161 |
| 35. | CONRAD IV AND THE GREAT INTERREGNUM | 165 |
| 36. | RUDOLPH OF HAPSBURG | 167 |
| 37. | ADOLPHUS I OF NASSAU | 173 |
| 38. | ALBERT THE ONE-EYED | 175 |
| 39. | HENRY VII OF LUXEMBURG | 179 |

| | | |
|---|---|---|
| 40. | LEWIS IV OF BAVARIA AND FREDERICK THE HANDSOME | 181 |
| 41. | LEWIS IV OF BAVARIA AND FREDERICK THE HANDSOME | 184 |
| 42. | CHARLES IV—THE STEP-FATHER OF THE EMPIRE | 187 |
| 43. | WENCESLAUS OF BOHEMIA AND RUPERT THE MILD | 191 |
| 44. | SIGMUND | 194 |
| 45. | ALBERT II | 200 |
| 46. | FREDERICK III | 202 |
| 47. | MAXIMILIAN I | 205 |
| 48. | CHARLES V | 211 |
| 49. | CHARLES V | 216 |
| 50. | CHARLES V | 220 |
| 51. | FERDINAND I AND MAXIMILIAN II | 226 |
| 52. | RUDOLPH II | 228 |
| 53. | MATTHIAS | 230 |
| 54. | FERDINAND II | 233 |
| 55. | FERDINAND II | 238 |
| 56. | FERDINAND III | 244 |
| 57. | LEOPOLD I | 246 |
| 58. | LEOPOLD I | 250 |
| 59. | JOSEPH I AND CHARLES VI | 253 |
| 60. | THE RISE OF THE HOUSE OF BRANDENBURG | 257 |
| 61. | CHARLES VII | 262 |
| 62. | FRANCIS I | 265 |
| 63. | JOSEPH II | 271 |
| 64. | LEOPOLD II | 275 |
| 65. | FRANCIS II | 276 |
| 66. | UNDER THE HEEL OF NAPOLEON | 280 |
| 67. | UNDER THE HEEL OF NAPOLEON | 284 |
| 68. | UNDER THE HEEL OF NAPOLEON | 288 |
| 69. | THE DOWNFALL OF NAPOLEON | 291 |
| 70. | DIVIDED GERMANY | 296 |
| 71. | DIVIDED GERMANY | 299 |
| 72. | THE STRUGGLE BETWEEN AUSTRIA AND PRUSSIA | 302 |
| 73. | WILLIAM I—UNITED GERMANY | 304 |
| 74. | FREDERICK THE NOBLE AND WILLIAM II | 309 |

CHAPTER 1

# ABOUT THE GOD TEW AND HIS CHILDREN

IN the dim days of very long ago there was a country called Fensalir. It was a low-lying country of rich green meadows and fair cornfields. Beside the slow-flowing streams trees drooped their branches laden with wondrous fruit. Upon the endless meadows countless herds of cattle browsed. It was a rich and peaceful land, but no man knew where it began or where it ended, for round the fair green meadows there hung ever a soft white mist, and any who strayed far were lost in its rolling folds. Weary of the quiet peace, stung by the longing to adventure and to know, some indeed wandered forth, never to return.

Over this strange land there rifled a beautiful giantess. Her hair was gold with the gold of the cornfields, her dress was rich and green with the rich green of the meadows. Only she knew the length and breadth of the fair country over which she ruled. Only she knew what lay beyond the rolling mists. All who remained under her rule found lasting peace and gladness. For she was to them a gracious, tender mother. She spread her hands abroad to bless her land with warmth and fruitfulness; she stretched forth her skirts to shelter her people from cold and frost.

So long years passed, and to this fair giantess there Tew came a son. This son she called Tew. He was bold and he was wise. To him was given victory in war. To him was given the wisdom of words. So it came to pass that if a man was very brave it was said of him, "He is as brave as Tew"; if a man was very wise it was said of him, "He hath the wisdom of Tew." And at length people made songs about Tew, in which they told of his deeds of valour and his wisdom.

And so as years went on, to the people Tew became a god, even as the sun and the moon. One day of the week was called after him, and to this day we still call it Tuesday.

Now Tew had a son, and he again had many children, so that soon the land was filled with people. Of these people there were many tribes, each taking its name from one of the grandsons of Tew; but the whole people were called Teutons, after the name of the great god himself.

This is a fairy-tale and an allegory. The beautiful giantess is a giantess we all know, for she is Mother Earth, and from her broad green lap there rose the god Tew, the father of the great Teutonic race. It is a race which stretches far and wide, and nearly all the peoples of Northern Europe belong to it. The Germans are but one of its many branches, and it is of them I mean to tell in this book.

They first got the name of Germans in Roman times. North of the Rhine dwelt the Teutons, south of the Rhine dwelt the Gauls. But there came a time when a wild horde of Teutons crossed the Rhine, and drove the Gauls out. The Gauls then gave to the wild tribe the name of Germans or neighbours, and by degrees the name was given to the whole race. We still call them Germans, but they call themselves die Deutschen. That is a much newer name, and they did not receive until the end of the ninth century.

It too has a meaning which is interesting. The Gauls and the Franks who had settled south of the Rhine; gradually began to talk Latin, or the Roman language, which later grew into French. It was the language of the learned. But the tribes on the north of the Rhine continued to speak the old language. It was the language of the common people. Thiod means "people"; theotisce means "of the people." So the language was called theotiscos, meaning "the people's language," and gradually it became changed from theotiscos to Deutsch.

So Deutsch means nothing less than "a son of the soil, a son of Mother Earth." And perhaps the little fairy-tale at the beginning of this chapter may help to make some of us understand better why we so often speak of Fatherland or Mother Earth. And it is interesting to find in the early story of the German people the dim outlines of this tale, for they more than any other people have given to their country the name of Fatherland.

But whence really came these Teutons or Germans? In the dim far-off days of the long-forgotten past, in a time so far back that neither history nor legend can tell us ought of it, they dwelt in Asia. But their home was never settled. They loved battle and hated labour. It was easier to conquer new lands than to till that they already possessed. So slowly they moved westward from country to country until they reached Europe. At first they settled along the shores of the Baltic, but by degrees they passed southward to the country of the Gauls.

These ancient Teutons were heathen, but not Druids like the Britons or the Gauls. They worshipped other gods. Wodan was chief of them all, but they worshipped also his son, Thor, the god of the hammer, and many a god besides. And when they died these old heathens believed that they went to Wodan's palace, the splendid hall of Valhalla. There, in company with all the gods and heroes of their race, they would lead, they believed, for ever a life of feasting and drinking, such as they had loved on earth.

They were fair-haired giants those Germans of old time—"Children with old men's hair," the Romans called them. Huge they were, strong of limb, and able to endure both cold and hunger. They cared nothing or gold and ornaments, and were clad only in a cloak of cloth, or the hide of some animal. This was held about their shoulders by a simple clasp or even by a thorn. They were armed with long spears and short javelins. Few wore helmets or armour of any sort.

As they dashed to war the very sight of them struck fear to the hearts of their enemies. Their fierce blue eyes and yellow streaming hair, their huge bodies, the shrieks of the women and children who surrounded the battle-field, and, above all, the hoarse sound of their war-chants, which rose and fell in harsh roar, all added to the terror of their attack.

These ancient Germans loved battle. They held it more honourable to win their daily bread by blood and conquest than to earn it by the sweat of the brow.

Yet even the best and bravest warriors in times of peace did nothing but eat and drink. "It is marvellous," says a Roman writer, "that the same men should so love sloth and hate peace."

CHAPTER 2

# TEUTONS AND ROMANS

BESIDES the Teutons we hear also in ancient times of the Cimbri, another wild tribe of the same Germanic family. These blue-eyed savages hated peace too. They were for ever wandering forth, clamorous for new lands, so again and again they came into conflict with the Romans. And even the world-conquerors could not stand against them. Many battles these Germans won, and for twelve years the Romans trembled before the "Cimbric Terror." Thrice the way to Rome lay open to the plundering hordes, but each time, why or wherefore we know not, they turned aside to Spain or Belgium, and Rome was saved. For the moment, it may be, they desired not conquest south of the Alps, but a home north of them.

At length, however, the German hordes decided to attack Rome, to waste all Italy, and lay the capital in ruins. An enormous host gathered. It was not merely an army of warriors, it was a whole people on the march. They came with their tents and their household goods, their wives and children, their slaves and servants, their cattle and dogs.

Slowly this enormous host wound southward, divided into two great bands, the Teutons under their King Teutobod and the Cimbri under their King Boiorix. The two hosts marched upon Italy by different routes, and it was the Teutons who first met the Roman army arrayed against them. For the Roman leader Marius resolved not to wait for Italy to be attacked, but crossed the Alps and marched to meet the foe.

It was at the mouth of the Rhone valley that the two armies met. Here Marius fortified his camp well, and dug a deep trench about it. Then he awaited the enemy. It was not long before the Teutons appeared upon the plain in numbers beyond all imaginings. On and on they came, hungering for battle. Soon their terrible war-song resounded, rising and falling in harsh roars. It was very awful to hear, for each man held his shield in front of his mouth, so that it acted like a sounding-board, and gave to his voice a strange unearthly tone.

Urged on by this wild music the warriors advanced. But Marius and his men lay still within their strong encampment. They refused to fight. For three days the barbarians raged around the camp in vain. From every attempt to storm it they were beaten back with great loss.

*On and on they came, hungering for battle.*

But if the barbarians raged without, the Roman soldiers raged within the camp. They were eager to sally forth, give battle to the foe or scatter them in flight, and they were made to sit still, or allowed at best only to throw a few arrows from the walls. "What does Marius take us for," they grumbled, "that he thus locks us up and will not let us fight? Is building walls and digging trenches worthy labour for a soldier? Are we not here to fight for our country?"

Marius was not ill-pleased to find his soldiers so eager for battle. He soothed them gently and bade them wait.

At length, weary of the useless attack, the Teutons resolved to march past the Roman army and reach Italy without further delay.

Marius allowed them to go. Growing bolder and ever bolder, they passed close to the camp, flinging taunts at the Romans. "Have you any messages for your wives and families?" they asked, "for we shall soon see them."

For six days the mighty host filed onward, horse and foot, men, women, and children, with numberless wagon-loads of baggage. Marius watched them calmly and did nothing. Then, as soon as the Teutons had passed, he left his camp and followed. And as they marched onward each night he encamped near to them in some strong, well-guarded position.

At length they came to a place named Aquae Sextiæ or Sextiliæ Waters, and here Marius resolved to give battle. He chose a strong position for his camp, but it lacked water. This was pointed out to him. Thereupon Marius pointed to a stream which flowed close by the camp of the enemy. "There," he said, "you can get water if you buy it with your blood."

"Why, then," asked a soldier wrathfully, "do you not lead us to it ere our blood is dried up in us?"

At that Marius smiled, well pleased, for he had only trained his men so that they might fight all the better when the right time came.

"Wait," he said quietly, "let us first fortify our camp"; and the soldiers were fain to obey.

Three days later the battle was fought.

Marius drew up his soldiers upon the summit of a little hill. Up this the barbarians rushed, and the fight began. It was long and bitter. For hours the Teutons fought with fierce, untamed bravery. When the foremost fell those behind took their place. But at length the wild northern savages, unused to the blaze of a southern sun, began to weary. Bit by bit the Romans drove them down the hill, and at length scattered them in flight.

The slaughter was awful, and so many thousands fell upon the field that it is said the people of Marseilles for many years after fenced their vineyards about with the bones of the slain Teutons. But the men did not fight alone. The women too joined, and when all hope of victory had fled, rather than fall into the hands of the conquerors, they slew themselves and their children. The Teuton host was thus utterly wiped out. Few escaped; those who were not slain were taken prisoner, the king among them.

Meanwhile the Cimbri had crossed the Alps into Italy. The snow and the cold of the high passes did not appal them. Almost naked as they were, they strode carelessly through the snowdrifts, and sitting on their shields they slid down the icy slopes with shouts of triumph. Thus, like an avalanche, they poured into the plain of Italy.

As the Cimbri advanced, plundering and wasting on every side, the Romans fled before them. Their leader was in despair when Marius, already victorious over the Teutons, came to help him.

The Cimbri, who knew nothing of the battle of Aquæ Sextiæ, wondered why the Teutons were so long in coming. Full of their triumphs, they now sent to Marius, and demanded land and towns for themselves and their brethren, so that they might make their home in the fair realm of Italy.

"Who are your brethren?" asked Marius.

"The Teutons," was the reply.

Then Marius laughed. "Do not trouble yourselves for your brethren," he said, "for we have already given them all the land they need, and which they shall possess for ever."

Soon the Cimbri learned that Marius mocked at them, and that the land their brethren had was but a soldier's grave. Then were they angry. "You will pay for this jest," they cried, and at once made ready for battle. It was a terrible fight, both fierce and long. But the discipline of Rome overcame at length the wild bravery the barbarians. The men fell in thousands, many of them slaying themselves rather than be taken prisoners. The women too fought. Clad in black robes, with wild eyes, and streaming hair, they seemed avenging furies as they defended the encampment. They fought the enemy, they slew the cowards who fled, they put their own children to death, and last of all slew themselves. So at length when night came there was no living thing upon the ghastly field, save only the faithful dogs, who howled dismally through the darkness over their dead masters' bodies.

Thus were the Cimbri wiped out. Seeking a home they found a grave in the sunny land beyond the Alps.

CHAPTER 3

# ARIOVISTUS, THE FIRST GREAT GERMAN

THE Germans and the Gauls were neighbours, the swift-flowing Rhine alone dividing them. Now two tribes of the Gauls, the Sequani and the Ædui, who dwelt along the borders of the Rhine, quarrelled, and after some time the Sequani asked Ariovistus, who was king over one of the tribes of Germans, to come to their aid.

This Ariovistus very gladly did. For the thought of battle, of rich plunder, and, above all, of the fair well-tilled fields of Gaul, drew his soldiers on. So a great army poured over the Rhine. But they did not come alone; they came with their wives and children, their cattle and their household goods.

The war against the Ædui was long, but at length they were defeated. Then the Sequani offered Ariovistus gold and precious booty as a reward, and bade him return to his own land.

But Ariovistus had no mind to go. The fields of Gaul were rich and fair, and he had a mind to make his home among them. So he subdued the Sequani and, taking a third part of their land from them, gave it to his own followers. As the years went on Ariovistus demanded ever more land and more tribute, until at length the people who had asked for a deliverer found that they had saddled themselves with a tyrant. It Was plain that Ariovistus had made up his mind to turn Gaul into a German kingdom.

The Gauls were too weak to drive him forth, so now they sought help from the greatest of all conquerors, the Romans.

Julius Cæsar had by this time been made governor of Southern Gaul. He hoped one day to bring the whole of Gaul under Roman sway. But he saw well that if Ariovistus was allowed to conquer at will there was danger that Gaul would become a German instead of a Roman province. He determined forthwith to make it Roman, and willingly came to help the oppressed tribes.

Caesar now sent a message to Ariovistus begging him to come to meet him, for there were weighty matters of state of which he wished to talk.

But Ariovistus received Caesar's messengers haughtily. "Tell Cæsar," he said, "that if he has aught to say he may come to me. I marvel what manner of business he has that may concern me, and I demand to know by what right he enters that part of Gaul which is mine by the power of the sword."

When Caesar received this proud reply he again sent a messenger to Ariovistus. This time he made known his terms. First, Ariovistus must promise that not another German should be allowed to cross the Rhine. Second, he must give back all the hostages he held. Last, he must promise to leave the Sequani and their friends in peace. If Ariovistus would keep these conditions then Rome would be his friend. If not, then let him look to himself.

Ariovistus again answered as haughtily as before. "I have conquered these people," he said, "and as a conqueror I have the right to treat my subjects as I will. I do not dictate to Rome how she shall treat her conquests, neither shall Rome dictate to me. If Cæsar desires war, he shall have it. He shall learn of what stuff the Germans are made, who have never known defeat and who, for fourteen years, have never slept beneath a roof."

So it was to be war, and Cæsar, gathering his army, marched to meet the haughty barbarians. But brave though the Roman soldiers were, as they marched to meet the German host their hearts sank. Such tales they had heard of these wild warriors, of their enormous size, of their lightning-flashing eyes, of their more than human courage. White terror shook the whole army; both men and officers were ready to flee.

When Cæsar heard of it he gathered his men together and spoke words to them, both brave and stern. He reminded them how fifty years before Marius had defeated the Teutons and the Cimbri; he bade them cease to tremble, and be true to their leader, for fight the Germans he would. If all the army deserted him, he vowed still to go forward with the 10th Legion alone, for they, he knew, were the bravest of the brave, and would never forsake him.

Cæsar's words put such heart into his men that they became ashamed of their fears, and from wishing to flee they became eager for battle. So the army marched onwards into the strange unknown country to meet this strange unknown foe.

At length the two armies came in sight of each other, and a great battle took place. The Romans were far outnumbered by the Germans; the Germans, too, fought fiercely and well, but in the end they were defeated. In wild panic the Germans fled towards the Rhine. Of the great army only a few reached and crossed the river in safety, among them Ariovistus.

Ariovistus is the first great German of whom we hear in history. But after he fled across the Rhine before the victorious Romans we hear no more of him. We know nothing of his after-life or of how he died.

This battle is one of the important battles of old times, but we do not know where it took place. It was, however, fought not far from the Rhine, and probably in Alsace, not far from the town of Besançon. By this one battle the Germans were driven back over the Rhine, and for hundreds of years the Rhine became the boundary of the Roman Empire against the Germans. But this boundary was not held without great trouble. Again and again the Germans overstept it. Again and again the Romans drove them back. Twice Cæsar himself crossed the Rhine, but he could not conquer the Germans. He could only show his strength, and by the terror of his name keep the barbarians to the right bank of the river.

Still better to shut the Germans into their own land, the Romans also built great walls along their frontiers. Upon these walls forts or watch-houses were built at short intervals, and in each a few soldiers lived to give warning of an attack by the barbarians. These walls were sixteen feet high, and they were further strengthened by a deep ditch twenty feet broad. There were about three hundred miles of them in all. Yet in spite of these tremendous barriers there was much coming and going between the Germans and the Romans. Roman traders came among the Germans, young Germans went to serve in the Roman army, and almost without knowing it the Germans began to follow Roman manners and customs and take on Roman learning.

Yet these years were not peaceful, for the Romans made many efforts to conquer Germany. The great Roman General Drusus made three expeditions into Germany, he overran the country as far as the Elbe, and won so many victories over the Germans that he received the surname of Germanicus. It is said that he would have crossed the Elbe and tried to carry his conquests beyond it. But upon the banks of the river there stood a wise woman. As Drusus and his host advanced she waved them backward. "Cross not the stream, great soldier," she cried, "for on the further side defeat awaits you. Death is not far from you, therefore be warned, and at the end of life do not darken your fame by defeat."

So Drusus turned backward from the Elbe, but he had not gone far before he fell from his horse and broke his leg. A few days later he died in the arms of his brother Tiberius, who sorrowfully carried his body to Rome, where it was buried with great honour.

CHAPTER 4

# HERMANN, THE HERO OF GERMANY

TIBERIUS succeeded to his brother Drusus, and under him, it seemed as if German freedom was to be lost. It was he who sent the triumphant message to Rome, "All the land between the Rhine and the Elbe is subdued." He had no doubt that Germany was at length become a province of Rome.

But the spirit of freedom was still alive. More than fifty years had passed since Ariovistus had defied Cæsar. Now there came to power a much greater man. This was Hermann, or, as the Romans called him, Arminius. He is indeed the German national hero.

Hermann was a prince. He was one of the many German princes who had learned Roman manners, and who had served in the Roman army. But although he had learned much from the Romans, he remained a German at heart. He loved his country, and longed to see it freed from the yoke of Rome.

Tiberius had by this time been recalled from Germany, and his place was taken by the Roman General Varus. He treated the free Germans as if they were slaves, and soon roused in their hearts hatred for himself, and an intense desire for revenge. Far and wide low mutterings of rebellion were soon heard. All that was needed to make it burst forth was a leader. And one in Arminius the people found. He was only twenty-five, but he was bold and ready and loved his country. At once the Germans began to plot to get rid of the Romans. Varus was told of these plots, but he paid little heed to them. How should base Germans dare to plot against Rome? he asked.

So the time passed, autumn came, and all was ready. Then, as had been arranged, a small and distant tribe rose in revolt. Varus marched to put down the revolt. This was the awaited signal. Hermann and the princes and peoples in league with him at once gathered and followed the unsuspecting Roman General. Varus believed he was marching to crush a petty tribe. He was marching to his own destruction.

Germany at this time was full of pathless forests, swamps, and marshes. Now Varus and his legions had to pass through a dense forest called the Teutoburg Forest. It was a terrible march, for the season was already late, there were no roads, the ground was sodden with autumn rain, the streams were swollen and impossible to ford. To make a path for themselves the Romans had to hew down trees and make bridges over rushing torrents. The rain poured down in floods, the wind roared in the mighty trees, as, heavily laden with baggage and provisions, the men toiled on through forest and swamp.

Then suddenly one day above the roar of the storm the fierce, wild war-cry of the Germans was heard. It seemed as if the forest around was alive with armed men, and a hail of arrows and javelins poured upon the Romans from every side. It was Arminius with his gathered tribes who had surrounded the Roman army. The Roman discipline was splendid, and desperately they fought.

All day the struggle lasted, the Romans slowly retreating before the foe, and when night came they encamped upon a small open space which they had reached.

When morning dawned, the fight and retreat again began. The Romans were now growing exhausted and thousands fell beneath the swords and battle-axes of their terrible foe, and all the way was marked with dead and dying. The retreat became a rout, and at length the Roman army of thirty or forty thousand men was utterly wiped out, only the shattered remnant, under cover of the friendly darkness, reaching the Roman fortress of Aliso.

Varus was not among these few. Rather than face the bitterness of defeat and disgrace he had thrown himself upon his own sword and died.

This is perhaps the worst defeat which ever fell upon the Romans. It is one of the great turning-points in the history of Europe. For that day it was made certain that Northern Europe would never be added to the Empire of Rome.

When the dire news was carried to Rome it was received with a cry of rage and fear. The Emperor Augustus was now an old man, and the news filled him with unutterable grief. He rent his robes in despair, he wandered frantically about his palace beating his head in helpless wrath against the gilt and marble pillars. With tears running down his furrowed cheeks he cried in anguish, "Varus, Varus, bring me back my legions." For a whole month long he neither shaved his beard nor cut his hair, vowing splendid offerings to the gods if they would take his kingdom once more under their care.

All Rome was filled with dire expectation. The Cimbric Terror once more laid hold upon the people, and every day they feared to see the wild barbarians at their gates.

But the Germans had no thought of conquest. For freedom alone they had fought. The desire alone of freedom had held them together. Now that the Roman power was broken they fell apart once more.

Almost at once the Romans made another effort to conquer Germany. Germanicus, the son of Drusus, who inherited the name Germanicus from his famous father, was the leader of the Romans. Arminius was still the leader of the Germans.

Many battles were fought, and in one Thusnelda, the wife of Arminius, was taken prisoner.

At that Arminius was mad with grief and wrath. Here and there he hurried among his people, urging them to war. "Before me three legions have fallen," he cried. "But not by treachery, not against women, but openly against armed men do I wage war. The standards which I took from Rome and hung up in honour of our country's gods may still be seen in the groves of Germany. One thing the Germans will never forgive, that is that the rods and axes and togas of Rome have been seen between the Rhine and the Elbe. If you prefer your fatherland, and your own peaceful life to tyrants and new laws, follow your leader Arminius to glory and freedom."

These words so stirred the people that from far and near they flocked to the standard of Arminius.

Meanwhile the Romans too had been stung to wrath by the sight of the fatal field in the Teutoburg Forest, where six years before so many of their kinsmen had fallen. As Germanicus and his men reached the spot it was a dreadful sight they saw. Everywhere the field was strewn with whitening bones, now piled in heaps where some brave stand had been made, now scattered wide as the men had fallen in flight.

As he walked sadly over the ghastly field Germanicus fought the battle again in his imagination. As he listened to the tale of one who had escaped from that dreadful day he seemed again to see the fight. Here he eagle was captured, here Varus was wounded, here again he died by his own hand.

Six years had passed, but the heart of Rome still bled from the wound. And now Germanicus was seized with a great longing to give honourable burial to these dead comrades. So he bade his soldiers gather the bones together, and lay them in one huge mound, and cover them over with earth. This the men did, not a soldier knowing whether or not the bones he laid on the pile might not be those of some dear kinsman. So they looked upon them all as their kinsfolk, and their anger against the Germans grew more bitter than before.

But in doing honour to his dead kinsmen Germanicus had given Arminius an opportunity. And in the wild rocky passes of the Teutoburg Forest Germanicus soon found himself surrounded even as Varus had been. The Roman soldiers were slain in thousands; but Germanicus was a far finer soldier than Varus, and he succeeded in cutting his way through the enemy, and retreated in good order to his ships.

With hearts enflamed with hatred and desires of revenge on either side the war went fiercely on. At length in A.D. 17 Arminius was defeated at the Maiden's Meadow near Minden. But, although Arminius was defeated, the Romans had lost so many men, that they dared fight no longer. They dared stay in Germany no longer. So they retreated to their ships which lay waiting for them on the river Ems, and set sail for the stormy North Sea on their way home.

At first the sea was calm, but soon a terrible storm burst forth. Soon with broken masts and torn sails the Roman galleys were driven helplessly hither and thither. Some were dashed upon the rocks and were splintered to pieces; others were swallowed by the angry waves; only a few, with broken spars and with shirts for sails, at length reached port.

Germany was still unconquered. But Tiberius, who was now Emperor, was jealous of the fame of Germanicus, and he would not allow the General to continue the fight and recalled him to Rome. After thirty years' fighting the Romans had gained nothing, and Tiberius now decreed that the Rhine should be looked upon as the German border.

Yet, although the war was thus made useless, Germanicus was given a triumph. And in the splendid procession there walked Thusnelda, the beautiful wife of Arminius, a prisoner, leading by the hand her little three-year-old son. The deliverer of Germany had not been able to free his own wife and child from the chains of Rome. Thusnelda never saw her home or her husband again, but died in Rome, when and how we know not. Let us hope it was soon, for life held only misery for her, and she was robbed even of her little son. He had been born in captivity, and as a tiny boy he was taken away from his mother. But what became of him we hardly know. He was perhaps trained as a gladiator, and taught to fight with wild beasts to amuse his captors. All that is certain is that he died while still quite young, and that he never saw his father or his fatherland.

So ended Rome's last attempt to conquer Germany by force.

But now there was war within German borders. Marbod, the king of the Marcomani, was after Arminius the greatest leader in Germany. He had never joined with Arminius in his war of liberty, he had instead made friends with Rome. His kingdom was the largest of all the German kingdoms. Now he began to try to take possession of still more land. It seemed as if he wanted to conquer all Germany and bring every part of it under his sway. This was not to be suffered, for was he not the friend of Rome? So now Arminius turned his sword against Marbod, and at length defeated him so utterly that he was obliged to flee the country and take refuge with the Romans. Thus Arminius a second time saved his country from tyranny.

After this very little is known of the life of the great Arminius. He had saved his country from the yoke of Rome, and his people were grateful to him. Yet there were those who were jealous of his greatness, and in the year 21 A.D. he was treacherously murdered by his own kindred. He was only thirty-seven.

"Truly he was the deliverer of Germany," said a Roman writer. "He defied Rome, not in her early days, as other kings and generals had done, but at the height of the glory of the Empire. He fought, indeed, undecisive battles, yet in war he remained unconquered."

To this day the Germans look upon Arminius as the saviour of their country. Not far from the town of Detmold a huge statue of him may be seen standing guard above the field where it is thought his great battle was fought.

CHAPTER 5

# THE HUNS AND GOTHS

FOR long years the Rhine remained the boundary of the Germans. But although the Romans made no further attempt to conquer the Germans there was no lasting peace with Rome, for the world was rarely at peace in those far-off days.

But as the years went on the Romans began to grow few and weak, the Emperors were either slothful or wicked, and to the once mighty Empire there remained but a shadow of its former greatness. The Germans, on the other hand, grew to be many and strong. Then the order of things was changed. It was no longer the Romans who crossed the Rhine or the Danube in order to conquer the Germans. It was the Germans who now crossed these rivers in order to conquer the Romans.

At this time, too, began what is known as the Wandering of the Nations. From their northern lands whole tribes of Germans began to move southwards, seeking new lands and new conquests. The warriors and the mighty men of battle did not come alone. They brought with them their wives and their children and all their goods. For they did not mean to return homeward. They meant to settle and found new homes in the southern lands.

These German tribes left their homes in search of new ones partly because their old lands had become too small to hold them, partly because they themselves had been driven out by the terrible Huns, who came upon them from the wilds of Asia.

These Huns were a wandering shepherd people. They had neither houses nor towns, but lived in tents. They spent their lives wandering from place to place, seeking fresh pasturage for their horses and cattle. They always rode on horseback, so their legs were feeble and bent, their bodies were short and broad, their arms very long and of great strength.

These misshapen barbarians, with their dark ugly faces, flat noses, and wicked eyes, struck terror into the hearts of the Germans. They seemed to them something less than human, they thought they must be the children of witches and of demons. So they fled before them in fear.

But even before these terrible Huns appeared the Wandering of the Nations had begun. It was the Goths who led the way. They came from the very north of Europe, and to this day part of Sweden is called Gotaland or Gothland.

The Goths were divided into two, the East or Ostrogoths and the West or Visigoths, and throughout their many wanderings they kept these names. It was before the might of the Goths that Rome at last fell.

But the story of how in 410 Alaric the Goth took and sacked Rome belongs rather to Roman than to German story. So too does the story of how, in 476, a German soldier deposed the last Roman Emperor of the West, Romulus Augustulus, and ruled in Italy as King.

But even before Rome fell the Roman Empire had been torn to pieces by these barbarians, and province after province had fallen under Germanic sway. That Germany, as far as the Elbe, should be a Roman province was for what the Romans had fought. And now, after six centuries of war, the end of the long struggle had come. Rome had fallen. Instead of Germany being a Roman province, Spain, Gaul, Britain, and Africa had all been conquered by wandering German tribes. In Spain the Suevi and the Vandals had settled; in Gaul the Franks, Burgundians, and Goths; in Britain the Anglo-Saxons; in Africa the Vandals.

But of all these newly-founded Germanic kingdoms it is with Gaul alone that we have to do. For of all the German peoples the Franks alone founded a lasting kingdom on the continent of Europe, and out of that kingdom grew the new Empire of the West. And for some centuries the history of the Franks is also the history of Germany.

CHAPTER 6

# WINFRID, THE APOSTLE OF THE GERMANS

BEFORE the Roman Empire fell, Christianity had become the religion of the people. The Goths, too, who overwhelmed the Empire, had heard the story of Christ. But many other of the German tribes who still dwelt in their old homes remained heathen. Some too, like the Franks and the Anglo-Saxons, who wandered forth, were also heathen, and where they settled they crushed out the religion of peace and gentleness, and instead of the cross they set up again their heathen idols.

But good and wise men were never wanting who were ready and willing to take their lives in their hands, and, unafraid at the thought of death or suffering, go to preach the story of Christ to the wild heathen.

Many were the brave and gentle men who went among the fierce German tribes, but the greatest of them all was Winfrid. Winfrid was an Englishman, and his home was a little Devonshire village. His father and mother were wealthy people of great importance in their own countryside. In those days, when there were no inns, all travellers were made welcome at the great houses of the nobles. And among the travellers who came and went in Winfrid's home there were many wandering priests and monks. And after the evening meal was over they would sit around the board, and in the glowing firelight they would tell of the distant lands they had visited, of the dangers they had run, and of all that they had suffered at the hands of the strange heathen folk, who had never, until they came, heard the story of Christ. And as the little boy listened to those tales a great desire grew up in his heart one day to become a priest, and to wander forth carrying the Good Tidings to heathen folk.

But Winfrid's father was rich, and he hoped that his little son would one day inherit all his wealth and his broad fair lands, and do great deeds in the world. So with all his might he tried to turn Winfrid's heart away from his desire. But it was all in vain, and so Winfrid had his way and he became a monk.

For many years he lived in his monastery, learning all he could of history and poetry as well as Bible knowledge. He became a great preacher, and was looked up to and beloved by all who knew him. But ever in his heart lived the desire to carry the Good Tidings to the heathen.

At last Winfrid had his desire, and he set sail with two monks for the land of Frisia.

They landed safely, but they found that they had come at an evil time. For there was a terrible war going on between the Frisians under their King Radbod and the Franks under Charles the Hammer.

Radbod was a fierce, wild heathen, and he hated Christianity and everything belonging to it. Yet once he nearly allowed himself to be baptized. For the Franks had defeated him, and there seemed little choice left to Radbod, he must die or become a Christian. For in those fierce far-off days the sword and the water of baptism went, as it were, hand in hand.

So Radbod allowed himself to be persuaded. He put off his armour and clothed himself in the white robe of a penitent, and stood before the Bishop ready to be baptized. One foot he dipped in the water, then he paused. He had been told the wonderful story of the love of Christ. He had also been told of heaven and of hell. So now he paused.

"Where are my forefathers?" he asked, turning to the Bishop. "Are they in heaven?"

"No," replied the stern Bishop, "they are in hell, for they were heathen."

"Then," said Radbod fiercely, withdrawing his foot from the water, "then will I never be baptized, for I would rather be with my forefathers than have all the joys of heaven without them."

So Radbod and his people remained heathens, hating the Christians and all their teaching. And now, when Winfrid saw the turmoil of the country, and how it was torn asunder with war and hate, he saw he could do no good, so he turned home again.

But Winfrid did not despair. Soon he set out once more. This time, however, he went first to Rome to receive the blessing of the Pope. Then, full of hope and faith, and having received the new name of Boniface, he crossed the Alps once more, and began his long labours among the heathen Germans, which have earned for him the name of the Apostle of Germany.

His deeds were bold and fearless. In one place there was a huge oak called the Thunder Oak. It was sacred to the god Thor, and because of its great age, its towering height, and mighty girth, it was looked upon with trembling reverence.

But Boniface made up his mind to show the heathen that there was nothing sacred in their tree. So, taking an axe in his hand, with only a few followers behind him, he marched to the spot where it stood.

In sullen wrath the heathen folk crowded round him. They dreaded the awful anger of the god Thor should Boniface insult his tree. They were ready to slay the bold and insolent priest. Yet some strange fear of him held them back. In shuddering awe they waited.

Boniface raised his axe. It fell and fell again and again. Then through the forest a muttering was heard. 'It was the distant rumblings of a storm. Louder and louder it grew, nearer and nearer it came. The heathen folk shrank trembling together. "Truly," they said, "it is the anger of Thor." But, undismayed, Boniface laboured on.

The storm grew ever wilder, the mighty wind roared among the trees, bending their strong stems, snapping their branches. Still Boniface toiled on, half his work done. Then suddenly a terrific blast swept the forest, and, amid the sound of rending timber, with an awful crash the gigantic oak fell to the ground, split asunder. Shrieking in terror, the heathen fled from the spot.

Thor had not avenged himself. Boniface and his followers stood unharmed, and the unknown God had helped them with His wind. So thought the heathen. It seemed to them that the unknown God was stronger than Thor. And when Boniface, cut up the huge oak into planks, and used it for the building of a church, no man hindered him.

And thus the work went on. Sacred groves were hewn down, gods of wood and stone were broken in pieces or burned. Throughout the country crosses were raised, and here and there little churches were built. Even to Frisia the Good Tidings were carried, for Radbod, the fierce enemy of Christianity, died, and Boniface once again turned his thoughts to that dark heathen land.

So for nearly forty years the Apostle of Germany laboured on, journeying far and wide over the land. At length, in the spring of 755, he returned to Frisia. He was grey and bent with age and many labours, and he felt that he had not long to live. But he was content that his end was near, for he knew that he had fought a good fight, and that he had been a good soldier of the Cross.

Old as he was, Boniface was still fearless, and he journeyed now through a land beset with heathen. Many of them, however, listened to his words and were baptized, and a day was arranged when these new converts should be confirmed.

When the day came a great crowd of people was seen coming towards Boniface and his followers. But as they came near, it was seen that this was no peaceful company, but an army of savage warriors, armed with swords and spears.

The followers and servants of Boniface at once made ready to fight. But Boniface gently forbade them. "We may not return evil with evil," he said, "but evil with good. The long-wished-for day is come, and our salvation is near. Be strong in the Lord, and He will free your souls."

Even as he spoke the heathen horde burst upon the little Christian band.

For one moment Boniface saw a sword gleam above his head. Quickly he raised the Bible which he held as if to ward off the blow. The sword descended and, cutting through the Book, gave Boniface his death-stroke. Thus did the Apostle of the Germans meet a martyr's death.

CHAPTER 7

# CHARLEMAGNE

AMONG the many German tribes which had taken possession of the Roman Empire were the Franks who invaded Gaul.

At first their kingdom was small, but after a time there came to the throne a King whose name was Clodwig or Clovis. He was a great soldier and conqueror. He fought and conquered tribe after tribe, and king after king, until at length he ruled over a great kingdom, which included part of what is now Germany.

But as years went on the Merovingians, as the line of kings to which Clodwig belonged was called, grew weaker and weaker, and at length their place was taken by a new line called the Carolingian. The Carolingians rose from a family which had at first been servants of the King. They had been Mayors of the Palace. To begin with, the Mayors of the Palace merely looked after the King's household. But by degrees they became very powerful, they led the army in battle, and were the King's chief advisers. Then, as time went on, the kings became ever weaker and weaker, until they were called Do-Nothing Kings. They indeed did nothing, and the whole power lay in the hands of the Mayor.

For many years this state of affairs lasted. The King in name sat in his palace and did nothing, while the Mayor ruled. Then at length the long pretence was put an end to. It was decided that the man who ruled should have the name of ruler. The last long-haired, blue-eyed, empty-headed Merovingian was sent into a monastery, and Pepin the Short, the first Carolingian King, was crowned.

Pepin was a great King, but his son Charles was far greater. Charles came to the throne in 768, and for a time shared it with his brother Carloman. But in 771 Carloman died. Then Charles ruled alone.

Charles became so great a King that he is known in history as Charles the Great or Charlemagne. When he came to the throne the Franks had not forgotten that they were Germans, and one of Charlemagne's great desires was to bring all German tribes under his rule. He wanted, too, to make his kingdom a great Christian kingdom. For the Franks who, when they first stormed over the Rhine into Gaul, had been heathen, were now Christian. But the Saxons and the Danes, in spite of Boniface and many other Christian priests who had come before and after him, were still heathen. They rose again and again in fury, slaying the priests and burning the new-built churches.

Hearing of these disturbances, Charlemagne marched into the land with sword in hand. His first attack was upon a strange idol called Irminsul or Irmin's Column. This is thought by some to have been merely a statue of the great Arminius, which the people had come to worship as an idol. The great hero, it is said, was shown in full armour. In one hand he held a standard, in the other a pair of scales, to show forth the uncertainty of battle. Upon his breastplate was painted a bear, upon his shield a lion resting upon a bed of flowers. The one was meant to teach the wild brave Saxon that death upon the battle-field would bring him sweetest rest. The other was an emblem of deathless courage.

Whether this mysterious figure really represented Arminius or not, it had at least grown to be a national idol, and Charlemagne cast it down, broke it in pieces, burned the wooden temples which surrounded it, and carried off all the gold and silver treasure which he found there. Then, taking with him many hostages, Charlemagne marched away to make war against the Lombards in Italy. But if he hoped the Saxons were subdued he was mistaken, for again and again they rose against him.

Meanwhile Charlemagne fought the Lombards or Longbeards. They, too, were a German race, who had come from their northern home upon the shores of the Baltic, and had taken possession of the sunny lands of Italy.

Now two great Frankish armies poured over the Alps into Italy, and soon the town of Pavia was besieged. Then, while the siege was going on, Charlemagne marched to Rome, where the Pope welcomed him with great honour. The people of the city came out to greet him as their deliverer, casting green branches before him and singing, "Blessed is he who cometh in the name of the Lord."

Then, having celebrated the solemn feast of Easter at Rome, and sworn friendship with the Pope, Charlemagne returned to Pavia.

Now at length the city was taken, and all the north of Italy yielded to the conqueror. The King, his wife, and daughter were taken prisoner and sent to end their days in Frankist convents. Only Adelchis, the King's son, would not yield; he held out to the last, and when at length no hope remained he fled in disguise.

Adelchis was very strong. In battle, instead of a sword, he used an iron staff, with which he felled his enemies to the ground. He could snap a hop-pole as easily as one might break a twig. And now it is told of him that as he wandered homeless and alone he came one day to the palace of Pavia, which had once been his father's, and where now Charlemagne held high state. There, as the custom was, he sat down to table as any might, none saying him nay. As the feast went on, Charlemagne was astonished to see him break up the bones of stags and oxen as if they were matchwood. He marvelled much who this stranger might be, who was so strong and had such a valiant air.

But ere the end of the feast Adelchis quietly slipped away. There were those, however, among the company who, even in disguise, well knew the Prince. So it was told to Charlemagne that the noble stranger was Adelchis, the son of the conquered King. When he heard that, Charlemagne was right sorry that he had allowed his enemy to escape.

Therefore, said a knight, "Sire, if you will give me the bracelet which is upon your arm, I swear to bring him back to you alive or dead."

So, as Charlemagne would most willingly have Adelchis a prisoner, he took the golden bracelet from his arm, and, giving it to the knight, bade him go and fetch back the Prince.

The knight sped away, and soon he came upon Adelchis as he sailed in a boat upon the river Ticino.

"Hold, sir knight," he cried. "Why did you leave the feast so secretly? The King sends to you his golden bracelet as a gift."

When Adelchis heard the knight call, he turned his boat and came towards the bank. But as he came near he saw that the knight held out the bracelet to him on the end of a spear. Then said he to himself, "There is treachery here."

Quickly then he buckled on his armour, and, standing in his boat a little way from the bank, he called out, "What you offer me at the spear's point I will receive at the spear's point. Even if your master sends me this gift falsely, so that you may compass my death, I will not be outdone. I too will send him a gift."

Thereupon he took off his bracelet, and, putting it on the end of his spear, held it out to the knight. The knight took it, but by no means could he persuade Adelchis to come nearer or leave his boat and follow him to Charlemagne. So in great sorrow for the oath which he had sworn, that he would bring Adelchis back with him either dead or alive, the knight was fain to return alone.

And when the knight came to Charlemagne he gave him the bracelet, and told him how he had fared. Then Charlemagne slipped the bracelet over his hand, but it was so large that it passed all the way up his arm to his shoulder. Then was Charlemagne greatly astonished. "It is no wonder," he cried, "that a man with such huge arms should have the strength of a giant."

And so it is said Charlemagne feared Adelchis greatly, and would very willingly have compassed his death. But Adelchis fled away to Constantinople. There the Emperor received him kindly, and gave him the rank of Patrician. There he lived quietly until he died at a good old age.

Meanwhile, with solemn ceremony, Charlemagne was crowned King of the Lombards. All the nobles of the land came to do him homage. He was girt with a sword of gold, a purple robe was placed upon his shoulders, and the iron crown of the Lombards was set upon his head. Henceforth he called himself King of the Franks and of the Lombards, and Patrician of Rome.

And now once more from his triumphs in Italy, Charlemagne was called back to fight the heathen Saxons. "It is hard to say," writes an historian who lived in those days, and who wrote the history of Charlemagne, "It is hard to say how often they were beaten, and humbly yielded to the king, promising him obedience. Sometimes they were so tamed as even to promise to give up their worship of idols, vowing that they wished to become Christians. But, ready as they were at times to promise all these things, they were always far more ready to break their promises."

At the very slightest chance of success they revolted, and of all Charlemagne's wars that against the Saxons was the fiercest and the longest.

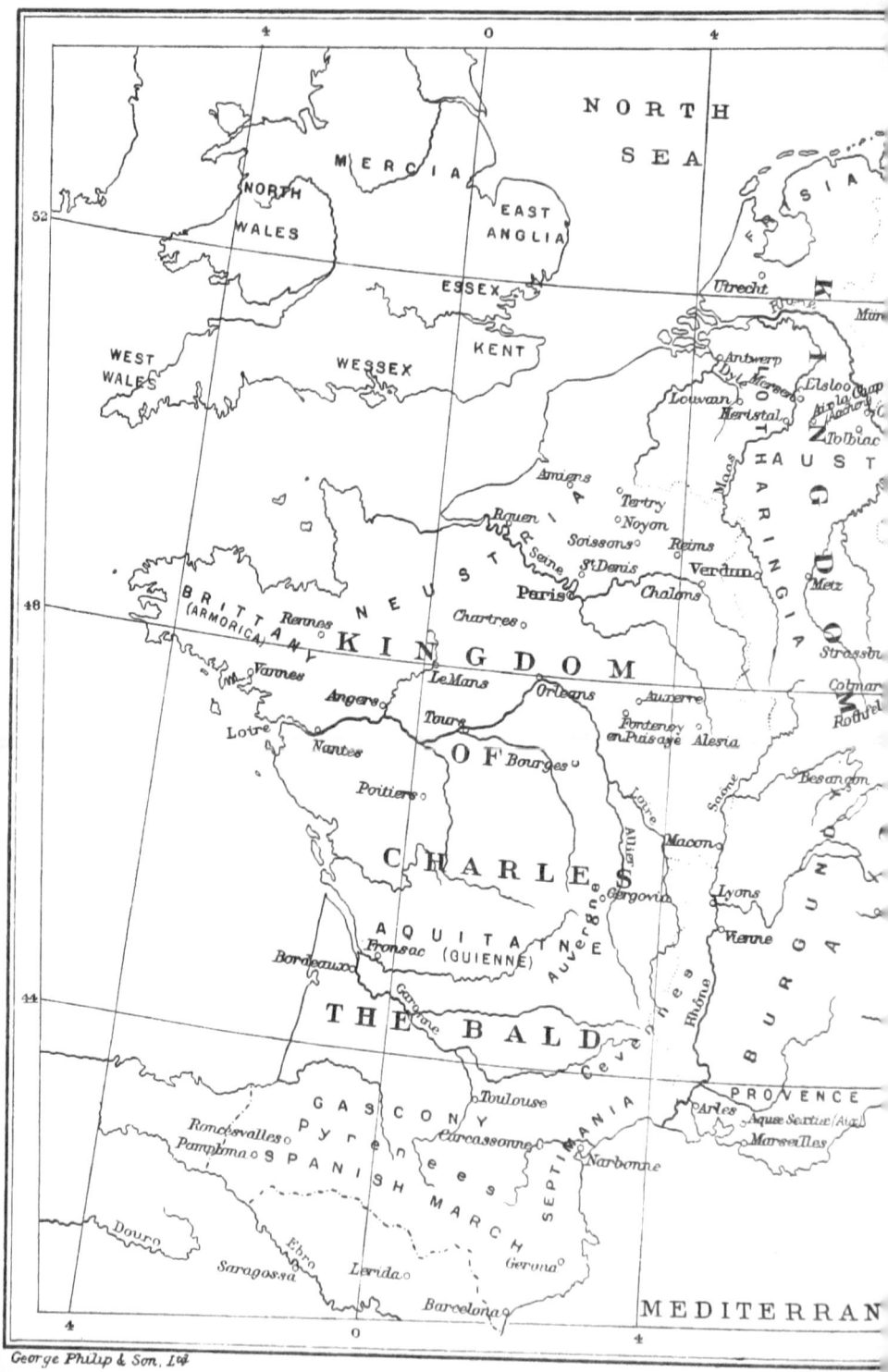

CHAPTER 8

# CHARLEMAGNE

TO Charlemagne the war against the Saxons was not merely a war of conquest. He fought against the Saxons for the love of Christ, and by war and hatred he meant to lead them to the religion of peace and love.

But beside the Saxons there were other heathen to fight. For Spain was in the power of the infidel Saracens. They had brought the teaching of Mohammed from Africa, and all but crushed out the Christian religion in Spain. But now the Saracens were at war amongst themselves, and there came to the court of Charlemagne an Arab, named Ibn-al-Arabi, to ask help of the mighty King against the Caliph Abderrahman.

Charlemagne gladly promised help, for he hoped to win back Spain to the Christian faith. So, gathering a great army from every part of his kingdom, he set out across the Pyrenees.

At first his march was victorious and easy. Town after town opened its gates to the conqueror, and, taking hostages with him, Charlemagne passed on his way triumphant until he reached Saragossa.

Ibn-al-Arabi had promised that as soon as Charlemagne arrived the gates of Saragossa should be opened to him. But Ibn-al-Arabi had promised more than he could perform, for the gates of the town remained closed. Worse still, the Arabs and Saracens, forgetting their own quarrels, now joined to resist the Christian King.

Charlemagne saw that he had been deceived. He had been beguiled by empty promises into the heart of a hostile land. He had no great engines of war with which to batter down the walls or force open the closed gates of Saragossa. To starve the city into surrender was not to be thought of, for already food for his own great army was growing scarce. So, seeing nothing else for it, Charlemagne turned homeward. With him went the unfortunate Ibn-al-Arabi, a prisoner.

All went well until the Valley of Roncesvalles was reached. Here the pass is so narrow that scarcely three men could walk abreast. But Charlemagne and the main part of the army passed safely through, and began to descend the farther slope into France. Roland, the beloved nephew of Charlemagne, followed next, in command of the rear-guard.

Now, as they marched, the sound as of an advancing army came to the ears of Roland's comrade, Oliver.

"I fear me, Sir Comrade," he said to Roland, "that we shall have battle with the heathen foe."

"God grant it," replied Roland proudly; "are we not here to fight for our King?"

But Oliver had not the careless pride of Roland, so he climbed to a height and looked backward the way they had come. And there, in the glorious sunlight, he saw the gathered splendour of the heathen host. Helmet plumes and many-coloured pennons waved in the breeze, and the sun was reflected from a thousand glittering points of steel. At the sight Oliver's heart was filled with dread. Well he knew that the rear-guard alone could not withstand that mighty host. Charlemagne must return to their aid. So it came to his mind that he would ask Roland to sound his horn. For Roland carried a wonderful horn of ivory, the sound of which could be heard many miles afar. Well Oliver knew that should Charlemagne hear it he would return to their aid. So hastily he came down from the hill and sought out Roland.

"I have seen the heathen," he said, "with their helmets and their shining hauberks, their lances and their gleaming spears. We shall have such a battle as never before. God give us courage, my lords of France. Stand firm or we shall be vanquished."

"Sorrow overtake those who flee," replied the peers. "There is not one of us who fears to die."

But although the peers were brave and ready to fight to the last, Oliver's heart misgave him. "The heathen are many, and our Franks are few," he said. "Friend Roland, sound your horn, and Charlemagne will hear it and return."

"Nay," said Roland, "I should act as a fool. I should sully the glory of gentle France. I will not sound my horn, but I will strike such blows with my good sword Durandal that it shall be dyed red in the blood of the heathen."

Then, as the heathen rode forward to the attack, they taunted the Franks.

"Felon Franks," they cried, "he who ought to defend you has betrayed you. The King who left you in this pass is a fool. To-day the realm of France will lose its glory, and Charlemagne his right arm."

But such taunting words only roused the Franks to greater courage, and recklessly they dashed against the foe. The fight was fierce and long, but the Franks were far outnumbered by the Saracens. Darkness at length closed over the dreadful field where the Franks to a man lay dead, among them wise Oliver and his proud friend Roland.

Real history has very little to say about this fearful fight in the Valley of Roncesvalles, and we know nothing more of Roland but that he fell there, and that he was Warden of the Marches of Brittany. But legend has made it famous, and some day I hope you will read the whole splendid story in the Song of Roland.

In the Song of Roland we are told that Roland at length sounded his horn, and that Charlemagne hearing it returned to help his army, and that he defeated the Saracens with awful slaughter. But that is not true to history.

Charlemagne never returned to Spain, and he never avenged the defeat of Roncesvalles. For, as soon as the battle was over, the enemy scattered, taking refuge among the forest-clad hills, and to follow them would have been difficult and dangerous, and would have meant a long and troublesome war.

Meanwhile Charlemagne had other needs for his army. For the Saxons, never truly subdued, had once more risen against him under the leadership of a chieftain called Wittekind.

CHAPTER 9
# CHARLEMAGNE

WITTEKIND seemed a second Arminius, and he fought Charlemagne as Arminius had fought the Romans. When other Saxons had yielded to Charlemagne, he had still defied him, and at length, when resistance was useless, he had fled to the court of the Danish King Siegfrid.

Now, knowing that Charlemagne was far away in Spain, he returned. With the desire for freedom burning in his heart, he called upon every Saxon who truly loved his country to join him and shake off the fetters of slavery.

Gladly the Saxons answered his call. They broke their oaths, they denied the waters of baptism which had been forced upon them at the sword's point. They cast down the crosses, burned the churches, and advanced through the country, filling it with terror and bloodshed.

As soon as Charlemagne heard of this revolt he gathered his army and marched against the rebels. Again many battles were fought, and all the land was filled with misery, and wasted with war. At length Wittekind gained a great victory over one of Charlemagne's generals.

When Charlemagne heard of it, his wrath was terrible, and, gathering another army, he marched against the rebels. The Saxons had fought bravely, but now when they heard that the mighty King was coming against them himself, their courage gave way. They laid down their arms, and scattered to their homes. And Wittekind, finding himself alone, fled once more to Denmark.

But Charlemagne, although he found no enemy in arms against him, was determined to be avenged. So he commanded the Saxon chiefs to appear before him. Not daring to disobey, they came. Then very sternly the King asked of them why they had revolted, and who was their leader.

With one accord they answered, "It was Wittekind."

But Wittekind was beyond the reach of Charlemagne's vengeance. Yet he was not to be baulked of it. So, threatening to waste the country with fire and sword were he not obeyed, he commanded that the chief of those who had helped in the rebellion should be given up to him.

And now the men who had fought so bravely in the absence of their conqueror quailed before his frown, and four thousand five hundred men were given into his power. Charlemagne condemned them all to death, and in one day all their heads were cut off. Those were rough times. But even in those days it was a deed of horror, and it remains as a dark blot upon the fame of Charlemagne.

By this terrible vengeance Charlemagne had hoped to crush the Saxons and to put an end to the constant rebellions. And indeed, for a short time, it seemed as if he had succeeded, for the Saxons were stunned with horror and grief. They seemed quiet, but it was only the dreadful quiet of sullen rage, and in spring it burst into wild rebellion.

Wittekind was recalled, and once more the land was desolated by war. Battle after battle was fought, again and again the Saxons were defeated, yet still they fought. Never before had they shown themselves so brave, and so determined. They were defeated, but not conquered. Winter put an end to the strife, but spring again renewed it, and so year by year the struggle continued.

Then one year Charlemagne made up his mind to remain in Germany all winter, and utterly crush the rebellion. This he did, and all winter long the wretched Saxons were harried and plundered. They were hunted from their hiding-places, and slain without mercy, until at length the spirit in them was broken, and they yielded to the conqueror. Wittekind alone, with a few faithful followers, held out beyond the Elbe.

At last even Wittekind yielded and was baptized. There is a story told, which, however, we fear is not true, of how Wittekind dressed himself as a beggar, and so found his way into the camp of Charlemagne in order to spy out its strength or weakness. He wandered about for some time, and at length came to the tent of Charlemagne, where Mass was being celebrated.

Wittekind, in his beggar's disguise, crept in among the worshippers, and, greatly wondering, watched the solemn service. It seemed to him very strange and beautiful. Then, as he stood watching in silent awe, a marvellous thing happened. It seemed to him, as he gazed at the lifted hands of the priest, that he saw in them a child clad in shining garments, radiant in beauty, such as never before had been seen on earth. And as Wittekind looked a sudden change was wrought in him. A wondrous peace seemed to fall upon his heart, and sinking on his knees he buried his face in his hands, tears of some strange unearthly joy running down his face.

When Mass was over, alms were given to all the beggars. When it came to Wittekind's turn he was so shaken by what he had seen that he forgot his danger, he forgot to act his part. It was soon seen that this was no beggar, but the great Saxon leader.

At once he was seized and led before Charlemagne. There he told of the shining vision he had seen, and of the wondrous peace which had come upon him.

And when it was told to Wittekind that he had seen a vision of the holy Christ-child, he begged to be baptized and received into the Church of Christ. Then he sent to his camp, and begged all his generals to come and be baptized even as he had been.

This story is very likely not true, and we do not really know how Wittekind was at length persuaded to become Christian. We only know that, weary of the hopeless struggle, he gave in at last, and promised to serve the God of Charlemagne who had proved himself the stronger.

Charlemagne rejoiced greatly over Wittekind's conversion. He stood as godfather for him, gave him the title of Duke of Saxony, and loaded him with many costly gifts.

After this we hear no more of Wittekind. It is believed that he lived quietly on his own estates until he died peacefully in some monastery.

CHAPTER 10

# CHARLEMAGNE

WITH the baptism of Wittekind the resistance of the Saxons was at an end for a time. For seven years the land had rest, and, in seeming at least, the Saxons yielded to the rule of Charlemagne. Saxon soldiers even served in the Frankish army, but it was easy to see that it was but a grudging service. They had no love for their leader, no desire to see him win. The old longing for freedom still slept in their hearts, the old hatred against their conqueror was still alive, though hidden. So, in secret, they plotted with every tribe unfriendly to Charlemagne, and at last, when he was fighting another foe, the Saxons once more broke out into wild rebellion. They refused to fight longer in the Frankish army. If fight they must, they resolved to fight for their own freedom. Once more they threw down the crosses, burned the churches, and slew the priests. Once more they turned to their old heathen ways, and wiped out the disgrace of baptism with the blood of their enemies.

So again, and yet again, Charlemagne marched against them. Again, and yet again, he cowed them, and wrung promises of obedience from them. These promises the Saxons gave because they needs must, or perish; but as soon as the conqueror was at a safe distance they broke their promises, and once more returned to heathendom and freedom.

But with iron determination Charlemagne returned to his task. He swept the country with fire and sword. He destroyed towns and villages, farms and fortresses, everything that would burn was set aflame, what would not burn was smashed to atoms and trodden under foot. Men, women, and children were slain or led into captivity. He settled these captives on Frankish lands, far from their own homes, and gave their old lands and possessions to Frankish soldiers and others whom he wished to reward.

Thus, at length, the unhappy country was subdued, but it was left desolate. So many of the people were slain that it was said the very colour of the earth was changed, and the brown fields were dyed red with the blood of its sons. So many had been carried away into captivity that whole tracts of country which had once been smiling corn-fields were now nothing but howling wildernesses, empty of inhabitants, given over to the wolf and the wild boar. Charlemagne, however, returned in triumph to his palace at Aachen. For he had sworn to convert the heathen or sweep them from the face of the earth, and he had kept his word. "He had done a work," says an old writer, "that even the Romans had failed to do. He had by a reasonable terror bent the savage and iron will of both Franks and barbarians." But when we remember all the blood which had been shed, all the thousands of women and children who had been driven forth homeless, fatherless wanderers, all the thousands more who had been led into bitter exile, we wonder if the terror of Charlemagne's name had indeed been "reasonable."

But before the Saxons were thus finally subdued, Charlemagne had reached his highest fame, he had become the first of the German Cæsars. Through all his wars Charlemagne had been friends with the Pope. He had sided with him against all his enemies, and looked upon him as God's representative on earth. "God," it was said, "had given two swords with which to rule the world, the one to the Pope, the other to the Emperor."

The great Roman Empire, you remember, had been split in two, so there had been one Emperor of the West, another of the East. But since the Goths had invaded Rome, since a German soldier had deposed the last weak Roman Emperor, there had been no Emperor of the West. But now together the Pope and Charlemagne agreed that the time to crown a new Emperor had come.

So Charlemagne once more journeyed to Rome. Here, on Christmas Day 800, all the people were gathered to hear Mass in the great Cathedral of St. Peter. It was a splendid scene. A thousand lights glowed in soft radiance upon gold and purple, upon gleaming gems and silken robes, upon glittering steel armour and waving many-coloured plumes. The deep notes of the organ rang through the lofty dome, and a thousand voices rose in songs of Christmas joy.

Mass was over. The Pope still stood by the altar; Charlemagne knelt on the steps in prayer. Then, suddenly, as Charlemagne was about to rise from his knees, the Pope took from the altar a splendid crown. He raised it high in his hands, then, stooping, he placed it upon the head of the kneeling King. "To Charles Augustus, crowned by God, great and peace-giving Emperor of the Romans, life and victory," he cried.

There was a moment of deep silence, then the gathered people took up the cry, and three times the mighty dome resounded with the words. Once more the solemn sound of chanting voices rose, and the Pope prostrated himself before the new Emperor.

Thus, after more than three hundred years had passed, during which there had been no Emperor of the West, a new Emperor was crowned. He was still called Emperor of the Romans, and his Empire was called the Holy Roman Empire. But although it was to be called Roman for many centuries to come, this was in reality the first foundation of the German Empire. The new Empire depended on the Germans as much as the old Empire had depended upon the Romans.

Charlemagne's Empire was very vast. It stretched from the Baltic to the Pyrenees and the Mediterranean, from the North Sea and the Atlantic to the borders of what is now Russia. From his father he had received only a small part, the rest he had won by his sword.

But Charlemagne was not merely a soldier and conqueror, he was a ruler and law-giver also. He made laws for his whole kingdom, taking an interest in everything, however small. But one man, of course, could not rule so great a kingdom alone, so to all parts of his Empire he sent officers who were called Missi Dominici or King's Messengers. These men were travelling envoys; they visited the different parts of the country, doing the King's justice. They listened to complaints, punished the evil-doers, protected the poor and feeble, and brought back to their Emperor an account of all that they had done.

This account they gave to the Emperor at his Parliament, which he held twice every year. In May he held a great Parliament, in autumn a small one, and because the chief meeting was held in May these meetings came to be called the Maifeld or Mayfield.

Charlemagne also took a great interest in learning. He founded schools throughout his kingdom, and caused not only the children of the rich but also the children of the poor to be taught. He gathered round him many of the learned men of the day, chief among them the Englishman Alcuin. He himself set the example of learning, and tried hard to learn to write. But although he mastered both Greek and Latin, he was never able to write well.

Charlemagne and the learned men at certain times used to meet together to talk. At those times he did not wish that they should speak to him as to a great and mighty ruler, but as to an equal. So he took the name of David. The learned men called themselves Homer, or Pindar, and such like, and the Court ladies also took other names. They used to write poetry or make up puzzles, and when they met together they would read them and talk about them, and criticise each other's work.

Charlemagne loved the German language, and he did what he could to make people use it in writing. For although people in those days spoke German, Latin was still the language of the learned. Everything which was written, either poetry or history, was written in Latin. Now Charles tried to induce people to write in German, and before he died he began to make a German grammar. He changed the names of the months, too, from Latin into German. January, for instance, was called Wintermanoth or Winter month; April, Ostermanoth or Easter month; December was Heilagmanoth or Holy month. But these never really came into use, and the Germans to-day still use Latin names for their months just as we do.

In speaking of German we must remember, however, that in those days there was as yet no German language as we know it to-day. But just as out of Charlemagne's great Empire there grew the Germany of to-day and the France of to-day, so there grew out of it the German language and the French language of to-day. In those days there were neither Germans nor Frenchmen, but only Romanised Franks and not Romanised Franks. The language which Charles the Great spoke and loved was the language of the not Romanised Franks, and that grew into German. But to a great number of his subjects Charlemagne's speech was like a foreign tongue. They spoke only Romanised Frankish, which, as time passed, became French.

Charlemagne ruled as Emperor for fourteen years. Then at the age of seventy-one he died. He had been ill for some days and felt he must die. Then at dawn one February morning, in 814, he felt the end had come. Gathering his last strength he feebly moved his hand to and fro signing himself with the sign of the Cross. Then folding his hands he murmured, "Into Thy hands, O Lord, I commit my spirit," and lay still.

The next day, with much pomp, he was buried in the great church at Aachen, which he himself had founded. He was not laid to rest as men usually are, whether kings or beggars. He did not lie taking his last sleep, but was placed in the vault sitting in a golden chair of state, with his royal robes around him, and a crown upon his head.

CHAPTER 11

# LEWIS THE GERMAN

ALL Charles the Great's sons died before him except one, the youngest and weakest of them all. This son was called by the Germans Lewis der Fromme, or the Pious, while the French generally call him Louis le Debonnaire, or the Good-natured. He was thirty-six when he came to the throne, and very soon it was seen that he held the sceptre of his great father with feeble hands. The whole Empire was filled with unrest when, about three years after he came to the throne, Lewis shared his Empire with his three sons. But this only brought confusion and warfare, for Lewis's sons were never satisfied. He divided and redivided his kingdom among them again and again, and they as constantly rebelled. At length they drove him from the throne, and thrust him prisoner into a monastery. Here the poor Emperor was humbled in every way possible. He was stripped of all his kingly dignities, and forced in public to read aloud a long list of crimes of which he was accused, and to do penance for them.

But the sons, who had united against their father, soon quarrelled amongst themselves. Once more Lewis was released and set upon the throne, but until his death he was never more than a mere tool in the hands of his scheming, passionate sons, who filled the Empire with strife. Meantime, while the kingly family fought within the realm, it was attacked on all sides from without. Northmen and Vikings came from out the northern seas, Moors and Saracens stormed over the Pyrenees or sailed across the blue Mediterranean from Africa. But Lewis paid little attention to them. At length, in 840, still at war with his sons, Lewis died.

As soon as their father was dead, his sons began to quarrel amongst themselves. To Lothar, the eldest, the title of Emperor had been given. But he grudged to his two younger brothers, Lewis der Deutsche or the German, and Charles, any share of the kingdom. So they joined together against him, and a great battle was fought at Fontenay-en-Puisaye. The battle was a terrible slaughter, huge numbers of knights and nobles being killed on both sides. Indeed, there were so few young nobles left, that for many a day great ladies were married to simple farmers, who were then made nobles, so that the great houses might not be altogether wiped out.

But the dreadful battle settled nothing. The hate and war between the brothers still went on.

In the following spring Lewis the German and Charles met near the town of Strassburg, and in presence of their armies took a solemn oath of friendship.

When the armies were gathered, Lewis the German, as being the elder, spoke first. "It is well known to you," he said, "how Lothar has persecuted and hunted this my brother and myself, and how he has sought utterly to destroy us. Yet out of brotherly love, and out of compassion for his Christian people, we desired not utterly to destroy him, and many times would we willingly have made peace with him. But he will not cease from pursuing me and this my brother as enemies. He is minded, by fire and sword, by robbery and murder, to crush our people to the ground. Therefore are we forced to come together against him. But not through any vile selfishness are we enticed to do this, but only for the well-being of our people, trusting that through your help God will give us peace."

Then Charles in his turn made a like speech, after which in very solemn fashion the brothers swore friendship with each other.

Now the soldiers of Lewis were Saxons from beyond the Rhine, while the soldiers of Charles were Franks or Gaulo-Romans. They spoke different languages. The Franks spoke a Romance language, which was no longer Latin, and which was not yet French, but which grew into French, while the Saxons spoke the Teutonic language, which has since grown into German. So that all might understand, Lewis the German spoke in the Romance language, and Charles spoke in the Teutonic.

This oath of Strassburg is very interesting to remember, for in it we see the beginnings of both the German and the French language.

And now Lothar found that his brothers, being united, were too strong for him. So he became willing to make peace. He sent messengers to his brothers no longer as bearers of proud defiance, but as ambassadors of peace. "I see," he said, "my guilt towards God and towards you, my brothers. I would end this fatal strife."

Lothar asked that he might be allowed to keep the title of Emperor and a third part of the kingdom. This the brothers were willing to give to him.

It was an old German custom that when two princes, who had been fighting against each other, wished to make peace, they met to talk of it in the middle of some river which bounded their lands. So now the brothers met on a little island in the middle of the river Saone. And here the great treaty, known as the Treaty of Verdun, was agreed to.

To Lothar was given Italy and a strip of land running right through the Empire, from the Mediterranean Sea to the North Sea; the land which lay to the east of that was given to Lewis the German; and the land which lay to the west of it was given to Charles. Thus the great Empire which Charlemagne had spent his life in building up was once more broken in pieces, and out of it were carved the three kingdoms of Germany, France, and Italy. But it is with Germany alone that we have to do in this book, and we may look upon that August day in 843, on which the Treaty of Verdun was signed, as the birthday of Germany. For, until now, the German lands had been merely a part of the great Frankish Empire, and the history of France was also the history of Germany. Now they were separate, although the kingdom of Lewis did not by any means contain all the wide lands which were to be gathered into the German Empire.

Now for thirty-three years Lewis ruled as King of Germany, but, although the quarrels of the brothers were at rest for the time being, those were no peaceful days. For all along the eastern boundaries of Lewis's kingdom were tribes who constantly fought against him, such as the Slavs, the Bulgarians, and many others. But Lewis conquered most of these peoples, and made his kingdom greater.

His northern shores, too, were attacked by the Northmen, those wild Sea-kings who came like storm birds, rejoicing in the wind and waves, who came not to settle, but to plunder and to burn. The Saxon land, however, was poor, and these robbers found little treasure or plunder of gold or silver to carry off. So they turned rather to the rich fields of Frankland, where the feeble Charles the Bald paid them great sums of money to be gone.

But suddenly one day the people of Hamburg saw the river Elbe grow dark with sails, and heard at their very gates the fierce war-cry of the Northmen. The wind was fair, and the swan-necked boats came sailing up the river with terrible speed. On and on they came, six hundred strong. The people were struck with despair, for the garrison was away, and the ships came in with such speed that they knew they would reach the town before the soldiers could arrive.

The Bishop tried to rouse the courage of the people, to make them man the walls, and hold the town until help could come. But it was in vain, they dared not face the wild freebooters. So, seeing no help for it, the Bishop gathered all the Church treasures together and fled.

The citizens too fled, but many of them fell into the hands of the Northmen and were killed or led into captivity.

For two nights and a day the Danes filled Hamburg with horror and bloodshed. They seized all the treasure they could find, and set fire to many of the buildings. Then once more they took to their ships and sailed homeward.

Lewis had not been able to stop the robbery at the time, but that summer he sent a messenger to Horich, the King of the Danes, demanding satisfaction.

Now, but shortly before this time another robber band had returned from France. There they had done as they would with the fair city of Paris, had seen the King tremble before them, and had returned laden with much treasure, flushed with triumph and swollen with insolence.

But not plunder alone had they brought with them. They had, unknown to themselves, brought also a terrible plague. And now, one by one, these haughty Sea-kings sickened and died, struck down in their pride by this dread disease. They knew not how to stay it. In vain they prayed to their gods. Their gods made no answer. At length a prisoner bade them become Christians, and pray to the God of the Christians for relief.

So Horich and all his warriors bowed their proud heads and humbled their high hearts. For fourteen days they fasted with tears and prayers, and at length the evil was stayed and the plague passed away.

Thus it was with a softened heart that Horich listened to the messengers of King Lewis. He promised not only to release all his Christian prisoners, but also, so far as possible, to give back all the stolen treasure. So there was peace on the Saxon shores, and the German King had rest from the Northern robber folk.

For more than ten years after the Treaty of Verdun there was peace between the brothers Then once more the war broke out, this time between Charles and Lewis, who had sworn everlasting friendship with each other.

Charles ruled his people ill, and he had neither wit nor strength to combat the fierce Northern pirates. They, finding him feeble, returned again and again in ever greater numbers, plundering and burning, murdering the people and carrying them away into captivity. So the people sent to Lewis, praying him to come and be their ruler and deliver them from the misrule and tyranny of Charles. "If you will not come," they said, "then must we turn to strangers and to the enemies of our faith for aid. And that will be a great danger to Christendom."

So at length Lewis listened to these prayers, and gathering his army he marched across Lothar's kingdom into that of Charles. And Charles, hearing that his brother was come against him, gathered his army and marched to meet him. Over against each other the brothers lay, both armies ready for battle. But no battle was fought, for as Charles gazed upon the glittering array his heart misgave him, his courage oozed away. In the night, with a few of his chief followers, he fled in secret, while the bulk of his army marched over to the enemy. Without striking a blow Lewis was thus master of his brother's kingdom. And so sure did he think his conquest, that he sent his own army homeward, and trusted himself entirely to the rebel army.

But Lewis soon found that to govern his new kingdom was no easy matter. Almost at once murmurs were heard against the new deliverer, as he had been called. Things had not gone as the people had expected. The Northmen still worked their evil will unchecked, the misery of the land was as great as before.

So the rebels rebelled a second time; they turned traitor to the new and went back to the old King.

Suddenly the news burst upon Lewis that his brother Charles was marching upon him with a mighty army. His own army had melted into nothing. He found himself almost alone, without a single follower. There was nothing left for him but to flee. So with all possible speed he fled back to his own land.

As a bubble that is burst Lewis's fancied conquest vanished into air, and Charles once more was master in his own kingdom. Ever afterwards, the day upon which his brother had fled before him, upon which the enemy had been "hunted forth and shattered," was kept as a solemn feast day.

Once again it seemed as if the land was to be torn asunder by the strife of brothers. But once again they met and vowed to forget all the evil they had done one to the other, and be at peace for evermore.

Long ere this Lothar the Emperor had died. He had, after the Carolingian fashion, divided his kingdom among his three sons. One, Lewis II, received the title of Emperor and the kingdom of Italy. Lothar II received the long strip of land which lay between the kingdoms of France and Germany, and Charles received Burgundy.

Now in 869 Lothar II died. At once his two uncles began to quarrel over his kingdom. For it lay between theirs, and they fought over it as two hungry dogs might for a bone. Lewis lay ill, sick nigh unto death at the time. So Charles at once seized upon the throne and with solemn ceremony had himself crowned at Metz.

From his sick-bed Lewis sent an angry message to Charles, bidding him at once to leave Lothar's kingdom. But to this message Charles paid no heed. He had been first in the field, and he meant to hold fast that which he had won. From town to town he journeyed receiving the homage of the vassals, and soon he was recognized as King in almost every part of his nephew's realm.

Again, as Charles was holding the feast of Christmas, came a threatening message from Lewis. To this Charles might have paid as little heed as before, but hard upon the heels of the message came the news that Lewis was well once more, and gathering his army. So Charles was forced to listen to his brother's demand or a share of the spoil. And at length, by the Treaty of Mersen in 870, they agreed to divide the kingdom.

By this Treaty of Mersen Lewis's kingdom was extended far beyond the Rhine. The Maas and not the Neser was the boundary on the north, the Saone end not the Rhine the boundary on the south. Indeed he boundary between France and Germany became now almost, though not quite, the boundary between he French-speaking and the German-speaking peoples.

For six years longer Lewis ruled. These years were hardly more peaceful than those which had gone before, for his three sons, Karlmann, Lewis, and Charles, all rebelled against him again and again. But he got the better of them always.

At last, bowed down with the weight of years, worn out by the labours and troubles of an eventful life, Lewis died in 876.

Lewis was no unworthy follower of his famous grandfather, Charles the Great. He was brave and wise, and those who lived at the same time have only words of love and praise to give him. And the Germans owed him love and loyalty, for under his sceptre for the first time the German-speaking peoples were united, and the foundations of their great nation laid.

CHAPTER 12

# LEWIS I AND CHARLES THE FAT

LEWIS was succeeded by his three sons Karlmann, Lewis, and Charles, and the kingdom was once more divided. Karlmann, however, did not live many years. He soon became very ill, and when Lewis heard that he could not get better he hurried as fast as he could into his brother's part of the kingdom and claimed it for his own.

Karlmann, the poor sick King, was powerless, but he commanded Lewis to come to him as he lay helpless in bed. Lewis came, but Karlmann could no longer speak. Only with his trembling hand he signed to him to have pity on his wife and his son. With beseeching eyes he prayed for mercy to them.

But Lewis's greed for land made him utterly hard-hearted. He cared little for the claims of his brother's wife or child, and he knew that they were not strong enough to fight him. He promised them, however, a little land and money, so that they need not become homeless wanderers. The rest of the kingdom he took as his own, and the dying King could only submit. Soon after he was thus deposed Karlmann died. There were thus only two kings left in Germany. But after adding to his kingdom with such hard-hearted greed, Lewis had enough to do to keep it safe. For there were rebel lords within the kingdom, and from without there threatened the old danger of the Northmen. They had harried the shores of England, they had wasted the fairest fields of France with fire and sword. Now they turned again to Germany.

But Lewis was resolved to drive these freebooters forth from his kingdom. So he gathered his army and marched against them. The Northmen had been plundering far and wide, and were on their way back to their ships with immense booty when the Germans fell upon them. A terrible fight followed, in which the Northmen were beaten. Five thousand of them lay dead, and the rest fled. But they carried with them in their flight Lewis's beloved son, sorely wounded. This son was young and brave and greatly beloved. When Lewis knew that he was wounded and a prisoner, he bade his soldiers cease from the pursuit of the foe, for he wanted at all costs to save his son. He sent messengers at once to treat for his ransom, not knowing that the Prince was already dead.

The Northmen were careful to hide the truth from Lewis. They were slow, too, to come to terms. Night came on fast, and Lewis was obliged at length to go back to his camp and, full of anxiety and sorrow, wait for morning.

But during the night the Normans fled to their ships, leaving behind them the dead body of the young Prince. When next morning the King found his dear son lying cold and pale upon the battle-field his grief was great. His anger too was great, for not only had he lost his son, but in the hope of saving him he has lost the chance of utterly destroying the robber horde.

But even after this great battle the Northmen Terror grew ever greater and greater. Again and again the sea robbers sailed up the rivers which opened to the North Sea. They plundered and destroyed at will, and town after town went up in flames. Added to this the harvest failed. A bitter winter followed on, and this hard winter seemed never-ending. Springtime came, but it brought no milder breezes, no early flowers. The earth remained frost-bound and barren, and the cattle, finding no fodder, died of cold and hunger. In this time of misery many of the great nobles, too, revolted against their King, and the whole land was filled with desolation.

But of all the troubles and sorrows which darkened the land, the Northmen Terror was the greatest. Again and again Lewis defeated the Northmen. But still they flocked down upon Germany in greater numbers than ever before. France, up to this time, had been their best-beloved hunting-ground. But King Louis of France had won such a brilliant victory over them that they now fled from that land seeking new battle-fields. They turned to Germany. And at length the sword which had kept them so long in check was still. For King Lewis lay sick to death. So, like ravening wolves, the Northmen stormed over the land. At Aachen they burned Charles the Great's famous palace, they stabled their horses in the great Cathedral, they burned the towns of Cologne and Bonne with their stately churches. Towns, palaces, convents alike were given to the flames, men and women to the sword. Behind them they left a track of blood and ashes.

While the horror of war came ever nearer and nearer to his palace doors Lewis lay helpless. He ordered his army forth. But without their King as leader they could do little to stem the flood of disaster. A comet now appeared in the sky, and to those ignorant folk of long ago it seemed an omen of evil, a warning of some terrible mischance. Shudderingly they gazed at the terrible apparition in the nightly sky.

While thus the black cloud of ruin hung over his kingdom, Lewis died on January 20, 882. And when the heathen folk heard that he was dead they burst forth into unmeasured joy; "they thought no more of war, but only of plunder," says a chronicler of the times.

Meantime Lewis's brother, King Charles, did nothing. He led an idle, aimless life, seeking only his own pleasure, and he is known as Karl III der Dicke, or the Fat. Besides being King of Italy he had also received the title of Emperor. In anointing him Emperor the Pope had hoped that Charles would help him against his enemies. But he had found himself deceived. The Emperor's chief policy was to sit still and do nothing.

And as he sat still it seemed fortune poured out treasures upon him. He had already been made Emperor without effort on his part. Now that his brother Lewis was dead he became ruler over all his kingdom, again without any effort on his part. For Lewis left no son to succeed him.

Charles was in Italy when the news of his brother's death was brought to him. But he made no haste to claim his inheritance, or defend it from the Northmen.

From all sides messengers came to him praying him to hasten to his kingdom, to save his people from destruction and from the scorn of the spoiler.

At last Charles the Fat set out from Italy, and after many delays reached Worms, where he was joyfully received as King by his new subjects.

Here many of the princes of the realm were gathered together to decide by what means the growing insolence of the Northmen might be checked. It was decided that a general attack should be made upon them, and soldiers were gathered from every part of the Empire. They came even from Italy. Never since the time of Charlemagne had Italian soldiers fought beside the Germans.

At length an enormous army was gathered, an army huge enough to strike terror to the hearts of any enemy, an army certain of victory, if only they had had a brave and clever leader.

But the first attack made upon the enemy failed. They had been warned, and already in the German camp there was talk of treachery.

After this the Emperor and his great army marched to Elsloo on the Maas, there to besiege the Northmen in their headquarters. A few days after the siege had begun there was a tremendous storm. It was brilliant summer weather, but one afternoon the sun was suddenly darkened by great clouds, until day became as black as night. Thunder growled and crashed, and sudden lightning lit up the darkness. Then hail came crashing down with such force that the noise of it was like falling houses. Such a storm no man living could remember. Some of the hailstones were so large that they could not be spanned by thumb and finger. They fell with such force that they shattered trees in the forest. Cattle in the fields were killed, and a great part of the wall of the town of Elsloo was broken down.

The breach was so wide that a whole troop in marching order might have ridden through it. The fortress lay at the mercy of the besiegers. One sharp assault was all that was needed, and the fortress was theirs. The soldiers clamoured to attack, for now they saw a speedy and glorious ending to the war. They saw before them a glorious vengeance on their foes.

But suddenly all their eagerness and joy were turned to wrath and shame. For a truce was ordered, and it became known throughout the camp that the Emperor was treating with the enemy. And they, the enemy, already hard put to it, already half-conquered, were making conditions!

A cry of wrath ran through the camp at the news, but the Germans were helpless. For hostages of peace had been already given, besides which Charles threatened with death or the loss of his eyesight any man who should lift his hand against the foe.

The insolence and knavery of the sea robbers now knew no bounds. As their custom was, they hung a shield upon the walls of their fortress in sign of truce, and threw open their gates. This they did to entice the Germans in. They came in numbers, either to spy out the fortification or to trade with the Northmen. Then suddenly, when many of the foe were within their gates, the Northmen shut them and pulled down the shield. Then with fierce war-cries they fell upon the unsuspecting strangers, slaying them at ease. And the slaughter only ceased when every man was slain or taken prisoner.

Yet in spite of this shameful treachery Charles completed his treaty with the Northmen in his safe camp, five or six miles away from the scene of battle. Godfrid, the King of the Northmen, gave a worthless promise that neither he nor his men would ever again invade Germany during the Emperor's lifetime. He was baptized, Charles himself standing as godfather, and giving him a christening gift of part of Friesland. Charles then married this speedily-made Christian to his niece Gisla. Thus in a day the heathen ravager, who had been a terror to the Empire, became a Christian and a prince of the realm.

Besides this, the Northmen were given an enormous sum in gold and silver upon their promise to go away and not return. To get this sum Charles was obliged to rob the churches and convents. So now these very treasures which had been fought for and defended so bravely, and which had cost so many lives to keep, were freely given over to the robbers by the spiritless Emperor.

At length, laden with spoil, dragging many prisoners in their train, the Northmen turned to their ships and sailed homeward.

Thus the great campaign in which every German tribe had taken part came to a shameful end. But the blame lay not with the soldiers, who were eager to fight for the freedom of their country, but with the cowardly Emperor. "Thereover was the army right sorrowful," says one who lived at that time. "They grieved that a prince had been set over them who was favourable to the foe and who robbed them of victory over their enemies. And right sadly they turned homeward."

But the shameful pact of Elsloo was quite useless The very next year hordes of Northmen, forgetting their promises, again appeared, harrying the coast sweeping up the rivers in their swan-necked boats plundering and destroying. Charles did nothing. Then under his weak rule the great nobles began to grow restless and unruly, and to fight amongst themselves. Charles let them fight.

Then, in 884, the young King of France died, leaving no son to follow him on the throne. So the nobles of France, although they knew Charles to be weak and cowardly, asked him to be their King. For, save for a child not yet five, he was the last descendant of the great Charlemagne.

Thus the great Empire was once more united under one sceptre. But with what a difference! The boundaries were indeed almost the same, but the sceptre was now in the hands of a ruler treacherous and idle, and neither a soldier nor a statesman.

Charles had won another kingdom as he had won the rest of his possessions, without effort on his part. He accepted the new kingdom, but he was not minded to do anything to make good his kingship, although the land was in sore need of help.

If the Northmen Terror was bad in Germany, it was still worse in France. "The Northmen never ceased," said a writer who lived at the time, "to drag these Christian folk into captivity and to murder them, to destroy the churches, to throw down the walls and burn the villages. On every road lay the dead bodies of priests and layman, of noble and peasant, of women, children, and babes. There was no way, no place, where the dead did not lie, and where wailing might not be heard."

And now, hearing of the death of the King, knowing the weakness of the Emperor, the Northmen returned to France in greater numbers than ever. You will read in French history how they sailed up the Seine and besieged Paris, how the people sent messengers to Charles beseeching him to come with all the might of Germany and Italy to save them; how he long delayed, but, coming at last, how he again made a shameful treaty with the foe, and marching away left Paris and France to its fate.

The siege of Paris ended gloriously for the French, disgracefully for the Emperor. The news of his folly and cowardice robbed him of the last semblance of respect from his people. In every corner of the realm mutterings of rebellion might be heard.

Then at length the anger of the people burst forth. Not, indeed, at first against the Emperor, but against his chief adviser and favourite Liutward. This Liutward was a man of low birth, but Charles had set him above all the nobles of the land, and heaped honours upon him. And Liutward's greed and insolence knew no bounds, until the people said he outdid Haman of whom we read in the book of Esther. For Haman, they said, with all his pride and insolence, was second to the King, but Liutward put himself higher than his Emperor, and was more honoured and feared than he.

The people blamed Liutward more than any one else for the disgrace of Elsloo; for was he not the Emperor's favourite and adviser, and could he not twist and turn him at will?

As the months went past the hate against this low-born favourite grew and grew. At length it burst forth. Liutward was accused of many wicked deeds. Neither he nor the Emperor knew how to deny them, and so in shame and disgrace Liutward was driven from the Court. And with a heart full of anger, and vowing awful vengeance, the fallen favourite went.

But now, without his friend and adviser, the Emperor felt absolutely helpless. He had long been ill. He was so stout that he could not move without help, and now his illness increased fourfold. He was sick both in mind and body, and without the guiding hand to which he had been used he felt utterly forlorn. His mind began to give way.

Then the nobles, seeing in his huge bulk nothing but a witless mass of flesh, resolved to thrust him from the throne and choose another ruler. So in 887 they held a great assembly and chose as their King Arnulf, the son of Karlmann, Charles's eldest brother, who, you remember, had died in 880. There was no fighting. At once every one flocked to the new King, and in three days Charles found himself utterly alone.

Without fighting a battle, without effort or trouble on his part, Charles the Fat had won a mighty Empire, until in power and riches he rivalled Charles the Great. Fortune had simply showered favours upon him, and now in a moment everything that fortune had heaped upon him was torn from him. One day he was Emperor, the next a beggar.

Humbly he sent to the new King begging for bread, and for the bare necessities of life. Arnulf granted his request, and the poor discrowned wretch crept into a monastery to die. And thus his miserable reign came to a miserable end.

CHAPTER 13

# ARNULF OF CARINTHIA

THE great Carolingian Empire was now once again broken up, this time never to be reunited, for Arnulf was chosen only as King of the Germans. The French and the Italians chose other kings, and a kingdom was also formed out of Burgundy. And although Burgundy, and Italy too, often again came under the same ruler as Germany, France and Germany were never again united.

Arnulf had won the throne of Germany almost without a struggle. But soon he had to fight, and that with his country's old enemy the Northmen. In 891 these riders of the sea appeared once again. Arnulf, when he heard of their coming, gathered his army, but before they were ready for battle the Northmen fell upon them and defeated them. They slaughtered every man who fell into their hands, and captured much booty, together with many wagon-loads of food.

When Arnulf heard of this defeat he was very sorrowful. He bitterly mourned the loss of his brave knights and men. He burned with wrath against the foe, and quickly gathering another army he marched against the Northmen.

It was at Louvain on the Dyle that the two armies met. At first King Arnulf hesitated to begin the battle, for on one side lay a marsh and on the other a river, and between the two there was no room for horsemen to fight. For foot-soldiers truly there was room enough, but his men were unused to fighting on foot.

In anxious thought the King swept the field with his keen eyes; he noted now this, now that; in his mind he weighed now one thing, now another.

Meanwhile from the Northmen's lines came sounds of mocking laughter and of scorn. With sneers and insults they accosted the foe. "Remember your last battle," they cried. Remember the little stream which we turned into a bath of blood. Soon we will show you such another."

The insults and mockery raised the King's ire, they roused his men to fury. "Men," cried Arnulf, turning to them, "commend yourselves to God. With His help you will be unconquerable in the defence of your country. Take courage. Think of all the blood of your kindred shed by these ruthless heathen. Think of the holy ones they have murdered, of the churches they have desecrated, of your homes they have ruined. Up and at them, soldiers. You have the felons before you. I myself will get from my horse and carry the flag before you. After me! It is not alone our own honour we defend, but God's honour. Up and at them, in God's Name!"

The King's words awoke a glow of courage in the hearts of all who heard him. As one man they leaped from their horses, old and young together, and from the ranks a battle-cry went up that seemed to shake the vault of heaven.

Shouting their battle-cry the Germans advanced. With a cry scarcely less loud, with rattling of bones and clash of sword on shield, the Northmen answered.

Thus the battle began, and fierce and stern was the fight. But the victory lay with the Germans. The Northmen turned and fled. And now the river, which had been to them a safeguard, proved their undoing. With the Germans raging behind them, they dashed towards the river, and hurled themselves into it in hundreds. On and on they rushed, until the bed of the river was choked with dead and dying. The German victory was complete, and of all the countless host of Northmen scarce a man was left alive to carry the news back to the ships. Among the dead lay two of the Northmen kings, and fifteen banners were captured, besides much spoil. On the German side it was said that only one man was killed.

As soon as the battle was over the whole army was formed into a procession, and singing hymns of thanksgiving and victory, they marched solemnly over the field. And for hundreds of years afterwards every year a festival was held in memory of this great victory.

This victory of Louvain gained for Arnulf lasting fame. But even yet the Northmen were not thoroughly beaten. Next year, knowing Arnulf to be far away fighting another enemy, they returned, sailed up the Rhine, and, unhindered, wasted and plundered the land in their usual fashion. A German army met them, it is true, "but they did nothing which might be called a brave deed," says a writer of the time. This was, however, the last time that the Northmen sailed up the German rivers. In autumn a famine swept over the land, and to escape the pangs of hunger the Northmen took to their ships and sailed away. They went to England, to fight with Alfred the Great, and never more returned to Germany.

Besides the Northmen, Arnulf had other enemies to fight. Chief of these were the Moravians. They had formed a kingdom on the eastern boundaries of Germany, and although their King was supposed to own the King of Germany as overlord, it was really a mere form. He did as he chose, so there was war between the two countries. In this way Arnulf was victorious, but he was helped by new and strange allies. These were the Hungarians.

The Hungarians were a heathen wandering people who had come from the steppes of Asia. They were fierce and wild, and splendid riders, and many people thought that they were descendants of the Huns, who long before had swept over Europe in conquering hordes. Like them they were little and ugly, with deep-sunk fiery eyes. Like them they seldom walked, but rode upon swift horses, dashing upon the enemy with terrible swiftness, and disappearing as rapidly as they had come. Arnulf made friends with these wild people, and they helped him in his war with the Moravians.

Arnulf also fought in Italy, for he wanted to be overlord of Italy and Emperor. The Pope too wished it, and when the Emperor died the Pope sent a message to Arnulf asking him to come to Rome to be made Emperor.

Arnulf went, but when he reached Rome he found, instead of the friendly reception he expected, the gates shut against him. The Pope was no longer master in his own city, for the Emperor's widow, Ageltruda, had taken possession. She had shut all the gates and garrisoned the walls, so that Arnulf should not be able to reach the Church of St. Peter. For she was determined that none but her son Lambert should be Emperor.

Deeply enraged, Arnulf drew back from the walls, and gathered his men to a council of war in a neighbouring church. First they heard Mass, then the King asked his followers what was to be done.

With a shout they replied as one man, "Let us take the city by storm." With tears running down their cheeks they once more swore the oath of fealty to their King, they confessed their sins, and marched out ready to do or die.

The King now rode round the walls to see how the assault might best be made. Meanwhile the watching defenders began to fling insults at the invaders, mocking them with scornful laughter. This made the Germans angry, and the soldiers clamoured to assault the city at once. Eager for battle, they rushed upon the walls.

Some threw great stones at the defenders, hurling them from the battlements. Others crowded to the gates, hacking them down with axes and battering-rams. Some dug mines beneath the walls, others laid ladders against them and climbed over. They worked with such heat and fury that all resistance was overcome. When the shadows of evening fell the great city of Rome was in the hands of the Germans, and the Pope was set free. The next day Arnulf held his triumphal entry. The Senate of Rome, in splendid robes, with many priests and nobles carrying flags and crosses, met the King; and singing hymns of praise, they led him into the city.

With fatherly tenderness the Pope received him, and led him into the great Church of St. Peter. There with solemn ceremony he placed the crown upon his head, and hailed him as Cæsar Augustus.

When they saw that their cause was lost, Ageltruda and her son fled. But Arnulf knew that although the crown was set upon his head his work was only half done. If his Empire was to be made safe, Lambert must be crushed.

So fourteen days later he marched forth with his army to do battle with him. But on the way he became very ill, and instead of fighting Lambert, Arnulf turned homeward with all speed. It was thought by some that he had been given poison by the Italians which by slow degrees killed him.

Arnulf lived for three years after he received the Emperor's crown, but his life was henceforth a sad one. He was ill, troubles crowded in upon him, and at last, worn out with sickness and sorrow, he died in December 899.

CHAPTER 14

# LEWIS THE CHILD

ARNULF was succeeded by his little son Lewis. He was, only seven years old when he came to the throne, so he is called Lewis das Kind, or Lewis the Child.

Lewis was, of course, too young to rule, so the power fell into the hands of the great churchmen of the realm. Chief among these were Bishop Adelbero and Archbishop Hatto. But these priests and bishops were more intent on making the Church powerful and themselves rich, than on governing the land well. Then the nobles, caring little for the weak rule of a child, began to do as they liked. As the King's power grew less theirs grew greater. They built themselves strong castles, they raised armies and made war, and ruled within their own lands as if they were kings, merely owning the King in a far-off sort of way as overlord.

These great lords, too, began to fight among themselves, and the whole land was filled with the noise of their feuds. The mightiest of these nobles were the Babenbergers, so called after their castle of Babenberg, and the Conradiners, who were related to the kingly house, and who took their name from their leader Count Conrad.

They were at deadly feud with each other, and they filled the land with bloodshed, now one side, now the other getting the better. But on the whole the Conradiners were the stronger, and the Babenbergers saw themselves being always more and more crushed by their great rivals.

Bishop Hatto had always been friendly to the Conradiners, and now he prepared to help them. Adalbert, the head of the Babenbergers, was commanded to appear before the royal council, to answer for his misdeeds. But he haughtily refused to come. Then an army was sent against him, and he was besieged in his castle of Theres on the river Main.

Adalbert made a brave resistance. But when his most trusted friend suddenly forsook him, and went over to the enemy, he had no more heart to hold out.

Then it was that Bishop Hatto, hoping to make Adalbert yield, came to him with fair words and promises.

"Follow my counsel," he said, "make peace with your King. I give you my word of honour that you may go to him without any fear. In safety and comfort as I lead you forth, so will I lead you back to your fortress. If you will not trust my priestly word, at least trust my solemn oath."

Adalbert believed the wily Bishop, and agreed to go with him. Very solemnly then the Bishop swore to be his safe conduct.

Before setting forth Adalbert begged the Bishop to partake of some food. But the wily Hatto, full of his wicked plans, refused. So together the Prince and Bishop left the fortress, Hatto leading Adalbert by the right hand.

But they had not gone far when Hatto stopped. "I grieve now," he said to Adalbert, "that I did not take your advice and have some food before we started, for the way is long and we are like to faint from hunger ere the end of it."

"Let us return, then, my lord Bishop, and have some food, so that you may not be wearied by the long fast," said Adalbert.

To that the Bishop agreed, and at once they turned round and went back to the fortress, the Bishop as before leading Adalbert lovingly by the hand.

When they were once more within the castle the Prince led his guest to the great dining-hall, and there feasted him with his best. Then once more together they set out for the King's camp.

Adalbert thought that he had gained a powerful friend, so little did he suspect the Bishop's treachery. But he was soon to be undeceived. As the little thirteen-year-old King sat in state Adalbert appeared before him to make his submission. Then an angry noble started up. "Hearken not to him, my lord King," he cried. "He does this only out of treachery. His submission is but a deceit and trick to save himself from a desperate situation. So soon as he receives your pardon he will return again to his rebellion. Let him die the death."

"For seven long years," cried another, "has this Adalbert disturbed the land. What blood has he not shed, what grief has he not brought upon the people by his wasting and plundering? Let him die the death."

Then, as with one voice, the assembled nobles condemned Adalbert to death for high treason.

But amidst the clamour and the rage Adalbert stood calm and unmoved. "Ye cannot touch me," he cried, "I have the Bishop's promise of safe conduct."

But the Bishop smiled a cruel smile, and was silent.

Then suddenly Adalbert's heart misgave him. "You are forsworn," he cried, "if you consent to my death."

"Nay," answered the Bishop, with a scornful laugh, "I have kept my word. Did I not promise that if you came forth from your fortress I would lead you back in safety? And have I not done so? Did I not, as soon as you came forth, lead you back in safety? I am absolved of my oath."

Darkly Adalbert looked upon his betrayer. "Would God," he cried, "that I had never come here. Too late have I learned your deceit, oh traitorous Bishop."

Then, loaded with fetters, he was led out before the assembled army, and his head was cut off.

Thus was the house of Babenberg crushed, and the house of Conrad became greater than ever. From that day Conrad the younger took the name of Duke, and henceforth he had no rival in the land.

But while within its borders the land was thus torn by the feuds of the great nobles, without a new danger threatened. This new danger was the Hungarians.

King Arnulf, you remember, had made friends with these wild people, and they had helped him against the Moravians. And so long as Arnulf lived, Germany had been safe from them. But they had overrun all the neighbouring lands. They had attacked the north of Italy, they had wasted all the countries along the western borders of Germany; they had utterly wiped out the Moravians.

And now that there was only a weak child-King to oppose them, they spared Germany no more. Great hordes of wild horsemen, more awful to look upon than wild beasts, it was said, stormed over the river Ems, and wasted the land with fire and sword.

Year by year they returned, year by year they stretched their plundering expeditions farther and farther. Bavaria, Thuringia, Saxony all felt the scourge, and the harvest-fields of Germany as far as the Rhine were trodden and destroyed by the hoofs of their horses. Without mercy they slew the old, both men and women; the young they carried away captive, in their savagery often fettering the women with their own long hair.

The whole land trembled before these terrible Hungarians. The people believed that the curse of God had come upon them, and they remembered the words of the prophet Jeremiah, "Lo, I will bring a nation upon you from far. It is a mighty nation, it is an ancient nation, a nation whose language thou knowest not, neither understandest what they say. Their quiver is as an open sepulchre, they are all mighty men. And they shall eat up thine harvest, and thy bread, which thy sons and thy daughters should eat: they shall eat up thy flocks and thine herds: they shall eat up thy vines and thy fig trees: they shall impoverish thy fenced cities, wherein thou trustedst, with the sword."

So great fear fell upon the people. But at length in 910 all the nobles gathered together a mighty army, and with the young King at their head marched to fight these terrible foes. Near Augsburg a great battle was fought.

In early morning, before the Germans were fully ready, the Hungarians attacked. But until midday the Germans fought bravely, with no sign of yielding. Indeed it seemed as if victory would be theirs. Then the Hungarians, as their habit was, tried trickery when force failed. They pretended to flee. Breaking their ranks the Germans pursued. Then suddenly the fugitives turned, the reserve was called up. The Germans were surrounded on all sides, and defeated with cruel slaughter.

The victorious Hungarians then marched farther into the land, and a few days later met another army, which had not been able to reach Augsburg in time to join in the battle. A second fight took place, in which again the Germans were defeated, and although the defeat was not so crushing as the first, the Hungarians were able to turn homeward triumphantly, laden with much spoil.

Lewis the Child is but a shadow King. This bootless campaign against the Hungarians is the only deed of his about which we know anything during his whole reign. "The weakness of the child who, nevertheless, bears the name of King," said one who lived in those times, "has deprived us this long time of a true ruler. His age is neither useful in battle nor fit to wield the laws. His weak body and lack of manly strength only excite the people to contempt, the enemy to insolence. How often I tremble when I think of those words, 'Woe to the land whose king is a child!'"

But the land was not much longer to endure the reign of a child. A little more than a year after the battle of Augsburg, at the age of eighteen, Lewis died, where and exactly when is not known. It was probably on September 24, 911. He had reigned, if reigning it could be called, eleven years. With him the German branch of the Carolingians came to a miserable end. He left the kingdom which his forefathers had made great utterly shattered within, and at the mercy of a relentless foe without. He left it far smaller than it was when he had received it from his father. For on the east side, during the many quarrels within, Lorraine had ceded from Germany, and the Duke now owned the King of France as his overlord, while on the west side the Hungarians had taken possession of great tracts of land which were lost to Germany for ever.

CHAPTER 15

# CONRAD I

LEWIS the Child left no son. There was indeed no direct heir to the throne. A Carolingian, it is true, still sat upon the throne of France. But never once did the German nobles think of offering the kingdom to him, and thus once more uniting the East and West kingdoms. No, they had grown too independent for that. So they met together to choose a new King from their own number.

Among the nobles there were two whose claims seemed almost equal, for they were both distantly related to the kingly house. One of these was Otto the Illustrious, Duke of Saxony; the other was Duke Conrad, of whom you have already heard.

Duke Otto was wise and good, and the first choice fell on him. But he was old, he felt that he had no longer the strength to bear the burden of the crown, that his arm which had often wielded a sword was no longer strong enough to hold the sceptre. That a greybeard should follow a child upon the throne would be a great misfortune for the land, he thought. The man who would save Germany from the foes within and foes without must not only be wise but strong. So Otto refused the crown, and the next choice fell upon the young and warlike Duke Conrad.

King Conrad I loved his country; he wished his people to be happy and prosperous. But somehow he was always unfortunate. He never succeeded in doing anything great for his people and kingdom until he lay on his death-bed. Then, as you shall hear, he did a great deed.

Meanwhile the new King was led into war almost at once. He fought with the French King, and tried, but tried in vain, to recover Lorraine from him. It was a sad misfortune for the new King that his first war should be thus unsuccessful. But a greater misfortune befell him. Otto the Illustrious died. He had given the young King good advice, and kept the bishops in check. For bishops and nobles looked upon each other with jealous eyes, each fearful of the growing power of the other. But now that Otto was dead the bishops were once more all-powerful. They soon made their power felt.

After Duke Otto's death his son Henry became Duke. But Conrad had begun to be afraid of this great vassal. It seemed to him that unless his power was checked the Duke would soon be as great as the King. So Conrad took part of Henry's inheritance from him, and gave it to Bishop Hatto.

At this the whole of Saxony was filled with wrath. How could the King forget that he owed his crown to Duke Otto? asked the people. They prayed their Duke not weakly to allow himself thus to be robbed, but to fight for his rights, and they gathered to him, both knights and barons and their followers, until he had a mighty army.

Now when Conrad saw how the people gathered to the Duke, and how they looked darkly on him, his heart misgave him. He dared not fight the Duke openly because of his great army, so he listened to the wily Bishop and sought to overcome Henry by treachery.

The Bishop, so the story goes, asked Henry to a great feast, promising him many favours and rich presents in order to entice him to come. Henry promised to come, and then the wicked Bishop went to a goldsmith and ordered him to make a beautiful chain of gold so cunningly contrived that it would be easy to strangle with it the person who wore it. This was to be Henry's gift at the feast.

All went well. As the day of the feast drew near the Bishop went to the goldsmith's workshop to see how he was getting on. As he watched the goldsmith work he sighed.

"Why do you sigh so deeply?" asked the gold-smith in surprise.

"I sigh," replied the Bishop, "because that chain must be dyed with the blood of a brave man, with Duke Henry's blood."

The goldsmith answered never a word. He told no man what he had heard, but as he worked his heart was sorrowful and heavy. When the chain was finished he took it to the Bishop, then he hurried away to Duke Henry.

As the goldsmith neared the castle he found Duke Henry mounted upon his horse, and ready to set forth as if on a journey.

"Stay, noble Duke," he cried, "whither will ye ride?"

"I am invited to a feast," answered Henry, "and to a great present-giving. I would even be on my way."

"Nay, but go not," cried the goldsmith. Then he told Duke Henry of the golden chain, and how it was wrought to cause his death.

And when he heard it Duke Henry was right ireful. He called the messengers to him who had come to bid him to the feast. Darkly he looked upon them so that they trembled before him.

"Go," he cried, "thank your master for his friendly invitation. Say to him that Henry's neck is no harder than Adalbert's. Say to him that I will not trouble him with my great train of servants, that I will rather sit at home and think how I may best serve him."

The messengers sped away. But no long time did Duke Henry sit at home and think. In great wrath he fell upon the Bishop's possessions in Saxony and in Thuringia and conquered them.

Shortly after this the Bishop died. We do not really know how he met his death. But the people hated him so that they said that the wrath of God had overtaken him in his wickedness, and that he had been struck down by a thunderbolt. Others said that he met with a still more terrible death which came about in this wise.

Many of the poor people were in great distress, for the land had been wasted by the Hungarians, and by the armies of the rival nobles. Their crops had been trampled and destroyed, their houses burned. Then followed a terrible year when the harvest failed and the winter was long and hard, so that the land was filled with starving, beggared people.

At length in their distress and hunger they came to the great Bishop, begging for bread, for well they knew that his vast granaries were still filled to overflowing with last year's corn. Hatto listened to their prayers coldly. Their poor weak bodies and pale thin faces, their trembling hands, awakened in his heart no pity. He saw in them only a crowd of useless beggars who could neither fight nor dig. Of what good were they? he asked. They were fit for nothing but to eat bread, and take it from the mouths of others. If they could only be put out of the way the famine would the sooner cease, and there would be more corn left for others who were of far more use in the world.

With such thoughts in his heart Bishop Hatto laid his wicked plans. He bade the people come to him on an appointed day, and he would satisfy all their wants. The day came. The joyful people gathered in crowds, and were all told to go into the Bishop's great barn.

In they went, more and more of them, till the barn was so full that it could hold no more. Then the Bishop locked the door and set fire to the barn, so that the wretched people were all burned up.

"A good riddance," said the Bishop. "They were just like mice, fit for nothing but to eat corn."

"But," says an old writer, "Almighty God, the just revenger of the poore folk's quarrel, did not long suffer this hainous tyranny, this detestable fact, unpunished. For He mustred up an army of mice against the Archbishop, and sent them to persecute him. So that they afflicted him both night and day, and would not suffer him to take his rest in any place."

Like a plague of Egypt were the mice. They followed the Bishop everywhere; they ate up all his corn; they swarmed in his bed and over his dinner-table. He could neither eat nor sleep for them.

At last he resolved to flee to his strong tower, which he had built for himself on a little green island in the river Rhine. There he would surely be safe from them. For, he said, The walls are high, and the shores are steep, And the stream is strong, and the water deep.

So in all haste Bishop Hatto set off. He crossed the Rhine, and reached his tower in safety. There he carefully barred the doors and windows, and stopped up every loophole. But all his care was of little use. "For the innumerable troupes of mice continually chased him very eagerly, and swumme unto him upon the top of the water to execute the just judgement of God. And so at last he was most miserably devoured by those silly creatures."

> For they have swum over the river so deep,
> And they have climb'd the shores so steep,
> And up the Tower their way is bent,
> To do the work for which they were sent.
> They are not to be told by the dozen or score,
> By thousands they come, and by myriads and more,
> Such numbers had never been heard of before,
> Such a judgement had never been witness'd of yore.
> Down on his knees the Bishop fell,
> And faster and faster his beads did he tell,
> As louder and louder, drawing near,
> The gnawing of their teeth he could hear.
> And in at the windows, and in at the door,
> And through the walls helter-skelter they pour,
> And down from the ceiling, and up from the floor,
> From the right and the left, from behind and before,
> From within and without, from above and below,
> And all at once to the Bishop they go.

Thus miserably, said the common folk, who hated him, perished the wily Bishop. And still to this day, among the vine-clad hills of the Rhine, there stands the Mäusethurm or Mouse Tower on its little green island opposite the town of Bingen.

Even after the death of the Bishop fierce war raged between King Conrad and his mighty vassal, Duke Henry. But the King could not subdue his vassal. For no knight in all Germany was so brave and splendid as Henry, no ruler more beloved of his people.

And Conrad could not give all his mind to conquering Henry, for other nobles too rose against him, and, worst of all, the Hungarians again laid waste the land. They burned the churches, slew the priests at the altar, and hewed down and insulted the crucifixes.

Conrad marched now here, now there, against his foes. Often enough he won a victory, but as soon as his back was turned the unsubdued enemy rose again. His reign was one long struggle. At length, sorely wounded, sick at heart and worn out by the long struggle, he lay down to die. "He felt," says an old writer, "that his lucky star had set."

In spite of all his mistakes and misfortunes Conrad loved his country, and now he gave his great proof of it.

As the King lay on his death-bed he called his brother Eberhard to him. "My brother," he said, "I feel that I can no longer bear the burden of life. It is God's will that I should die. Now what shall become of the kingdom lies with you. Therefore take counsel with yourself, and listen to my advice, the advice of your brother. We have, my brother, troops and armies, we have towns and weapons in our hands, we have the crown and the sceptre. We have all that belongs to royal state, save only fortune and kingly puissance. Fortune, my brother, together with this kingly force, stands ever on Duke Henry's side, and the salvation of the state lies in his hand. Take, then, the sacred lance, the golden brooches, and the royal mantle, the sword and the crown of the old King. Go to Henry, greet him as King, and make your peace with him, so that you may have him henceforth as a friend. For he will be a true King and a ruler over many peoples."

And when Conrad had ceased speaking Eberhard promised him with tears running down his cheeks that all should be done as he wished.

Conrad then called the great nobles about his bed. He bade them to think of peace. "After my death do not be torn asunder by jealousy and greed of power. Choose Henry for your King, set him over you as lord. For he is wise and knows well how to hold the sceptre. I do not only counsel you, I beg and pray of you to obey him."

Then, having done the greatest deed of his life, Conrad folded his hands and died, at peace with all the world.

CHAPTER 16

# HENRY I THE FOWLER

EBERHARD was true to his word, and as soon as his brother was dead he, with others of the great nobles, set out in search of Henry. With them they carried the crown and sceptre. But Henry was not in his castle, and after some search they found him among the mountains, amusing himself with catching birds. He was dressed like a simple hunter, and with his children about him he was busy with bird snares and nets.

And from this he received his name der Vogler or the Fowler. But I must tell you that many people think that this is a fairy-tale, and that Henry only received his name of the Fowler long afterwards.

At first Henry, like his father before him, refused the crown. But Eberhard asked to be left alone with the Duke, and when the nobles had withdrawn he threw himself on his knees before him, and begged him to accept the throne.

So Henry yielded. Then the nobles gathered round him with great joy. Standing upon his shield they raised him shoulder high, and with loud shouts acclaimed him King.

Then from the midst of the nobles an archbishop stepped forth, and would have led Henry to the altar so that he might be crowned and anointed, and blessed by the Church, as the custom was.

But Henry waved him back. "Nay," he said, "it is enough for me that I am chosen King, and that I bear the name of King, which before me no Saxon of my house has borne. I thank your love and God's grace for it. And let that suffice. Let the anointing and the crowning be for one better than I. Of so much honour I am not worthy."

This Henry did, not because he despised the Church, but because he knew how powerful the great churchmen had become, and he wished to show that he did not mean to be under their rule. His words pleased the assembled nobles well, for they too disliked the growing power of the priests. And raising their right hands to heaven once more they swore fealty to their King, crying, "God save King Henry, God save the King," till the sound echoed and thundered afar.

With Henry the story of the Saxon rulers of Germany begins. For until now the rulers of Germany had been Frankish, descendants of that great Frankish Emperor Charlemagne, who had fought and conquered the Saxons. Henry himself was a true Saxon, and his wife Mathilda was descended from Wittekind, the great Saxon leader. So in Henry the Germans felt they had a true German King once more, and that the dominion of the Franks was at an end.

But although many of the nobles had chosen Henry for their King all had not done so, and soon he had to fight against his revolted vassals, even as Conrad had done. But Henry was more fortunate than Conrad, and first one and then another of the rebels yielded to him. For Henry did not try to crush the great nobles altogether. He left them much power in their own lands, but forced them to own him as overlord. He fought when needs must, but he used peaceful means too.

One of the nobles whom Henry had to fight was Arnulf, Duke of Bavaria. But the King had no desire to fight. He thought that much horrible bloodshed might be avoided, that the lives of many gallant men might be spared, if only their leader would listen to reason. So he sent a messenger to Arnulf asking him to meet him alone.

To this Arnulf consented, and, thinking that it was single combat the King offered him, he went alone, but fully armed, to the place appointed. What then was his astonishment when the King stepped towards him unarmed, and greeted him with kindly words.

"Why will you fight against God's will?" Henry asked the astonished Duke. "It is by His will that the voice of the people has called me to be King. Why then out of jealousy will you shed the blood of all these Christian people? Had they raised you to the throne no one would have been more ready to acknowledge your right than I."

When Arnulf heard the King's words he hung his head in shame. In deep thought he turned upon his heel and went back to his camp. There he gathered his chief knights and nobles about him, and took counsel with them. They counselled him to make peace with the King.

Then Arnulf listened to this wise counsel, and coming to Henry he knelt before him, put his hands within the King's hand, and swore to be his man.

Besides overcoming the great nobles Henry won Lorraine back. He struggled long for it, both by peaceful and by warlike means, and at length cunning helped his sword.

It is told how in those days there lived a man in Lorraine called Christian. He saw that King Henry was fortunate in everything. He saw that although he had sometimes to fight long for a thing, he, in the end, was ever victorious. So he cast about in his mind for a way to win favour of this powerful and fortunate ruler. At length he fell upon a plan.

Christian pretended to be very ill and about to die, and begged Duke Giselbert of Lorraine to come to him, so that he might place his inheritance in his hands. Suspecting no evil, Giselbert came to Christian's castle, where he was at once seized and cast into prison. Then, bound and securely guarded, he was led before Kind Henry.

Henry greatly rejoiced when he thus found his bold and dangerous enemy in his power. But he knew that Giselbert was a brave soldier and a wise man, so he treated him with all honour. Soon by his kindness he won Giselbert's heart, and from being a prisoner Giselbert became a friend. Henry gave him back his dukedom and married him to his daughter Gerberga. So at last Lorraine was again united to Germany, and it remained a part of the Empire for many hundreds of years.

Thus after six years' reign Henry had succeeded in doing what Conrad had struggled in vain to do. He had peacefully united all the German peoples under one King. He had done it, too, more by statesmanship than by war and bloodshed.

And now that Henry had won peace within his kingdom, he had another and deadly enemy to fight. The Hungarians, who, as good luck would have it, had spared the German lands during the first years of Henry's rule, now descended upon them with all their old fury. Far and near they scattered devastation. Towns and villages, convents and churches went up in flames, so that the track of the marauders might be traced by the ruins and the ashes, by the smoke clouds that darkened the sky by day, and the flames which made night terrible. Young and old, men, women, and children were slain, or fled in terror to the mountains and the forests, there to die in hunger and nakedness.

Brave though Henry was, he dared not meet these wild horsemen in open field. For well he knew he had no army fit to stand against them. His foot-soldiers were few, badly armed, and badly drilled; horsemen he had none. Then fortune again was kind to him. His men, by chance, took a great Hungarian noble prisoner and led him bound before their King.

Henry was much rejoiced, but there was great sorrow in the Hungarian camp, for this noble was of high honour amongst them. They at once sent messengers to Henry offering untold sums of gold and silver for his ransom. But Henry treated all their offers with scorn. It was not gold he wanted, but peace, and peace alone he would have. As ransom for their noble he demanded from the Hungarians a nine years' truce. He promised also to pay them a yearly sum of money.

To this the Hungarians agreed; their noble was set free, and they marched homeward.

But to pay tribute to these heathen folk was surely a shameful and a useless deed. Right well Henry knew how the Carolingian kings had suffered from the Northmen and the Danes from such bargains. But Henry did not make his bargain out of cowardice, but out of prudence. He wanted time in which to prepare for the hour of need, which he surely knew would come. And from the first moment of the peace which he thus bought he laboured to make his country strong against the heathen enemy on its borders.

In these days there were no walled towns in Saxony. Only on the banks of the Rhine and the Danube, when the Romans had long ago lived, there were a few fortresses But these had nearly all been ruined by the Northmen or the Hungarians. Here and there, indeed, rose in frowning grandeur a fortress of some great lord, a castle of some bishop, a monastery or convent with its clusters of little houses built beneath its protecting walls. But for the greater part the people lived in lonely farms and small unprotected villages, a prey to every foe.

Henry made up his mind to change all that. And now, day by day, the sound of hammer and trowel was heard. All along the borders of the land strong fortresses were built. Unprotected villages were turned into walled and fortified towns, places of refuge in time of need. And in order to hold the people together and make them live in the towns, Henry ordered all courts of justice, all markets, indeed gatherings of every kind, to be held within the walls of the towns.

So gradually round the palaces of princes and bishops, round churches and cloisters, walled and fortified towns arose.

Henry I is remembered as the founder of German cities. And by degrees all the life of the kingdom began to centre in those towns, and a new class arose, a class of merchants and townsfolk. And in days to come the Kings and Emperors had cause to thank him, for many a time these burghers fought for them against the mighty nobles.

But meantime to defend these towns and fortresses men were needed. So Henry chose out every ninth man, and made him become a soldier. These men were drilled and taught how to fight. They were also taught how to ride, so as to be a better match for the Hungarians. And Henry's horsemen were soon so fine that they became the very backbone of the army, and as years went on the foot-soldiers became less and less, the horsemen more and more, important.

Henry drew all sorts of men into his service. There were many freemen who in those wild times found a living by wandering from court to court, and offering their services to any great lord who might be at war with another. These Henry gathered into his army. Others there were who infested the highways, robbing and plundering unprotected travellers. To such Henry offered a free pardon if they would become his faithful soldiers, which they did. "Thus," says an old writer, "an army was made out of robbers. For King Henry willingly pardoned thieves and robbers, if they were only courageous and strong in war."

But the nine years' truce sped fast, and war with the most terrible of all their enemies again threatened the people. So Henry gathered his lords and barons together and spoke to them.

"Well you know," he said, "what confusion ruled in your land. But through God's help, through labour and care on my side, through bravery on yours, we are now peaceful and united. But one thing yet remains for us to do. We must rise like one man against our terrible enemy, the Hungarians. Until now I have, perforce, robbed you, your sons and daughters, to make rich their treasury. Now nothing more remains to us. Now if we must still pay tribute, must we rob the churches and the altars of God, for nothing more is left to us but our bare lives. Therefore take counsel together and choose what we shall do. Shall we take the treasure which belongs to the service of Heaven and give it to your enemy and God's? Or shall we take the tribute which we have hitherto paid to the heathen and dedicate it to the service of most high God who has created and redeemed us?"

And when Henry had ceased speaking a great shout went up from the people. "May the true and living God, who is faithful and right in all His ways, and holy in all His works, make us free from our bonds," they cried.

Then, raising their hands to heaven, the people swore to stand by their King, and to help him against the heathen folk. And having thus sworn, the people went to their homes until the King should have need of them.

Soon after this the messengers from the Hungarians came as usual for the promised tribute. But this time they were received with scorn, and sent away with empty hands. When the Hungarians heard of it they were filled with wrath, and hurriedly gathering a great and powerful army they marched on Germany. Burning and wasting, they strode through the land. Then after a time the army divided in two, one part marching west, one north.

So soon as this happened Henry saw his chance. He fell upon one part of the enemy's force, and a terrible battle was fought in which the Hungarians were defeated. Many were slain, others were scattered through the land, where they died of hunger and cold, or were taken into captivity by the Germans, and ended their lives miserably as slaves.

But the second and larger part of the Hungarian army was still to fight. When, however, they heard that their comrades had been utterly defeated, and that Henry was marching now upon them, great fear took hold of them. In haste and terror they broke up their camp in the night and fled. When morning came, Henry quickly followed the fleeing foe, and another great battle took place near Riade in Thuringia.

"The Hungarians are our enemies, but they are, too, the enemies of the whole Christian world," cried Henry to his soldiers. "Put your trust in the grace of God, and avenge our fatherland."

Their hearts beating high with hope, their eyes bright with the lust of battle, the Germans rushed to the attack. Joyfully they watched their King as he rode now in the front, now in the middle, now behind, encouraging and commanding, while the great banner with the fighting archangel Michael fluttered ever before him.

The fight was not long. Soon the Hungarians fled, and fled so fast that although the Germans pursued them for eight long miles scarce a man was killed, scarce a prisoner taken. Their camp, however, with all its rich plunder and many prisoners fell into the hands of the victors, who set all the captives free.

The joy over this victory was great. Through the length and breadth of Germany Henry was greeted as the father of his country, and never more while he lived did the Hungarians molest his kingdom. And the tribute which had been paid to them was given to the Church for the benefit of the poor and needy.

But Henry's wars were not yet at an end. The Northmen were still terrible as of yore, so now Henry marched his victorious army against them. But their King, Gorm the Old, did not dare to meet the victor of the Hungarians in open fight. So he made peace.

The war with the Northmen was the last of Henry's wars. It was victorious and splendid as all his wars had been from first to last. And now his work was done. Germany stood high among the nations, and kings and princes sought Henry's favour. In the whole realm, both within and without, there was peace.

And now in this time of peace Henry turned his thoughts to Rome. He, who had refused the kingly crown at the hands of a bishop, thought that, like other rulers before him, he would cross the Alps to receive the blessing of the Pope, and the title of Emperor.

But Henry never reached Rome, never received the title of Emperor. For sickness struck him down. Then, feeling his end near, he called his wife, Queen Mathilda. "My dearest and best beloved wife," he said, "I thank our Lord that I go out of life before you. No one has ever had such a wife as I. How often have you calmed my anger, how often given me wise advice, and when I wandered you have ever brought me back to the paths of righteousness. I thank you for all you have been to me."

In deep sorrow the Queen replied, thanking the dying King for all the love and truth he had shown her. Then, bowed down with grief, she went into the church to pray for her husband.

And as she knelt in prayer the sounds of loud wailing came to her. Then a great horror of darkness fell upon her, for she knew that the King was dead, that she was a widow, and the people a fatherless people.

CHAPTER 17
# OTTO I THE GREAT

WHEN Henry I died the lords and nobles gathered together to choose a new King. Before he died Henry had prayed the nobles to choose his son Otto for their King. But Otto had been born while Henry was only Duke of Saxony, and so Henry's younger son, who had been born after his father became King, thought that he had a better right to the throne. "Nobler blood runs in my veins," he said, "than in the veins of my brother; for I am the son of a King, he but the son of a Duke." The nobles, however, were true to their word, and Otto was chosen as King.

So in Aachen, where Charles the Great lay buried, there was a great and solemn ceremony. Clad in splendid robes, surrounded and followed by lords and nobles, Otto went to the great Cathedral. There at the door he was met by the Archbishop of Mainz with all his bishops and priests around him.

Holding his crosier in his right hand, the Archbishop led the young King by the left into the middle of the Cathedral, which was crowded by an eager throng in glittering holiday array. Turning to the swaying crowd of people the Archbishop cried aloud:

"See, I bring Otto to you, whom God has chosen for your King, whom Henry pointed out, and whom the princes of the realm have acclaimed. If the choice pleases you, raise your right hand to heaven."

All raised their hands, and a thundering shout rang out, "All hail to our new King and ruler."

Then with slow and solemn steps the Archbishop led the King to the altar, where lay all the splendour of royalty, the sword and the mantle, the golden bracelets, the crown and sceptre.

First the Archbishop raised the sword, and, turning to the King, he cried, "Take this sword, and with it drive forth all the enemies of Christ, all heathen, all bad Christians. For God has given the realm into your keeping so that you may make it a sure refuge for all the Christian world." Then he placed the golden bracelets upon the King's arms, and the splendid robe upon his shoulders: "Let the wide flowing folds of this robe," he said, "remind you to be zealous for the Faith, and to continue in peace until death." Next in his hands he placed the sceptre and the staff. "Let these be a sign to you," he said, "that you shall be a father to all those who are under you. But above all, stretch out a merciful hand over God's servants, over the widow and the orphan." Then anointing him he cried, "May the oil of compassion never dry from your head, and may you at the last be crowned with an everlasting crown," and with these words the Archbishop placed the crown upon the head of the kneeling King.

Then clad in all the kingly splendour Otto arose, and mounting the steps sat upon the golden throne prepared for him. When the long service was ended, the King, with all his lords, passed back again to the palace, where a splendid feast awaited them. And so in feasting and rejoicing the great ceremony came to an end.

Never before at the crowning of a German King had such splendour been seen as at the crowning of Otto I. The greatest lords in the land acted as his servants, and served him at table as his cupbearer and butler, as groom in the bed-chamber, in the stable as master of horse. And it was with no empty form that these great nobles put their hands within those of the King and swore to be his men, for well they knew that this young and warlike prince was indeed their master.

Yet hardly was Otto upon the throne than there were rebellions against him, and his whole reign was filled with wars. He had to fight outside enemies, he had to fight rebellious nobles, he had to fight his own sons and kinsmen. But he fought well and bravely, and in the end he was victorious.

Quarrels soon broke out among the great nobles of the land. And for this, perhaps, the Saxons were mostly to blame. For, says an old writer, "the Saxons had become so proud that the royal honours had fallen to them, that a Saxon could no longer bear to serve any other man. If a Saxon had an overlord belonging to any other State, he would not do homage to his overlord but acted as if he had no overlord save the King only." And because of this Saxon pride many quarrels arose between Saxon vassals and Frankish overlords.

Such a quarrel arose between the great Frankish Duke Eberhard and a great Saxon vassal Bruning, who refused him obedience. In fierce wrath Duke Eberhard gathered his army and attacked Bruning in his castle. He took it and burned it to the ground slaying all within the gates.

But when King Otto heard of these lawless acts he ordered Eberhard and all the nobles who had helped him to appear before him, to answer for their misdeeds. Eberhard and his friends came. They came without fear, for they declared they had done nothing against the King. They had but used the right which was theirs of punishing a rebellious vassal.

The King, however, did not see it thus. Eberhard, he said, had broken the King's Peace, and he was ordered to pay one hundred pounds in silver. For his friends was reserved the light but shameful punishment of having to lead dogs in broad daylight to the King's palace. It was considered a great disgrace for a noble to have to do this. The Frankish nobles bowed their proud heads to the King's will and performed their punishment, and when they reached the palace Otto received them kindly and graciously, and sent them home laden with many and rich presents.

In this way Otto hoped to win peace within the realm, and to bind these princes to him. But Bruning the Saxon, whose pride had been the cause of all the strife, remained unpunished, and the Frankish nobles returned homeward with bitterness in their hearts. The King's graciousness, far from reconciling them, filled their hearts with deeper wrath against him.

So it came about that while the King was in Bavaria fighting another rebel lord, Duke Eberhard, despite the King's commands, once more attacked Bruning. Soon the whole country-side was ablaze with war. Crops were destroyed, towns and villages were burned to the ground. Murder and bloodshed were everywhere rife. The King's brothers, too, joined in the struggle, Thankman, the King's step-brother, taking sides secretly with Duke Eberhard; Henry, his younger brother, fighting openly against Eberhard.

When Otto heard of this renewed war and bloodshed he was deeply grieved, and he called his unruly vassals before him. But Eberhard and his friends had no mind a second time to lead hounds to the King's palace. They refused to obey, and openly declared themselves to be rebels.

Then Otto offered them free forgiveness if they would lay down their arms. He hoped by gentleness to put an end to this deadly strife which seemed to endanger the whole kingdom. But this gentleness only made the rebels more angry still. Many saw in it not policy but merely weakness. Instead of laying down their arms they fought with increasing bitterness, and day by day the horrors of war spread farther and farther throughout the land.

It seemed as if the evil days of King Conrad had come again. The throne seemed shaken to its foundations, and King Otto knew not which way to turn for help.

Thankman now openly joined with Duke Eberhard and marched against his brother Henry. He besieged the young Prince in his castle, took it and destroyed it, and took Henry prisoner. Bound with cords' like any common fellow he led him captive to Duke Eberhard.

Things looked ill for the King. But now fortune favoured him, for Eberhard quarrelled with some of his followers, and they, from wrath towards the Duke rather than from any love towards the King, went over to the King's side.

And now Otto, thus strengthened, would no longer shut his eyes to the part his step-brother Thankman played. And gathering his army he marched to besiege the town of Eresburg, where Thankman was. But when the people of the town learned that the King had come against them with a great army they opened their gates to him freely, hoping thus to appease his wrath. Thankman, however, dared not face his brother's anger, and he fled for refuge to the Church of St. Peter. There, with his hand upon the altar, he felt himself safe. But even there he was pursued. The door of the church was thick and strong; it was bolted from within with huge heavy bars of wood and iron. But nothing stopped the infuriated soldiers. With mighty blows they smashed the door to splinters and stormed into the church, axe in hand.

Thankman stood near the altar, upon which he had laid his weapons and the golden chain, which was the sign of his nobility. Now as the savage horde rushed in upon him Thankman seized his sword, and made ready to defend his life to the last.

Hurling insults at him a bold Saxon rushed upon his foe. But with calm courage Thankman met the blow, and a moment later, uttering a terrible death-cry, the Saxon fell dead upon the steps of the altar. One foe was dead, but others followed thick and fast. Hotter and hotter grew the fight; man after man went down, and still Thankman, though sorely wounded, stood fighting for his life upon the altar steps. But at length a javelin was hurled through the window behind the altar. It struck Thankman in the back, and without a groan he sank dead upon the ground.

But of all this struggle the King knew nothing. Although he had come against his brother with sword and spear he had never meant that he should be slain. When at length the news of his brother's death was brought to Otto his grief and wrath were great. He bitterly blamed the passion of his unruly followers, but in this time of civil war he dared not punish them severely, lest they should forsake him and join his enemies.

If the King was sad at the death of his rebellious brother, Duke Eberhard was also sad, for in him he lost his great supporter. His courage sank within him. He looked this way and that and saw no hope or help anywhere. It seemed as if there was nothing left for him but to make his peace with Otto. Then he bethought him that the King's brother Henry was still his prisoner. He remembered that Henry had laid claim to the throne, and he resolved now to try to persuade the Prince to join him in rebellion against the King.

So Eberhard went to the imprisoned Prince, and throwing himself on his knees before him, begged forgiveness for all the evil which had been done to him. The Duke reminded Henry that once he had laid claim to the throne, that he had himself said that he was of more noble blood than Otto. And Henry, who was very young and very fiery of temper, and who longed for greatness and power, listened to the flattering words of the Duke. He forgave all the wrongs and insults of his imprisonment, and swore an oath of friendship with his jailor, promising also to help him against the King.

Then the Prince, who had been dragged thither on foot half-naked, and with a rope about his neck, returned homewards clad in splendid robes, and laden with rich gifts. With treachery in his heart he returned to Otto; who, little guessing at that treachery, received him with joy.

Soon afterwards Duke Eberhard followed Henry. He came to the King, and upon his knees humbly begged for pardon, vowing once more to be his man, and to serve him truly with all that he had.

And Otto forgave his rebellious vassal. Yet he dared not leave his rebellion altogether unpunished. Nor did he dare to punish it heavily. So Eberhard was only banished from his dukedom for a little time. Very soon, however, he was received back into favour, and was given once more all the honours that had been his before. But still he hid hatred and treachery in his heart.

Meanwhile, in silence and in secret, Henry plotted. In one way or another, through promises or bribes, by awakening the jealousy of one noble, by flattering the pride of another, he won many to him, until far and wide throughout the kingdom men were eager to follow him.

At length all was ready, and on a sudden the fires of rebellion burst forth. And so secretly had the preparations been made that no one was more astonished than Otto.

Quickly, however, the King gathered his army, and marched to meet the foe. The first town he attacked was Dortmund. This was defended by Hagen, one of Henry's vassals. But the garrison no sooner heard that the King had come against them than they opened their gates. So without any hindrance Otto rode into the town and took possession of it. Then calling Hagen to him he bade him ride swiftly to his master, and try if by any means he might turn him from his evil purpose. "But, if you cannot so turn him, swear to me that you will come back hither, and yield you my prisoner," said the King.

So Hagen swore a great and solemn oath that he would do the King's bidding, and if he could not turn the Prince from his purpose he would come himself again, and yield him to the King as a prisoner.

In haste Hagen set forth. He found Henry, however, in no mood for peace, but already marching against his brother, and so, true to his oath, Hagen returned to the King.

Meanwhile Otto had marched towards the Rhine, meaning to cross over it. But only a small portion of his army had crossed when Hagen arrived.

At first Hagen hardly dare confess the ill success that he had had. Humbly he knelt before the King in greeting. Then rising, "Your brother, my overlord, greets you, O King," he said. "He wishes you long life and health to rule over your great kingdom. He bids me tell you that he will shortly be with you."

"Comes he in peace, or comes he in war?" asked Otto.

But even as he spoke a great army appeared in the distance. In a long and glittering line they came with banners fluttering in the breeze, advancing, as the King well saw, towards that part of the army which had already crossed the river.

The King sprang from his seat. "What crowd is that?" he cried. "What people are these?"

And quietly Hagen answered, "It is my lord your brother. Had he listened to my advice he would have come in different guise. But at least I have returned, as I swore to you that I should."

When the King heard that he was sorely distressed. Quickly he mounted, and back and forth upon the river banks he rode in vain seeking help. Bridge there was none, ships there were none; the stream was too wide and swift to swim. What then was to become of the little company on the farther side? Only certain death awaited them.

At length in his agony and distress the King sprang from his horse, sank upon his knees, and raised his hands to heaven. "O God," he cried, "Thou art the creator and ruler over all. Look down upon Thy people at whose head Thou hast set me, and save them from the hand of the enemy, so that all the earth may know that no mortal man may withstand Thy will. For Thou art almighty and livest and reignest to all eternity."

But while Otto on the one side of the river lifted despairing hands to heaven his soldiers on the other side were making ready to fight, and to sell their lives as dearly as might be. With the courage of despair the little company, scarce one hundred strong, divided its ranks, and one half attacked the enemy in the rear, while the other met them in front.

This Henry had not expected. He did not know the strength or the weakness of the foe; he did not know from which side to expect the fiercest fighting; and his ranks were thrown into confusion. Quickly the Royal army saw their advantage. A few of them could speak the Frankish language, the language of many of Henry's soldiers. So seeing the confusion and trouble of the rebel army they called out in the Frankish tongue, "Flee, flee! all is lost. Save yourselves who can."

Then the enemy, believing that it was their comrades who cried out, were seized with fear and fled. They fled in utter rout, pursued by a mere handful of victorious Saxons. Many were the slain, many the prisoners, Henry himself barely escaping with his life.

The victory was complete. But it seemed to the King that it was by no earthly power that it had been gained, and that God Himself had fought for him in answer to his prayer.

Still the war went on. From battle-field to battle-field, from siege to siege, from one side of the kingdom to another the King sped. He fought bravely and well, but enemies rose thick and fast around him. Yet the greater the danger the greater seemed Otto's courage. He fought on when all seemed hopeless. When it seemed as if every noble in the land was against him he still did not despair.

At length in a great battle Duke Eberhard was killed. The King was not at this battle and knew nothing of the death of his stubborn enemy. But one morning he mounted his horse at daybreak in order to go to church to say his prayers, as his custom was. As he rode along he saw a man in the distance who was hastening towards him at great speed. The King soon saw that this was a messenger, and a messenger too of good tidings. For as soon as the man saw the King he made signs to him and shouted aloud in joy.

The King and the nobles around him rode speedily forward eager to hear the news. In their impatience it seemed years ere the short distance which lay between them and the messenger was passed. But even when they reached him the messenger would not at once address the King. It was not fitting, he thought, that he should appear before his ruler in dusty and disordered garments. So he turned aside to shake the dust of his journey from his clothes.

The King and nobles waited impatiently. At length he was ready, at length he knelt before the King and began a long and respectful greeting. But the King looking round at his impatient courtiers bade him cease.

"Enough," he cried. "Say wherefore thou art sent. Tell us shortly the good news. Relieve my people here of their anxiety and fill their hearts with gladness. Afterward we will listen gladly to thy fine speeches."

Thus admonished the messenger told his news. "Duke Eberhard is dead;" he said, "and his army scattered."

Then, as the messenger would have continued to tell how it happened, the King signed to him to be still. Quickly dismounting from his horse and kneeling on the ground he gave thanks to God for this victory. Then mounting again he rode onward to the church. Again it seemed to the King that God Himself had fought for the right.

CHAPTER 18

# OTTO I THE GREAT

THINGS now went better for the King. Many of the rebels yielded to him, but his brother Henry still held out. He fled now to a strong castle called Chevremont, which was in the hands of his sister. But his sister would not open her gates to him. "Do you want to have me besieged in my castle?" she asked. "For when it is known that you are here the King's wrath will spread like a flood over the land. I will not suffer it, I will not bear it. I am not such a fool as to pay for your misdeeds."

Thus denied a refuge in his own land Henry fled to the King of France. Otto, however, followed him there, and the war was carried into the very heart of France. And now Henry, weary of the struggle, sought to make peace with Otto. And Otto pardoned his brother, and gave him again the dukedom and all the titles and honours which had been his before.

Yet the anger and rebellion had not died out of Henry's heart. Soon he grew discontented, soon he plotted once more against his brother. And at length, tempted by evil men, he even made up his mind to murder the King. All was ready when Otto discovered the plot. But it was now Easter time, and he was unwilling to disturb the peace of the holy feast. So he resolved to wait until after Easter and then lead the traitors to justice. Meanwhile he was content to surround himself day and night with true and trusty followers.

Seeing these precautions the conspirators became uneasy, yet they could not believe that the plot was discovered. So they waited patiently, plotting and planning afresh. Then suddenly one day after Easter the ringleaders were seized upon and hanged or imprisoned, Henry alone escaping.

For a long time no man knew whence Henry had fled, or how he lived. But at length true grief for his misdeeds grew in his heart, and he made up his mind to cast himself once more upon his brother's mercy.

It was Christmas Day. King Otto in his splendid robes sat in the great Cathedral listening to the songs of joy and praise. He was surrounded by a glittering throng of knights and nobles, the great church was filled from end to end, a thousand lights glimmered, the organ rolled and the voices of the choir rose and fell in the well-known words, "Peace on earth, good will toward men."

As Otto listened he looked down the long aisle of the church, and there he saw a man come slowly towards him. His head and feet were bare, and he was dressed in the robe of a penitent. With bent head and clasped hands he came right up to the throne, where he threw himself at the King's feet.

It was Prince Henry, who came to beg forgiveness. With pitying eyes Otto looked upon his penitent brother. "Thy rebellious folly deserved small pity," he said. "Yet now that I see thee humbled at my feet I will not add to thy misery."

Then stooping the King raised his brother, and taking him in his arms freely forgave him all the evil that he had done.

And from that day Henry rebelled no more, and there was peace and loving-kindness between the brothers as long as they lived.

Still Otto had little rest. One after another all the great nobles in the land rebelled against him. But one after another the King conquered them. He took the dukedoms from these rebels, and gave them to men of his own family, until at length all the power lay in the hands of the King and of his near relatives. Thus the power of the crown became stronger than it had ever been.

But Otto had not only to fight rebellious nobles at home. He had also to fight many enemies abroad. Northmen once more attacked the shores of Germany. But Otto fought and conquered them and forced Harald Blue Tooth, their King, to do him homage and swear to be his man. He overcame the Duke of Bohemia, and made his land into a German dukedom. The Duke of Poland too yielded to him and paid him tribute. Everywhere Otto was victorious. But greatest of all was his victory over the Hungarians. They, taking advantage of the troubled state of the kingdom, burst once more over the land in far greater numbers than ever before. They came a hundred thousand strong, threatening to drink every river in Germany dry; swearing that unless the earth swallowed them, or the sky fell, they would conquer the land from boundary to boundary.

Burning and wasting in their old terrible fashion, they swept through the land until they closed round Augsburg.

Augsburg was a large and wealthy town, but it was surrounded only by a low wall, and in no fit state to resist the terrible enemy. But by good fortune it was governed by the brave Bishop Ulrich.

He bade the people strengthen the walls as speedily as might be. And while the men worked, white-robed nuns marched through the streets in solemn procession, singing hymns and praying for God's help against the heathen host.

The good Bishop himself spent the long night on his knees praying before the altar. As soon as the first streaks of dawn reddened the sky he gathered his soldiers to hear Mass. He bade them be of good courage and fight for their faith and country, and think that day upon the words of Scripture, "Yea, though I go through the valley of death yet will I fear no evil, for Thou art with me, Thy rod and Thy staff they comfort me."

So when in the early morning light the fierce Hungarians appeared before the walls they found them manned by brave stern men ready to die rather than yield.

And as the Germans looked down upon the surging heathen host they saw that the men were unwilling to attack. They saw that they were driven onward by whips, and their courage and hope rose high.

Suddenly a trumpet sounded loud above the noise of battle. The onward march of the Hungarians ceased. Then the whole army faced about and marched away from the walls of Augsburg.

News had come to the Hungarian leader that Otto was marching to fight him. So he turned about to meet the King. He would, he thought, first defeat Otto and then take Augsburg.

Beneath the burning August sun a fierce battle was fought. From all parts of Germany men had gathered to the King's standard. Yet the army was far out-numbered by the Hungarians. It seemed as if the Germans must be swallowed up by the foe.

But Otto did not despair. Proudly he rode at the head of his army, the splendid banner of St. Michael fluttering before him. "See," he cried, "we have need of strength and courage, for the enemy lies before us. But have no fear. Everywhere in foreign lands we have fought and conquered. And here on our own native land shall we fail? Shall we turn our backs to the foe? Yes, I know it well, the enemy surpasses us in numbers, but not in courage or in skill. Many of them are ill-armed, and none of them have our best weapon, God's help. Truly, it would be shameful if we, after having conquered Europe, should give our kingdom into slavery to a heathen people. No, it is better to die in battle than to live shamefully in slavery."

Then, having thus spoken, Otto seized his shield and spear, set spurs to his horse, and dashed upon the enemy. After him stormed his whole army. The hurled themselves upon the foe with such force that soon the Hungarian ranks were broken, and the enemy fled in mad disorder.

Many were killed in the flight and pursuit, many were drowned in the river Lech, many were taken prisoner, and the whole army was utterly shattered.

Many, too, of the noblest of the Germans lay among the slain. But, in spite of all, the victory was complete and never again did the Hungarians attack Germany. Indeed, after this they ceased their wild wandering, and settled down in the land which they had already won. So in this battle of Lechfield we may see the beginnings of Austria as a settled country. And for many centuries the kings of Hungary were, in name at least, subject to the German King.

When the splendid victory became known, the army and the people of Germany greeted Otto with great rejoicing. They called him the Father of his country and Emperor, and as he passed through the land they crowded to bless and cheer him. And not only Germany rejoiced, but the whole of Europe, which was now freed from the raids of these terrible heathen.

In their joy over the defeat of the Hungarians the German people called Otto Emperor. But he was not really Emperor, no King of Germany since Arnulf having borne the title.

But now Otto turned his thoughts towards Italy, and his desires towards the Imperial title. Otto had already fought in Italy, and forced the King Berengar to own him as overlord. But Berengar soon threw off his yoke, and he also quarrelled with the Pope and fought against him. Then at length the Pope, finding himself well-nigh a prisoner in his own city, sent to Otto begging for help. In return for his help the Pope promised to make Otto Emperor of the West.

Very glad was Otto when he received the Pope's message, and gathering an army he marched into Italy. But he had not gone far before he found the way barred by a huge army under King Berengar.

Berengar, however, was a tyrant, and his people hated him. At the last minute they refused to fight unless he would abdicate in favour of his son. This Berengar refused to do, and his army scattered, and Otto marched unhindered on his way.

His march was a triumphal progress. Towns opened their gates to him, governors and people welcomed him with every sign of gladness. And so through a rejoicing land he passed until he reached the gates of

Rome. Here, with crosses and with banners, and all solemnity and high state, the senate and people came forth to greet him. Kneeling before him they kissed his feet. Then, mounted on a splendid horse sent to him by the Pope, he rode in triumph to the great Church of St. Peter.

Here, clad in magnificent robes, seated in a golden chair, the Pope awaited the chosen Emperor. As Otto slowly mounted the marble steps the Pope rose. And having kissed him the Pope took him by the hand, and led him through the silver gates, into the church beyond, while the choir sang, "Blessed is he who cometh in the name of the Lord."

A few days later, with great and solemn ceremony, Otto was crowned and anointed Emperor. But the Pope soon found that in seeking for a friend he had found a master. Otto indeed fulfilled all his promises to the Pope, but he showed that he did not mean the title of Emperor to be merely an empty title, but that he meant to rule his new kingdom with a firm hand.

The Pope was very young. He was greedy of power, and soon he was right sorry that he had helped to set this powerful German so high. But so long as the Emperor remained in Rome the Pope dared do nothing against him. As soon, however, as the Emperor had gone he turned traitor, sent messages of renewed friendship to Berengar, and began to plot to place him on the throne once more.

Otto soon heard of these plots, but he found it hard to believe them. He also heard that the Pope was leading a wicked life, but to that too he paid little heed. "He is but a boy," he said, "the example of good men may make him better." He turned back, however, to Rome, and when he reached it he found the gates shut against him. But the Pope had no courage to fight, so he fled, and a second time Otto entered the city, this time as a conqueror.

Otto at once called the clergy together. They came in numbers, all loudly accusing the Pope of many evil deeds.

When Otto had heard all these accusations he sent a message to the Pope asking him to come to defend himself against them. But the Pope would not come. His answer to the clergy was short and sharp. "I have heard that you wish to choose another Pope," he said. "If you do, I will excommunicate you all in the name of Almighty God, so that you will no longer be able to say Mass or ordain any one."

But Otto cared little for these proud words, and as the Pope would not come to defend himself he deposed him and appointed a new Pope.

It would seem now that the Emperor was at the very height of his power. He had forced the Roman people to bend to his will; he made and unmade Popes at pleasure. But he was soon to find that he could put no trust in the faith of the fickle Italians, and again and again they rebelled against him. While he was among them they were obedient. As soon as his back was turned they rose in rebellion.

The crowning of Otto as Emperor is perhaps the greatest event in his reign. For it was an event which had important results for Germany in aftertimes. For after this the German kings claimed the title of Emperor, and the crown of Lombardy as their right And by being emperors, the German kings became mixed up in quarrels with which their own land had nothing to do. The Germans poured out their blood and wasted their gold in quarrels not their own, and although by being Emperor the German kings won some glory abroad, they lost much real power at home. For while the Emperor was away fighting in far-off lands the great nobles ruled each in his own state almost as a king. And when the Emperor returned from these far-off wars he often found it impossible to overthrow the power of these petty kings. So while France, which had been at one time merely the western portion of the great Frankish Empire, grew into a united whole under a despotic king, Germany, the eastern portion, continued to be only a collection of states, more or les independent of one another, although governed in name by one ruler.

Otto spent much of his last years in Italy trying to rule his new and disordered kingdom. He died in 973, having reigned thirty-six years. Already during his lifetime he was called Otto der Grosse, or the Great, and he had well earned the title. For he had quelled the civil war; he had conquered all outside enemies, and forced them to pay tribute to him; he had conquered a great part of Italy and been crowned a Emperor; he had, in short, placed his country at the head of all the countries in Europe.

CHAPTER 19

# OTTO II THE RED

OTTO I was succeeded by his son Otto II, who was but a lad of eighteen. Already, in his father's lifetime, Otto had been crowned as King and Emperor, and, young though he was, had reigned as co-Emperor with his father. So now he succeeded to the throne without any trouble. His face was very red, and from that he took his name of Otto der Rothe, or the Red. Otto was a small man. But although he was small he knew well how to wield a sword and spear. He was a brave soldier, and he was very wise and learned too. He was married to Theophano, the beautiful daughter of the Emperor of the East, and both she and his mother had great influence in ruling the kingdom.

Otto came to the throne quietly and without any opposition. But it was not long before troubles and rebellions arose. Henry, Duke of Bavaria, the son of that Henry who had rebelled so often against Otto the Great, soon found cause for rebelling against his cousin the Emperor. This Henry was called the Zanker, or the Quarrelsome.

Henry the Quarrelsome was defeated and taken prisoner, and Otto took away his Duchy and gave it to Otto of Swabia. But Henry was not thus easily subdued. He escaped from prison, and soon he gathered another army, swearing to overthrow Otto. But Henry was again defeated and fled into exile. Once more, however he returned, and through all Bavaria the flame of rebellion spread anew. Henry the Quarrelsome was helped now by his cousin Henry the Younger, and by Bishop Henry of Augsburg. Otto of Swabia and Otto of Carinthia fought for the Emperor. So it was a war of Henries against Ottos. The Ottos won, and the Henries were banished from the land.

Otto had other battles to fight with the Poles and the Danes, but at length after five years of strife there came a lull. With his beautiful Queen Theophano, Otto then journeyed to Aachen, there to hold the feast of St. John. He meant to stay to rest some time in the splendid palace of Charlemagne, and in peace attend to the ruling of his kingdom.

But what Otto planned did not come to pass. For the French King Lothaire II had long wanted to win back Lorraine for France. Now it seemed the time had come. So, gathering his army, he marched rapidly towards Germany.

Lothaire's lords and barons had sworn either to slay Otto or take him prisoner. And when, having crossed the river Maas, they heard that Otto was at Aachen, not many miles distant, with only a few followers, their joy was great. They decided to march direct upon Aachen and take Otto by surprise. And this they might have easily done; for with such secrecy did the French King make his preparations that Otto had not the slightest suspicion that a hostile army had crosses his boundaries.

But now, instead of hurrying onward with all speed, Lothaire waited until all his baggage was across the river. Instead of hurrying forward at once he wasted time in arranging the order of march. So Otto was warned in time.

One day as Otto and his Queen were about to sit down to dinner, a hot and dusty messenger dashed into the palace. "My lord Emperor," he cried, "the French King is upon you with a mighty host. He is even at my heels."

"That cannot be," answered the Emperor calmly, "Lothaire could never do such a thing. He could never invade my land, for he has no army large enough, and he dare not trust his people."

But messenger after messenger now hurried in, heated, breathless, terrified. "Lothaire is here," they assured the Emperor. "He is at the very gates."

"That I will never believe, unless I see it with my own eyes," replied Otto.

So horses were called for. The Emperor mounted and rode out to see for himself this great and hostile army in which he could not believe.

And lo, the thing was true! Otto had not ridden far before he saw a great army of thirty thousand men marching towards him. So close they marched that their spears seemed like a vast moving forest.

Well knew Otto that with his little company it was impossible to resist this oncoming host. The only hope was in flight, if he and his would escape imprisonment and death. So, with tears of anger in his eyes, he turned his horse, and with his wife and the nobles who surrounded him he fled to Cologne, where he arrived in safety.

The Emperor had escaped none too soon. Scarcely was he well beyond the walls of Aachen when the French stormed into the city, into the palace. And the dinner which had been prepared for Otto served as a feast of triumph for Lothaire.

Otto had fled in haste, leaving jewels and great riches behind. Now the soldiers plundered the town at will. The crown jewels, rich robes and ornaments, and all the splendid furnishings of the palace were carried away as booty. The huge iron eagle with outspread wings which Charlemagne had placed of the tower of his palace, and which was turned toward the east, the French now took down and turned toward the west, as a sign that Aachen once more belonged to the Western kingdom.

But Lothaire was cheated of his greatest triumph. The prize had slipped through his fingers. He had hoped to take the Emperor prisoner, and thus gain an easy victory, and a treaty of peace which would give him Lorraine.

But now that Otto had escaped him Lothaire dared do nothing more, and having sacked the town of Aachen he turned homeward. Meanwhile, however, Otto had not been idle. He was filled with wrath and desire of vengeance. In all haste he gathered his army, and ere Lothaire reached the borders of his kingdom a herald from the Emperor overtook him.

"Treachery and cunning are abhorred of the Emperor," announced the herald proudly. "Openly he declares war against you, O King. On the 1st of October he will be in France, and hopes for ever to put an end to your lordship." With these proud words ringing in his ears Lothaire continued his way.

The German nobles flocked round their Emperor eager to wipe out the disgrace of flight, till at last an army was gathered such as for many a day had not been seen in Germany. Sixty thousand strong, half of them knights, steel-clad from heel to helmet, the mighty host rolled onward, and, true to his word, on the 1st of October Otto marched into France.

He swept everything before him. His vengeance was so terrible that for many a day the "German terror" was a byword. Right through the land he passed in triumph until he reached the Seine, until he reached Paris.

Upon the hill of Montmartre the army encamped, and the siege began. But Paris was well defended, and although the people suffered tortures of cold and hunger they held out bravely. Otto could not face a long siege, for winter was drawing near, already sickness and death were thinning his ranks. Towards the middle of November, therefore, he resolved to raise the siege and turn homeward. But he meant to show the French that he went as a conqueror, not as one defeated. So, before he set forth, he held a festival of triumph upon Montmartre. He would let his cousin of France hear a Te Deum such as never before had he heard, said Otto insolently.

To Montmartre Otto gathered all the priests and clergy who could be found far and wide. Then he bade them sing aloud with all their hearts a song of triumph. So there rose to heaven such a burst of song that the sound was carried far. And the stricken people in the streets of Paris paused to listen and wonder. What might these sounds mean? they asked with sinking hearts. Had reinforcements reached the enemy? Had their last hour come?

But the sound of singing ceased, there was great commotion in the German camp, and with lightened hearts the French saw them march away.

Lothaire was now so filled with awe and wonder by the might and power of Otto that he longed for nothing better than to make peace with him. So in the following summer the two Kings met together, and peace was made, Lothaire giving up for ever all claim to Lorraine.

Now hardly was Germany at peace than Otto, with his beautiful wife Theophano and his little baby son, set out for Italy. Otto the Great had added all Italy as far as Rome to his Empire. But he had by no means put an end to war and strife there, and now the whole state was in confusion, and many wild and lawless deeds were done.

All Southern Italy was still supposed to be under the rule of the Grecian Emperor, but it was really in the hands of the Arabs.

Otto now determined to free Southern Italy from the power of the Arabs and Greeks, and add it to his Empire. And having brought order into disordered Rome, he marched southwards.

At first Otto was successful, and the Greeks and Arabs fled before him. Then on July 13, 982, a great battle was fought. With tremendous force the German knights dashed upon the white-robed, brown-faced foe. They fought with fury, but they could not withstand the onslaught of the steel-clad Northerners. The Arab leader fell beneath the stroke of a German sword, confusion filled the ranks, and they fled tumultuously. After them stormed the Germans in the joy of victory.

But this joy was short-lived, for as the German soldiers dashed after the fleeing foe a second army of Arabs fell upon them and cut them to pieces. It was a terrible slaughter which now began, and in a short time the victory became a defeat. The German army was almost wiped out, and "the flower of Christendom was trodden under the feet of the heathen."

All the best of the German nobles lay dead upon the field, the Emperor himself barely escaped with his life. In the midst of the noise and clamour of battle a young Jew brought a horse to him urging him to save himself, and, seeing all was hopeless, the Emperor sprang upon it and fled towards the seashore. There, in the distance, he saw a ship, and spurring his horse into the waves he made towards it. But the ship with wide-spread sails sped onward, and took no notice of the Emperor in his need and danger. So Otto was obliged to turn back to the shore, where the young Jew watched anxiously, filled with fear at his master's peril.

The Emperor gazed towards the land, and saw the enemy fast approaching. "Alas!" he cried in agony, "what will now become of me?" Nothing but certain death or a more dreadful imprisonment awaited him on land, he knew, so again he gazed towards the sea. There, to his joy, he beheld a second ship appear. Then a second time he urged his horse into the waves, and this time reached the ship and was drawn on board. It was, however, unfortunately, a Greek ship, so Otto seemed only to have escaped one danger to fall into another. But, happily for him, there was on board a young soldier who knew and loved him.

This young soldier tried to help the Emperor. He told the captain that he knew him, that he was, indeed, a high officer in the Emperor's household, and that if he would take him to Rossano he would be well rewarded.

But the captain was suspicious. He did not believe that this young and splendidly dressed noble was merely an officer of the Emperor's household. "Are you not the Emperor himself?" he asked.

At first Otto would have denied it, but seeing that this was useless he at length answered, "Yes, I am the Emperor. For the punishment of my sins I am come into this plight. I have lost the best of my kingdom, and stung with sorrow and pain I will no more tread the land nor see the friends of the dead. Take me, therefore, to Rossano, where my Queen awaits me with much treasure, and you shall surely be well rewarded for your pains."

These words well pleased the captain, and turning about he made all haste to Rossano, hoping for great rewards.

As soon as they came to land the Emperor sent the young soldier, who was called Zolunta, with a message to the Queen. She received him with joy, for having heard that the army had been utterly defeated, and that the Emperor had disappeared, she already sorrowed for him as dead.

Otto bade Theophano send at once mules laden with gold and treasure to the shore as his ransom. This in all haste she did, sending also the Bishop of Metz with a fine horse for the Emperor.

Accompanied only by two knights, the Bishop came on board the vessel. As he greeted his master tears, both of joy and sorrow blinded his eyes. The Emperor was now eager to land. But the captain's greed was roused. Knowing well the value of his guest, he had no mind to let him go easily. Seeing this, and fearing delay, the Emperor suddenly ran to the side of the vessel and sprang overboard. Even as he did so a Greek soldier laid hold of his robe, but one of the Bishop's men struck him down and the Emperor leaped free. Quickly he swam to the shore, and there waited the coming of the Bishop and his two knights, who, with drawn swords, held back the angry crew until the Emperor was in safety. Then lightly springing upon the horse which stood ready for him, Otto rode towards the town, and soon was safe within its walls, where the sorry remainder of his army speedily gathered to him.

The Emperor had been defeated, but the victory was of little use to the Saracens, for they had lost their leader. Without him they had no more heart to fight. So they turned back to Sicily whence they had come, leaving all the rich booty, all the armour and weapons, upon the battle-field. And for many a long day the south of Italy was left in such peace that the people came to look upon the battle of Colonna as a victory and not as a defeat.

And now Otto too turned sadly homeward, with the shattered remains of his army. But the news of his defeat sped before him far over Europe. In every country around the borders of Germany the news was received with joy. Danes, Poles, Hungarians, and every German enemy seizing their swords rose in a body, ready to shake off the hated yoke of Germany.

But in Germany itself the news was heard with grief. The nobles there, so often ready to rebel, now united to help their Emperor. Soon a great army marched into Italy. At Verona, Otto called all the nobles of Germany together to a Parliament. It was a glittering assembly of bishops, counts, dukes, the great, indeed, from every state in Germany. From Saxony, Franconia, Bavaria, Lorraine, Swabia, and Italy they came to gather round the throne of the Emperor, eager to show their loyalty to him. And seeing this Otto persuaded the nobles to acclaim his little three-year-old son Otto as King. This the nobles promised to do.

Then Otto once more prepared to fight the Saracens, and wipe out the disgrace of his defeat. But it was with heavy hearts that some among the gathered nobles saw him go. One holy abbot, who could see, people said, into the future, seized the Emperor's hand and tried to hold him back. "Go not to Rome," he said, "for if you do, you will never see your fatherland again. There will you find your grave."

But Otto paid little heed to such warnings. His hopes were high, his mind was full of great plans. He went southwards, while the nobles turned northwards across the Alps, taking with them the little baby Prince in order to crown him at Aachen.

But Otto went no farther than Rome. For death met him, and with the arms of his Queen about him he closed his eyes for ever on December 7, 983. He was only twenty-eight, and he had reigned for ten years as sole King and Emperor.

Otto II died in Rome, and in Rome he was buried. Of all the German Emperors of the Holy Roman Empire he is the only one who found a resting-place in the great city whence they took their title.

At Otto's birth his grandmother said of him, "He will far surpass in fame any man of our house, and he will add new lustre to the glory of his forefathers." This prophecy was not fulfilled. He lives in history as one of the most able, but at the same time one of the most unfortunate, of German Emperors.

CHAPTER 20

# OTTO III

ON Christmas Day 983 the little four-year-old son of Otto II was crowned at Aachen. It was a splendid and gorgeous ceremony, although the child, who was the centre of it, hardly understood what it was all about, or why the white-haired priests should anoint him with oil, and place a crown upon his head.

After the ceremony, days of feasting followed. But the rejoicing and feasting were hardly over when dire news reached the city, news of the death of the Emperor. Then all the laughter and joy were turned into weeping, and the city of mirth became a city of sorrow.

There was cause truly for sorrow. The Danes and other northern tribes were in rebellion, Italy was torn asunder with war and discord, the Empire was exhausted and the Emperor a child. But now added to all this there was another trouble. For a child of four could not reign, and at once quarrels arose as to who should be Regent. According to old German customs the young King's nearest male relative had that right. But according to the custom of the Grecian Empire the young King's mother had the right.

Now Queen Theophano was a Grecian princess, the daughter of the Emperor of the East, and she claimed the right to rule for her son. Henry the Quarrelsome too claimed the right, for he was the King's nearest male relative.

So the choice lay between the Queen, who was woman and a stranger, and the Duke of Bavaria, who was indeed a man and a German, but who was hated by many. For many feared that if he became Regent he would try to win the throne for himself. The Queen was still in Italy, Henry still an exile and a prisonor. But now the Bishop who held Henry captive set him free.

Soon many of his old friends joined him, and marching quickly to Cologne he seized the young King and declared himself Regent.

But soon it became plain that Henry was not content with the title of Regent. Soon it became plain that wanted to be King. He held the Easter festival with all the state of a sovereign, and received the homage his followers as their King.

After this Henry thought that the throne was won. But he was greatly mistaken. Many of the nobles were still true to the King, some because they hated Henry and others because they loved the house of Otto. Immediately after Easter these nobles met together. Solemnly they denied all allegiance to Henry, swore fealty to Otto III, and armed themselves to defend his rights. And they were so strong that Henry was forced to flee from Saxony. But he found himself no better received in the other states of Germany. Not even in his own Duchy of Bavaria did the people receive him as King.

Henry had not expected so much opposition, and his courage began to give way. He found himself surrounded by enemies on all sides, and at last he was forced to promise to give the little King back to his friends on a certain day at a town called Rara. Meanwhile the Queen was hurrying from Italy with all the speed she might. Upon the appointed day she too reached Rara ready to receive her son.

True to his word, Henry came, surrounded by his train of knights and nobles. But he would not willingly yield up his prize, and long and loud were the arguments on this side and that. At length one day, we are told, in clear noontide a great star appeared in the sky. And when they saw it the people cried out that it was the young King's lucky star, that it was a sign sent from heaven. They greeted it with hymns of joy, and such was the enthusiasm that even Henry himself could hold out no longer.

Humbly he gave back Otto to his mother, he renounced the name of King, and solemnly freed from their oath of allegiance all those who had sworn to be his men.

With great joy Theophano received her son. Henry and all who had joined in his rebellion were forgiven. Humbly acknowledging his fault he knelt before his overlord, and placing his hands within those of the little King swore to be his man. Then peace was made. Henry was again given his dukedom of Bavaria, and ever after remained a true and faithful vassal to his King. Soon the people forgot his old name of the Quarrelsome and called him the Peacemaker. No state was so true to the Emperor as Bavaria, and when ten years later Henry lay dying, he called his son to him. "Never rebel against your King and lord," he said. "Deeply do I rue me that ever I did it."

And now for seven years the wise and beautiful Grecian lady Theophano ruled in Germany. Then on June day in 991 she suddenly died.

Otto was still only eleven years old and could not yet rule. So his grandmother, Queen Adelheid, became Regent. But she did not really rule as Theophano had done, and the power was almost entirely in the hands of the great princes of the realm, with the good Archbishop Willigis at their head.

And now the power of these dukes and princes which Otto the Great had done so much to lessen began to grow great again. The states began again to choose their own dukes, and in many ways to show their independence of the Crown.

Meanwhile Otto was growing up learned in all the arts of Greece and Rome. He spoke Greek and Latin as well as German. He was so learned and so clever that although still a child he knew far more than any grey-haired man. So they called him the Wonder of the World. His mind was full of splendid ideas and beautiful dreams. He loved all that was lovely and poetical in life, and he rather despised the rough Germans who were his chief subjects. He had splendid dreams of a perfect Empire and a perfect Church. But Rome, not Aachen, should be the centre of his Empire Italy, not Germany, was the subject of his dreams. There Emperor and Pope should live in perfect friendship, together wielding a great and undivided power together working God's will on earth.

But while the Emperor was dreaming glorious dreams and building splendid castles in the air, Germany was almost constantly at war. The Poles and Dane had never been at rest since the defeat of Otto II in Italy. The sea-kings of the North again sought the shores of the Baltic, and Sven Forkbeard sailed in his dragon-headed ships far up the German rivers.

The young Emperor now began to march with his armies against these enemies. But although he could use a sword and spear right well he was no born soldier and leader of men. These endless battles with heathen folk soon wearied him. He found no pleasure in long tramps through woods and marshes, in the taking of miserable villages and towns, in the slaughter and destruction of war. He thought that the high title of Emperor called him to something better than this.

So when at length the good Archbishop Willigis told the Emperor that the time had come when he must go to Italy to be crowned, and also to help the Pope to put down the rebellions which had arisen there, Otto went right gladly.

A splendid train of knights and nobles and bishops went with him. But before he reached Rome Otto heard of the death of the Pope. He at once appointed his own cousin, a young man of twenty-four and both learned and fiery-tempered, as the new Pope. This Pope took the title of Gregory V, and he was the first German to sit upon the papal throne.

Gregory V crowned the young Emperor, who was now sixteen, and having put down the rebellions he went back to Germany.

But a year later Otto returned to Rome, for once again that restless city had risen in rebellion. Gregory V was driven from the papal throne, and another Pope crowned in his stead.

Otto reinstated his Pope and punished the rebels with terrible cruelty. The ringleader and many of his followers were beheaded. The false Pope, cruelly mutilated, was led through the streets riding upon a mangy donkey, and was then thrown into a dungeon there to die a slow and painful death.

Gregory V once more sat upon his throne, but not for long. He died suddenly in 999, poisoned, it is thought by the angry Romans. Otto then made a Frenchman named Gerbert, who had been his teacher, Pope.

From now on Otto seemed to forget Germany more and more, seemed more and more to make Italy the centre of all his thoughts. He built a palace for himself there, which even Charles the Great had never thought of doing. He gave his nobles Italian titles and Italian names. All of this little pleased the Germans, who, with their rough tongues, stammered over these high-sounding foreign names. They murmured loudly that the seat of Government should be beyond the Alps. But the Romans were pleased, and they dreamt once more of seeing their beloved city mistress of the world.

Otto loved high state and kingly splendour, and clad himself in magnificent gold and purple robes like Caesar. He ate at a table alone, his dishes were of gold and he was served by great nobles.

But although Otto loved splendour he was a strange mixture. His restless fanciful spirit drove him from change to change. So at times throwing off all state he would humble himself in penance, he would shut himself into a narrow cell, and give himself over to silent thought; or again with bare feet and head would visit the shrine of some saint and martyr.

He was filled with thoughts of the glory of Charles the Great. And, driven by some uncanny curiosity, caused the vault in which he was buried to be opened There, strange to say, the great Emperor still sat in stately death as he had been buried so long before, only the nose had fallen from his face. And when Otto saw the calm old figure sitting so strangely still he threw himself upon his knees in prayer.

Otto caused a golden nose to be put on the old Emperor's face, took a tooth from his mouth as a relic, and shut up the vault once more.

In such strange doings did Otto spend his time during his last short visit to his fatherland. Then he turned again to his beloved Rome.

But again the Romans rose in rebellion. For three days Otto was besieged in his palace, then he fled from the city, never to return.

Otto now sent Henry of Bavaria to Germany to gather an army, while for nearly a year he himself wandered from place to place in Italy. At times he fought, trying to subdue his rebel people. At times he shut himself into some lonely cell, spending his days in fasting and prayer.

But when Henry reached Germany he found the nobles little inclined to march into a foreign land to fight for an Emperor who neglected and despised his own country. So only a very small company gathered at length to their Emperor where he lay sick unto death in the town of Paterno.

This town was all that was left to him of the splendid Empire of his imagination. For his German subjects, through long neglect, had grown weary of him and were ready to choose another Emperor; his Italian subjects were in open revolt.

And here at Paterno, shut out from, but almost within sight of, his beloved Rome, he died, a disappointed broken man, on January 23, 1002. And so ended the great house of Otto.

When he died Otto was scarcely twenty-two. For eighteen years he had borne the title of King. For twelve of these years, others had ruled for him wisely and well. During six he had undone much that they had done; he died leaving his Empire on the verge of ruin.

Otto III had loved Rome and Italy. But as he lay dying he begged that his body might be buried not in Rome but in Aachen, beside the great Emperor Charlemagne. And so the faithful German princes who surrounded him resolved that his wish should be fulfilled. But the whole country was swarming with rebels in arms. Through them the Germans were obliged to cut a path for the dead Emperor with their swords. Day by day they fought around the bier they carried. At length they reached the Alps and passed into German land. In sad procession they marched onward, and at length laid the body of their Emperor to rest in the Cathedral at Aachen, beside that of Charlemagne, as he had desired.

CHAPTER 21

# HENRY II THE HALT

OTTO III had never married, and he left no son to succeed him. There was indeed no near heir to the throne, and at once three of the great princes of the Empire claimed it. These were Henry, Duke of Bavaria, son of Henry the Quarrelsome; Eckard, Marquess of Meissen, the bravest soldier of his time; and Hermann, Duke of Swabia.

The last, Hermann of Swabia, only claimed the throne in a half-hearted way. He was led on by the persuasions of others more than by his own desires, for he was already an old man and cared little about the throne. So the real struggle lay between Henry and Eckard. They were both young and warlike, and they both meant to win.

Even before Otto was buried Henry seized the crown jewels as belonging to him by right of inheritance, for he was related to the royal house. Eckard was not. He could claim nothing by right of inheritance, but he hoped to win support by his fame as a warrior. "He was," says a writer of the time, "the flower of the kingdom, the pillar of the Fatherland, the hope of the people, and the terror of his foes." So he had great hopes of the throne. For after all the right of inheritance counted for little, as the German peoples had never given up their right to choose their ruler. And Eckard was so sure of being chosen that he began keep great state as a king.

But although Eckard had many friends he had enemies too, and one night as he journeyed through the Hartz Mountains these enemies set upon him and slew him. It was never known by whose orders this was done, or who was at the bottom of the plot. It by been suspected, however, that Henry knew of it. If so it leaves a dark blot upon his story. Certain it is the murderers were never punished.

After the death of Eckard the princes of the Empire hesitated no longer, and Henry was chosen and anointed as King. But although Henry was acknowledged a King it did not bring peace to him or to the Empire The weak rule of Otto had left the Empire in confusion. Both within and without were enemies ready to take advantage of that confusion, and many were the battles Henry had to fight ere he could bring order out of disorder.

First upon the East there was the great and warlike Boleslaw, Duke of Poland, surnamed the Glorious. It irked his proud spirit to be a vassal of the Emperor, and he vowed to make himself King of Poland. So again and again he rose in rebellion. Far and wide through the land he swept with his warriors. Against him Henry waged three fierce wars lasting for fourteen years. And in the end, although Boleslaw owned himself a vassal, he was not really conquered. He bowed the knee indeed to the King, paid him indeed an empty show of homage, but for this empty show he received in fief those German lands which he had already conquered and which Henry was powerless to wrest from him. And so, in name a vassal, in reality an independent King, Boleslaw ruled as a tyrant, and none dared oppose him, not even Henry himself.

But besides his war with Poland, Henry had to fight in Italy. Henry did not wish to make Italy the centre of his Empire as Otto III had done. He loved Germany first; he had, however, no mind to lose Italy. But already before the Germans had decided who should be their King, a noble named Arduin of Ivrea had seized the throne of Italy and been crowned at Pavia. So Henry marched across the Alps to wrest the crown from him.

His descent into Italy was rapid and unexpected. Fear seized upon the troops of Arduin and they fled in all directions, and town after town opened their gates to Henry. Almost without striking a blow all Lombardy was conquered. It seemed as if the cause of Arduin was utterly lost, and with solemn ceremony Henry was crowned King of Italy at Pavia.

But as the King and his nobles sat at the feast after the coronation, cries and shouts were heard, and clash of arms. Nearer and nearer came the noise, until at last the palace where the King sat was surrounded by a furious mob, and a hail of stones and arrows crashed and rattled upon its walls. It was Arduin's followers who had rallied and who now attacked the new-crowned King.

A fierce fight followed. Night came on, but still the fight lasted. Then, in order to see and the better to defend the palace, the Germans set fire to some of the houses near. So, lit up with the glare of burning houses, the battle raged all through the night. But the town was mostly built of wood, and from street to street the fire leaped with devouring fury, until Pavia was a sea of flames. From burning street to burning street the battle surged and swayed, and those who escaped the sword fell fearful victims to the flames.

At length even the palace was alight, and the King only saved himself by leaping from a window. He fell, hurt his thigh, and all his life after he limped, so that he was called Henry the Halt.

When morning came it showed a fearful sight. The royal city of Lombardy was a heap of ashes, and among the charred and blackened ruins thousands of its citizens lay dead. Those who still lived, the victorious Germans hunted and slew mercilessly, until at length the King bade the slaughter cease.

For ten days Henry stayed by the smoking ruins of the once splendid city. And there to him in fear and trembling came messengers and hostages from many a rebel lord. For the burning of Pavia had struck terror to the hearts of the people. Fear conquered them. The Italians bowed the knee to their German master, but they had no love for him, and when a few weeks later he recrossed the Alps he was followed by the curses of the people.

Arduin, who had fled before Henry, was not yet subdued. Scarcely had the King recrossed the Alps when once more Arduin appeared, and the people began to flock to him. But many remained true to Henry, and so there were two kings in Italy.

Eight years later, however, Henry once more marched into Italy. And now, as before, in terror at his coming the people forsook Arduin, and towns and cities yielded to the German. Even Arduin humbled himself, and offered to do homage to Henry as his King, and to give up his claim to the crown of Italy in return for a countship.

But Henry now paid no heed to Arduin and marched onward victoriously to Rome. There on February 14, 1013, he was crowned as Emperor. Then, having once more received the homage of the people, and set the affairs of Italy in order, Henry returned homeward.

But again, as soon as he was gone, rebellion broke out. This time, however, Arduin found his friends were few, his enemies many. Weary of the struggle, sick in mind and body, he fled to a monastery. There he laid down the crown and sceptre, shaved his head, and became a monk. And there, little more than a year later, he died.

Henceforward Henry was undisputed King of Italy. He took the title of King of the Romans. And after this all the German kings took this title until they received that of Emperor.

But although Henry took the title of King of the Romans, he did not try to make Rome the capital of his Empire, as Otto had done. Aachen was his capital, and to the Court at Aachen Italian nobles came to attend the Parliament of the Empire, and do homage to their King.

On the western boundaries of the kingdom Henry had also to fight. There was war with Flanders, there was fighting in Luxemburg, but chiefly there was war with Burgundy.

The King of Burgundy, Rudolph III, was Henry's uncle. He had no children, and Henry was looked upon as heir to the throne. But Henry was not content with that, he wished to add Burgundy to the Empire at once. Rudolph was weak and yielding, and was quite ready to give up his throne to his nephew. But the nobles of Burgundy were angry, and rose in arms against Henry. And although Henry twice led an army into Burgundy, he could not conquer the proud Burgundian nobles. At last he was forced to make peace, to give up all claim to the throne during his uncle's lifetime, and content himself with the promise of it at his death.

Besides all these wars upon the borders of his empire Henry had many battles to fight within its borders. For noble after noble rebelled. It was not only the great dukes, as in the time of Otto the Great, who rebelled, but many lesser nobles too rose, eager to show defiance to the Emperor. And so for twenty years Henry ruled, sword in hand. Yet in Henry's reign the meetings of the Parliament or Diet were frequent. For Henry found that it was no longer possible for him to rule by his own will alone as Otto the Great had done. The nobles had grown so powerful that he was forced to ask their advice in all the great affairs of the nation.

But as a check on the ever-growing power of the nobles Henry tried to increase the power of the clergy. He gave great gifts to the Church, and half the land in Germany now belonged to it. He was himself, too, very good and pious, and when he died he was made a saint.

For the time being the power of the clergy seemed to safeguard the King against the power of the nobles; but in the long run the clergy became as dangerous to the crown as the nobles; and in later times, when the Pope and the Emperor quarrelled, the clergy nearly always took the side of the Pope.

Henry's last war led him again into Italy. He went to fight the Greeks and Saracens, who again and again attacked, and who had now gained possession of much of Southern Italy. Henry won victories and took towns from these foes, but he was not able quite to drive them out of the country. For the summer came on, plague and sickness attacked his northern soldiers, unused to the heat of Italy, and with a sorely diminished army the Emperor turned homeward.

But although the Greeks and Saracens still harboured in Southern

Italy, the North and middle were at peace, and secure to the Empire. Germany too was at peace within, when on July 13, 1024, Henry died after a reign of twenty-three years as King, and eleven as Emperor—a reign filled with many wars. He was the last of the Saxon Emperors, for he left no son to succeed him on the throne.

## CHAPTER 22

# CONRAD II

HENRY II died and left no heir to the throne; and so the lords and freemen of the Empire gathered together to choose a new ruler. On a great plain in the broad valley of the Rhine, between the towns of Mainz and Worms, they met. It was a glittering assembly. Dukes and bishops, nobles great and small, knights and freemen all mingled together. The plain was white with their tents, and the autumn sun glowed warmly upon many-coloured banners and rich robes, and was reflected in a thousand shining points from helmet and hauberk.

Earnestly the nobles talked together. Now one or another of their number was proposed and rejected. One seemed too old, another too young, another lacking in valour or in wisdom. At length the choice was narrowed down to two. They were princes of the noble house of Franconia, both brave men, and both named Conrad. To distinguish them one from another the one was called Conrad the Elder and the other Conrad the Younger.

It seemed as if most would choose Conrad the Elder, for he was a strong and fearless man, generous and wise, and skilled in every knightly art. Yet some hesitated, for Conrad the Younger was very powerful. He himself had great hopes of the throne, and there was danger of strife between the two parties.

Then Conrad the Elder took his young cousin aside, and spoke to him long and earnestly. "Let us not quarrel," he said. "If by the voice of the people you are chosen King, I will not try by any treachery or lying to turn that fortune away from you. I will, indeed, rejoice more than any other. But should I be chosen, I do not doubt that you on your side will rejoice with me."

"That is my desire," answered Conrad the Younger; "and if you are chosen I promise, my dear cousin, to honour you as my King."

At these words Conrad the Elder bent down and kissed his cousin tenderly. And when the princes and nobles who had looked on at a distance while the cousins talked saw that, they rejoiced greatly. The news that the cousins had come to a friendly understanding spread like lightning through the camp. The nobles resolved to hesitate no longer, but to put an end to all doubt and choose a King. In a huge circle stood the nobles and freemen, the prelates and knights, behind them, row upon row, thronged the eager people. A tense silence of expectation fell upon them, only the rustle of the wind in the trees was heard.

Then into the open space stepped the Archbishop of Mainz, clad in splendid robes. He raised his hand, and in a clear and sonorous voice he cried, "I, Aribo, Archbishop of Mainz, do choose Conrad the Elder to be my Lord and King, to be the leader and protector of our Fatherland."

After him followed, one by one, the bishops and abbots, and, as with one voice, they chose Conrad the Elder to be their King.

Then first of all the nobles Conrad the Younger sprang forth, and in his ringing boyish voice he cried, "I choose Conrad for my King and Lord."

Then Conrad, with a joyful smile, stretched out his hand to his young and generous cousin, and drew him to his side.

The die was cast, the choice was made. Noble after noble stepped from his place and made known his will. To Conrad the Elder every vote was given.

Cheer upon cheer broke the stillness, and with thundering applause the people greeted their new King. Then Kunigunde, the widowed Empress, stepped into the open space. In her hands she carried the crown, and sceptre, and kingly jewels. These she presented to Conrad, vowing in noble words to honour him as her King.

And thus the crown of Germany passed from the house of Saxony to the house of Franconia.

In joyful haste the chosen King was hurried to the Cathedral of Mainz, there to be crowned. All along the way the people thronged about him, shouting and rejoicing. The priests marched before him chanting hymns of praise and thanksgiving. Never in the memory of man had there been such a gladsome scene. Had Charles the Great returned to earth in all his might and glory he could hardly have been received with greater joy, it was said.

But as the procession passed merrily along, three poorly-clad, miserable figures thrust their way through the glittering throng of knights and nobles who surrounded the King. They were a peasant, a widow, and an orphan, who, casting themselves at the King's feet, cried aloud for justice.

The nobles would have thrust them forth, angry that they should disturb the King at such a moment. But Conrad forbade it. He commanded the procession to stop until he had heard the complaint of the poor people.

Provoked at the interruption, one of the bishops urged Conrad to hurry on to the Cathedral. But the King answered him calmly, "How often have you said to me that not the hearer of the law but the doer is blessed? It is a heavy office that I have taken up, and surely I must walk in the paths of righteousness." So he refused to move from the spot until he had judged the cause of these poor and needy folk.

And it seemed to the people that happy days must be dawning for them when their King began his reign with deeds of mercy, when he seemed more eager to do justice to the oppressed than to adorn himself with robes and crowns.

The whole Empire, however, did not at once accept Conrad as ruler. As soon as Henry II died the bold and rebellious Duke of Poland at once threw off all pretence of vassalage, and proclaimed himself King of Poland. He would not bend the knee to Conrad, but in little more than a year he died. He was succeeded by his son Mesco, who also took the title of King. Conrad looked upon this as rebellion, and war began.

But it was only after many defeats and much bitter warfare that Poland was again subdued. At length, however, Mesco was forced to submit, and although his heart was still filled with hatred to the Germans he gave up his title of King and swore to be Conrad's faithful vassal. Soon afterwards he died. Then the land was torn asunder by civil wars. Noble fought against noble, town against town, until the land was filled with blood and ashes, and the kingdom which Boleslaw the Glorious had built up was scattered to the winds.

There was trouble too in Italy, and plots to seize the throne there. But they came to nothing. It 1026 Conrad was crowned King of Italy, and a year later Emperor in Rome.

It was a very grand ceremony, and among the glittering throng of kings and nobles there was Canute the Great, King of England and of Denmark, and also Rudolph III, King of Burgundy.

With Canute the Great Conrad had made friends and had even given up to him the Mark of Schleswig which Henry I had wrested from the Danes. And to make the friendship more secure, Canute married his daughter Gunhilda to Conrad's young son Henry.

Rudolph III, too, was friendly, although at first he had been unwilling to recognise Conrad as his heir, for he said he had promised his throne to

Henry II personally, and not to the King of the Germans. But Conrad had no mind to give up Burgundy, and he forced Rudolph to acknowledge him as his heir. And when in 1032 Rudolph died Conrad took possession of his kingdom. This included the land we now call Switzerland, and the valley of the Rhone, right to the Mediterranean.

Thus Switzerland became, and remained for many a long day, part of the German Empire. But the Emperor had really little sway over the country. For the nobles were very powerful, and they ruled the land much as they liked.

It is well to remember that this kingdom of Burgundy did not include the Duchy of Burgundy. That belonged to the French King.

Of all Conrad's enemies his stepson, Ernst of Swabia, was perhaps the most dangerous and troublesome. He thought that he had a better right to the throne of Burgundy than had Conrad, and so, soon after Conrad came to the throne of Germany, Ernst rose in rebellion. He was joined by many other nobles, among them Conrad the Younger. For he very quickly regretted his generous deed on the day of election, and quarrelled with the King.

Conrad, however, easily overcame this rebellion. One after another the conspirators fell away from their comrades. Duke Ernst came to the King and humbly begged forgiveness, others crept away to their castles in fear of his wrath.

Conrad forgave Ernst and his companions, but it was not long before they rebelled a second time, and many others who feared the Emperor too much to rebel openly, joined them in secret. Among these were his nearest relatives, even his mother.

Now Conrad, seeing the danger in which he stood, called a Parliament to Augsburg, and commanded Duke Ernst to appear before him to answer for his deeds.

Ernst came, but in no humble mood. He came full of insolence and pride. He was ready to treat with the Emperor as with an equal, to bargain for the throne of Burgundy. And if the Emperor did not willingly give all he wanted, he trusted to the swords of his many followers to win it for him.

But when at length the Duke's vassals understood that he had called them to arms to fight against their Emperor, many of them refused to obey him.

"We do not deny," they said, "that we have sworn an oath of fealty to you, that we have sworn to fight for you against every foe. But our faith to our lord the King and Emperor is the highest protector of our freedom. If we fight against him we forfeit our freedom, which is the one thing a brave man will fight for to his last breath. Ask us to do what is right and honourable, and we will obey you. Ask more than that, and we are free of our oath, and we will return every man to the Emperor, who is above us all."

Such being the mind of his vassals, Duke Ernst saw no hope for his cause. So he yielded, and threw himself upon the Emperor's mercy. This time the rebel was not so lightly forgiven, but was cast into prison.

Others too yielded. Some were deprived of all their lands and imprisoned, Conrad the Younger among them. Others were forced to become monks. But Count Werner of Kiburg, Duke Ernst's greatest friend, would not yield. For three months he held out in his castle of Kiburg, and when at length the castle was taken he escaped.

But although Conrad punished the rebels severely he did not long nurse his wrath against them. Many were soon again set at liberty, among them Conrad the Younger, who ever after remained true to the throne. Even Duke Ernst was given his freedom, and the Emperor promised to return to him his dukedom if he would betray his friend Werner and deliver him up to justice.

But Ernst proudly refused to betray the friend who had shared every danger and hardship with him. In vain Conrad pleaded with him. "It is your twofold duty," he said. "As my son I command you no more to keep company with your father's bitterest enemy. As a German Prince I command you never more to harbour a disturber of the peace."

"Call it what you will," cried Ernst wrathfully, "it is not faith, it is not friendship, it is not gratitude. All forbid me to do this thing. I am not yet so broken down by long imprisonment as thus to betray my only friend."

In wrath Conrad replied. Then with still more bitter words of scorn and anger Ernst hastily left the Emperor's presence, followed by a few companions.

This haughty refusal to do his will roused the Emperor's anger against Duke Ernst more than all his rebellion. He deprived him for ever of his dukedom; he proclaimed him to be an outlaw and enemy of his country; he caused him to be excommunicated. Even the Empress was forced to give up her misguided son, and in the presence of the assembled nobles she swore solemnly never to avenge any ill that might befall him, never to punish any one who might lift up his hand against him.

And now, forsaken by all, with the hand of every man against him, Ernst joined his one remaining friend Werner. Together they fled to the wildest district of the Black Forest. Here they gained possession of a fortress, high perched upon a stony height, and here for several months they lived a wild life of raid and robbery, defying the laws of the Empire.

But not for long were these outlawed nobles left to lead their lawless life. The news of their deeds soon reached Conrad, and ere long the outlaws found their castle surrounded by soldiers of the Empire.

The rock-bound fortress was too strong to storm, so Count Mangold, who led the Emperor's troops, resolved to starve the outlaws into surrender. But rather than die like wild animals caught in a trap, they made up their minds to make a desperate dash for freedom, and die, if need be, sword in hand. So from their rocky fortress the gallant little band of desperate warriors sallied forth. A terrible struggle followed. Like a very angel of death Werner smote with his sword. It flashed and fell now on this side, now on that, until the foe lay in heaps about him, and the ground was sodden with blood.

Like a lion at bay fought Ernst. For he and his few comrades had nothing to lose. They sought but to sell their lives as dearly as might be.

So stubbornly did the little band of outlaws fight, that for long the victory seemed doubtful. They were, however, far outnumbered by the Emperor's soldiers, and in the end numbers told. But not till Duke Ernst, Count Werner, and nearly every man of their comrades lay among the dead did the fighting cease. Thus ended the greatest rebellion of King Conrad's reign.

But the common folk had loved Duke Ernst. In their hearts they took sides with him against his stern step-father and Emperor. Now they grieved for him, and made great tales about his sorrows and his bravery. For hundreds of years minstrels sang of his great deeds and of the love that there was between him and Count Werner. So all through the ages his memory has lasted, and the Song of Duke Ernst is one of the great poems of old German literature.

With a strong hand Conrad curbed the pride of the nobles, and wrought peace in the land.

Towards the end of his reign there were once more disturbances in Italy, and a second time he crossed the Alps to quiet the unruly Italians. For so long as he remained in Italy the fear of his might and wrath subdued them.

It was while Conrad was in Italy that he issued a famous Edict. By this Edict he proclaimed that all fiefs should be heritable, and descend from father to son. He also decreed that no overlord should dispossess a vassal of his fief for any cause, except by the judgment of his peers. And should the vassal consider himself wrongfully treated he was given the right of appeal to the Emperor. This law was meant to curb the power of the great nobles and help the lesser vassals by making them feel that the Emperor was their friend, and mightier than their overlords. At first this law only held good in Italy, but it soon extended to Germany, and greatly strengthened the Emperor's power there. Conrad also befriended the burghers, and did all he could to make them look upon their Emperor as their protector against the tyranny of the nobles. In this way too he strengthened the power of the Crown.

About two years after Conrad's last visit to Italy he died. We are not quite sure of his age, but he was about forty when he was chosen as Emperor. He had reigned fourteen years.

CHAPTER 23

# HENRY III THE BLACK

A week after Conrad died his cousin and rival, Conrad the Younger, also died. Of all the great house of Conrad there remained only one—Henry, the young son of Emperor Conrad.

The right of choosing the Emperor lay with the nobles of the Empire. But in his lifetime Conrad had done all he could to make the throne hereditary in his family. During his lifetime Henry had already been chosen and crowned King of Germany and of Burgundy, and he now succeeded to the throne without any trouble.

Henry was only twenty-two, but from a child he had been trained in all the duties of a King, as well as in all the knightly arts and learning of the times. So when he came to the throne he was more fit to rule than many an older man. He was humble and good, yet noble, brave, yet peace-loving, wise, yet willing to listen to the advice of others.

Like his father, Henry was tall—a head and shoulders above his fellows, it is said. But his handsome face was so dark that he is called Henry the Black. He was a gallant soldier and a fervent Christian. Often on the field of battle he was seen to kneel in prayer. Dressed in kingly splendour, surrounded by pomp, he dashed proudly over the battle-field. But when a victory had been won he never failed to give thanks to God. Barefoot, then, and clad in a hair shirt, he went from church to church, giving praise and humble thanks to the Lord of Battles.

In every way Henry seemed fitted to be Emperor, so no one challenged his right to the throne. But although so far as the Emperor was concerned there was peace, the land was not really at rest. For the great nobles were constantly quarrelling among themselves, and the whole kingdom was full of bloodshed and robbery from their private wars.

It was now that in the neighbouring kingdom of France the Truce of God was proclaimed. By this men were forbidden to fight from Wednesday evening until Monday morning, all through the year, and during Lent and Advent they were altogether forbidden to fight. It was not the King of France but the churchmen of France who first instituted this law, and they chose those special days and times for peace because they were the days and times upon which He who had come to bring peace and goodwill on earth had suffered and died.

Henry saw what good the Truce of God worked in France, and he resolved to command a like peace in his own kingdom. In October of 1048 he called his nobles together in Constance. There upon the fourth day of the assembly, when they were all gathered in the Cathedral, the King, accompanied by a bishop, went to the high altar. Standing there he spoke long and fervently to the people, urging them to forgive their enemies and live in peace together. "I as King," he said, "will show you the example and forgive all those who have done aught against me." This he solemnly did. Then by persuasions and by threats he forced the assembled nobles to follow his example.

After this through all his Empire, on both sides of the Alps, he proclaimed the King's Peace, commanding his subjects everywhere to cease from private feuds and warfare.

And so great had the power of the Emperor become that everywhere he was obeyed. Over the land there spread a peace such as had never been known before, such as was not to be known again for many long years. And in this peace the land prospered. The peasant tilled the fields at ease, and the merchant passed through the land without fear.

But it was not alone in worldly things that Henry showed his power. He showed it too in things of the Church. He was a good and pious man, and he saw with pain and grief the evil ways into which the highest churchmen had fallen. He saw bishoprics and archbishoprics and all the high offices of the Church given, not to men best fitted for them, but sold to the highest bidder. He saw the most hallowed office of all—the office of Pope—sold by one wicked Pope to another for a thousand pounds of silver. He saw three Popes at one time all fighting for the sacred throne. Such things filled him with horror, and he resolved to end them.

Already he had made a law that throughout the whole Empire no priestly office should henceforth be bought or sold, and that any one doing so should henceforth be excommunicated. Now, when he heard of the shameful struggle in Rome, of three Popes all fighting for the sacred throne, he set out for Italy resolved to cleanse the Church from so much wickedness.

At Sutri a great Synod was called together, and all three Popes were deposed, even Gregory VI, who was the best of them. For it was he who had bought the office for a thousand pounds in silver. And although he had meant to use his power well, he had won it sinfully, and was adjudged unworthy to hold it. He was now made to speak his own condemnation. "I, Bishop Gregory," he said, "the servant of the servants of God, declare that, because of the abominable barter and simony which have crept into my election I must be deposed from the bishopric of Rome. Is that your opinion?" he asked, turning to the bishops.

"It is," they replied.

Then Gregory stepped down from the papal throne, and taking his robe strongly in both hands he tore it asunder as a sign that he gave up his office.

All three popes being thus deposed, they were banished from Rome. Gregory sought a refuge in Germany, and with him went a monk named Hildebrand, the son of a poor carpenter. It is well to remember his name, for we shall hear more of him.

Henry now elected a new Pope. He was a German, and a man of holy life, a man as eager as Henry himself to see the Church kept pure. But he did not live long. When he died Henry, however, chose another Pope, also a German. It gives us some idea of Henry's power when we remember that he elected no fewer than four Popes one after the other. Two were relatives of his own, and all were Germans.

In the meantime Clement II, as the new Pope was called, crowned and anointed Henry as Emperor. It was on Christmas Day 1046 that the ceremony took place. And never since Charlemagne had been crowned on the same day nearly 250 years before had a German Emperor been received so joyfully. It was not only the German nobles who acclaimed him, the Roman citizens too joined their voices to the general applause. What Otto I had wrung from them by force they gave to Henry III gladly.

Besides taking the title of Emperor Henry revived the old title of Patrician, and almost always wore a green mantle and a golden band about his brows as signs of his office.

Henry was now at the very height of his power, and he was not yet thirty years of age. He was the most powerful ruler in Europe, and the Pope was his vassal. But his brilliant reign did not pass altogether without war. One bitter enemy he had within the Empire, and that was Duke Gottfried Longbeard.

Gottfried was the son of Gozelo, Duke of Lorraine. Already during his father's lifetime he had received the title of Duke, and never doubted that at his father's death he would receive the whole dukedom as his inheritance. But, it is said, the old Duke wished otherwise, and before his death he begged Henry to divide the duchy, as it had been before, into Upper and Lower Lorraine, giving half to his younger son Gozelo.

Henry was glad of anything which might lessen the power of the great nobles. So he willingly consented, and when the old Duke died in 1044 he divided his duchy, giving Gottfried Upper, and Gozelo the Lazy Lower Lorraine.

But Gottfried had no mind to lose half of his inheritance. He appeared before the King, and with hot and angry words demanded the whole of his father's dukedom. The King would not listen, and Gottfried left the Court in wrath, vowing to regain by the sword what had been taken from him.

But Henry had no mind to leave this unruly vassal unpunished. Gottfried was accused of high treason, and commanded to appear before the Emperor to answer for his misdeeds.

Gottfried came, and was condemned to the loss of his dukedom and to imprisonment. And when in a short time he was set free he was obliged to leave his son as hostage.

This treatment, far from breaking Gottfried's spirit, turned him into the Emperor's bitterest enemy. Soon through all Lorraine he marched slaying the people and burning the towns in vengeance.

But Henry, too, marched into the land, and ere long Gottfried was utterly defeated, and forced to flee for his life. Then, though wrath still burned in his heart, Gottfried, seeing no help for it, yielded to Henry. One day as the young King sat upon his throne the worn and hunted rebel, already a grey-haired man, appeared before him. He demanded justice. He demanded that his cause should be judged by his peers, the princes of the realm.

He had his wish. But once more the sentence went against him, and he was adjudged a rebel, and condemned to be imprisoned. So he was cast into the strong tower of the castle Giebichenstein, the same tower in which once Duke Ernst had been confined.

Next year, however, Gozelo the Lazy died. This softened the King's heart towards Gottfried, and he set him free. Gottfried thought that he would now be given the whole of his dukedom once more. So he bowed his proud head, and with every appearance of sorrow and penitence he threw himself at Henry's feet begging forgiveness.

Henry forgave him, and restored to him his dukedom of Upper Lorraine, but Lower Lorraine he gave to another.

That was too much for Gottfried to bear. Every sign of sorrow vanished from his heart. He resolved on revenge, and he only waited for the right moment to come.

Soon it came. Henry went to Italy, and while he was gone Gottfried plotted with the nobles of Lorraine, with the King of France, and with the Dukes of Flanders and of Holland. Then soon after the Emperor returned a great rebellion burst forth. Through all the land Gottfried marched, fighting and destroying, burning palaces and cathedrals, cottages and farms, till the people fled in terror at his approach.

When Henry heard of it he marched against Gottfried, proclaimed him an outlaw, and once more deposed him from his dukedom. Then fiercer than ever burned Gottfried's wrath against the Emperor, more furiously still he raged through the land.

But he could not long withstand the might of the Emperor. Excommunicated by the Church, outlawed by the State, forsaken by many of his friends, he at last threw himself once more upon the King's mercy. Henry granted him his life, but cast him into prison.

And now, once again in prison, under the curse of the Church, Gottfried's proud spirit seemed to be broken. He gave himself up to penance and good works, and openly declared his sorrow for his rebellion.

Then Henry, willing to believe in his repentance, once more set Gottfried free and, to show his trust, sent him to fight against the Duke of Flanders. But Gottfried had no heart to fight against his old friend, and the war had little success.

Two or three years went past, Gottfried, deposed and neglected, leading a miserable life at the Court of Henry. At length one day he quietly slipped away and sped over the Alps to Italy.

There lived Beatrix, a Princess of Lorraine, the widow of a powerful Italian count who had been lately murdered. She saw herself and her children surrounded by enemies. She wanted a brave man to protect her and them. And so when Gottfried, a noble of her own country, appeared, she gladly married him. For, rebel though he was, he was still one of the bravest soldiers of his day.

Thus the Emperor's great enemy became the most powerful prince in Italy. Among a people always ready to revolt he might with ease stir up rebellion. To the Emperor this was plain. And when in the following year Henry once more journeyed to Italy, Gottfried knew well that it was against him he had come. So he did not wait to meet the Emperor but fled away to Flanders.

Beatrix, however, felt that she had done nothing but what she had a right to do, and so, taking her little daughter with her, she boldly went to meet the Emperor.

But Henry was full of wrath against Gottfried. He bitterly reproached Beatrix with having married, without his knowledge and counsel, an enemy of the Empire. He forbade her to leave the Court, so, a guest in seeming—in truth a prisoner—she was forced to follow the Emperor back to Germany.

And thus a prisoner she remained until Gottfried again made his peace with Henry. And now the Emperor's mood was softened. This time no punishment fell upon the fiery, untamed vassal. He received back his wife and step-daughter, and was allowed to depart in peace.

It was not until after Henry's death, however, that Gottfried received again his dukedom, for which he had fought so hard.

Besides Henry's long strife with Gottfried he had to put down rebellions in Burgundy and in Bohemia. But the great war of his reign was carried on against Hungary.

King Stephen of Hungary, also known as St. Stephen; had made the people Christian, and had done much for the land. But when he died the people drove his nephew, King Peter, from the throne. He in his need fled to Henry begging for help.

Henry granted him the aid he asked for, and set him upon the throne again. But in return he made him give up to Germany all the land as far as the March and the Leithe which had once before belonged to Germany. He was also forced to acknowledge the overlordship of the Emperor, and accept his throne as a fief of Germany.

Before all the assembled people King Peter came to Henry with a golden lance in his hand. This he gave to the Emperor, and with it he gave his kingdom. Then with solemn ceremony Henry restored again his kingdom to Peter, but only as a fief of Germany. Thus did Henry add yet another kingdom to his already great Empire.

The wild Hungarians, however, were little minded to be under the rule of mild King Peter, or to be vassals of the Empire. In little more than a year they burst forth in fierce revolt against their King, and against this Christian religion. Churches were destroyed, priests were slain with many horrible cruelties. King Peter was first blinded and then banished from the land, and the pagan Andreas set upon the throne.

But in spite of this wild revolt Andreas soon saw that only a Christian could wear the crown of St. Stephen, and it was not long ere he made his peace with the Church. He found himself forced, too, to bow to the Emperor, and receive his kingdom from his hand. Yet Andreas was no obedient vassal, such as King Peter had been, and again and again during the last years of his reign Henry marched into Hungary, in a vain endeavour to quell Andreas and his unruly people.

Henry's reign had been brilliant and successful, but now troubles gathered thick about him. The princes had grown weary of his stern rule, and many of them rose against him. Revolts and wars beset him on every side, defeat instead of victory followed his armies. In the midst of these troubles he fell ill and died. He was only thirty-eight, and had worn the crown for nearly seventeen years

CHAPTER 24

# HENRY IV

HENRY III was one of the greatest of German rulers. Never perhaps has the power of the Empire stood higher than in his days, but unfortunately he left a child only six years old to succeed him.

Already in his father's lifetime the baby Prince had been chosen and crowned as King, so now he succeeded without opposition, and his mother the Empress Agnes was chosen as Regent. This was not the fair-haired English Princess Gunhilda to whom you remember Henry had been married as a boy. She had died before he became King, and later he married the beautiful and wealthy French Princess Agnes of Poitiers.

But although the little King succeeded without opposition his throne was surrounded by many dangers. For with only a child and a woman to withstand them, the powerful, discontented nobles now saw their chance of gaining all they desired. Soon the Court was full of plots and conspiracies, the land of desperate feuds and bloodshed.

The Empress tried to make friends with the unruly nobles by giving them lands and money. But she could not buy their faith, she only made them more powerful against the Crown. Every man sought his own greatness not that of the Empire. There was not one among the selfish, grasping crowd that the Empress could trust. But her greatest enemy, the soul of all the plots, was Hanno, Archbishop of Cologne. He was a man of low degree, but he was wily, haughty, and greedy of power. And when the little King was about twelve years old he decided to get possession of him.

Henry and his mother were staying at Kaiserswerth on the Rhine, when one day Archbishop Hanno and his friends, together with a great company of soldiers, came sailing down the Rhine in a splendid ship.

They had come, it seemed, to pay the King a friendly visit. The Queen received them courteously, and made a great feast for them. The meal was right merry, every one was in the gayest of moods, for the April sun shone brightly, and spring was in the air.

After dinner Hanno asked the King if he would like to come on board his ship, and see all the fine things there. The King was delighted. It was just what he longed for, and without more ado they set off for the ship.

By the way Hanno and his friends smiled and jested with the King. But once on board all was different, their faces grew stern, orders were shouted, men hurried to and fro, and the ship steered out into midstream.

It seemed to the little King as if he were forgotten. His heart sank. These big, splendidly dressed men who a few minutes before had been his friends, were changed. Suddenly he knew them to be his enemies. He was afraid of their stern faces, afraid of their sharp swords. He felt sure they meant to kill him, and with a scream of wild terror he leaped over the side of the ship into the river.

The Rhine is deep and very swift, and the King was borne rapidly down stream. His death seemed certain. A cry of fear and anger rose from the ship. But quick as thought Count Ekbert, one of Hanno's companions, sprang into the water. He was a strong swimmer, manfully he battled with the stream, and at length he reached the boy, and, well-nigh exhausted with the effort, dragged. him on board the ship.

At once the little King was surrounded, made much of, flattered and coaxed. And in spite of his struggles and entreaties the ship was rapidly rowed up stream. The Empress upon the balcony of her palace wept and cried aloud in grief, and followed the ship with streaming eyes. For a long way, too, it was accompanied by crowds of angry people who ran along the bank cursing the robbers. But tears and curses were alike in vain, and the little King was borne away.

Hanno's plot was quite successful. The Empress, though she wept and wrung her hands, made no effort to get her son back again. Her spirit was utterly broken. She was tired of the troubles and hardships of ruling. So she went away to live quietly on her own estates, and took no further share in the government.

Hanno would now have liked to become Regent. But the other bishops had no desire that he alone should have the power. So it was proposed that the King should live with each Bishop of the kingdom in turn, and that the Bishop where he stayed should be Regent for the time being.

Thus it was arranged. But it was nearly always with friends of Hanno that the King lived. The King, however, hated Hanno, for he could never forget how he had stolen him from his mother. So he did all he could to make friends with another powerful man, Adalbert, Archbishop of Bremen. Of noble birth, he was even more haughty than Hanno, and no less greedy of power.

Adalbert taught the King much that was wicked; he also gave way to his evil passion and flattered him. So Henry liked him much better than the coarse and stern Hanno, who made him do his will. The two Archbishops pretended to be friends, but really they hated each other, for each wanted all the power. "Their tongues spoke friendship," says a writer of the time, "but their hearts fought against each other in deadly hate."

So between them the King grew up with bitterness and mistrust in his heart.

Thus the years passed, the King remaining ever in the power of one or other of these greedy, self-seeking prelates. But at length, when he was fifteen, Henry was declared to be of age to rule. He was made a knight, a sword was girt about him, and a staff of office placed in his hand.

It was chiefly Adalbert who brought this about. For he believed that he had gained such power over the young King that he would now be able to do as he liked with him. But he was mistaken, he was soon thrust from power and died in misery.

And now Henry began to show that he would be no King in leading-strings, but that he indeed meant to rule. One of the first things he determined to do was to tame the Saxons, who were in a state of wild revolt. In order the better to do this he built strong castles throughout the land, and filled them with soldiers. But such terrible deeds were done in these castles—the King's soldiers harried the country, and oppressed the people so brutally—that the whole of Saxony, princes and people alike, rose in revolt like one man.

With an army 60,000 strong they marched against the King. The castle where he was was strongly built, and perched upon a high hill. The path up to it was steep and difficult. Behind it stretched a vast uninhabited forest, crossed and recrossed by a wilderness of narrow pathways.

The castle was too strong to take by storm, but the rebels lay around watching every outlet, for well they knew that they had the King in a trap, and that soon hunger would make him yield.

But the King too saw that. He knew that his only safety lay in flight, and he resolved to escape.

The rebels kept a strict and constant watch; but it was impossible to guard all the many paths through the forest, and by the forest the King made up his mind to escape.

A huntsman who knew every path in it promised to behis guide. Then one August night, with a few followers, he silently and secretly left the castle. Before he left he gave the castle into the keeping of his faithful soldiers, and bade them pretend to the enemy that he was still there, and hold the castle against them as long as possible. Then, with a last murmured farewell, the little company slipped silently away, and were swallowed up in the darkness of the wood.

For three days they wandered by unknown paths without food or shelter. One behind the other along the narrow ways they went, in anxious dread, now pausing to listen, now hurrying onward. In every thicket they feared to see the lurking foe. Even the rustle of the wind in the trees, or the cry of some wild beast, startled them.

But at length, on the fourth day, worn out by hunger and want of sleep, utterly exhausted by the long tramp, they reached a small town in safety. Here they refreshed themselves with food and sleep. Next day they set out again, and at length reached the Abbey of Hersfeld.

Henry now called upon the princes of the Empire to gather their vassals, and march with him against the rebel Saxons. But the princes refused to come. They would fight against the enemies of the Empire, they said, but not against their brothers and comrades.

This answer filled Henry with bitter wrath, but he was helpless. His very crown seemed in danger, and he could do naught to save it. Hated and despised by all, there was none to whom he could turn for help.

Sick at heart, worn out by disappointments and hardships, he fell ill. For some days it seemed as if he would die. The princes waited, hoping that he might, for his death would end the strife. But Henry did not die. Quickly he recovered, and wearily he set forth once more upon his journey towards Worms, a town he knew to be still true to him. And now it was that Henry, forsaken by the nobles, found help in the burghers and townsfolk.

The Emperors Conrad II and Henry III had befriended the towns, and protected them against the greed and oppression of the nobles. As a result the merchants and townsfolk had grown rich and prosperous. Now they repaid the friendship which the Emperors had shown them. First Worms declared for Henry. The citizens there armed themselves and flocked to his banner, and one after another many rich and prosperous towns followed this example. Once more Henry had an army.

Meanwhile the Saxons had been doing as they would. They took and razed to the ground many of Henry's castles, shouting with joy as these signs of tyranny disappeared. But they did not stop there. They were mad with a desire of vengeance, and in their madness they sacked and burned the churches, they desecrated the churchyards, and scattered the ashes of the dead to the winds.

These deeds of violence lost the Saxons many friends. The Saxon nobles, too, were no longer all united, some of them went over to the King's side. And when at last Henry marched against the rebels he had an army behind him such as had never been seen before.

The Saxons were cowed. Willingly now would they have made peace. But it was too late; Henry's wrath was kindled against them, and war he would have.

At Langensalza a great battle was fought. It was a terrible fight. The foes dashed upon each other with fury. Their spears were shivered to atoms. Then they gripped their swords, and it became a hand-to-hand fight. It was with swords that the Saxons were most used to fight, and often they went to battle with two or three girt about them, and they used them with so much skill and strength that their enemies were filled with admiration as much as with fear. Right good service now they did, many a marvellous sword stroke was given, many a brave deed was done.

At twelve the battle began, at nine it still raged fiercely, the victory still uncertain.

But at length the Saxons wavered, they turned, they fled. The victory was the King's.

In wild triumph the victors pursued the fleeing foe. They sought shelter in their camp. There was none there; for the pursuers were upon their heels and drove them forth. And so for many miles the flight and pursuit lasted, all the way red with blood and strewn with dead and dying. At length night put an end to the slaughter, and the victors returned to plunder the rebel camp. There they found such costly food and drink, such rich clothing, so much gold and silver, that it seemed to them as if the Saxons must have come forth, not to do battle, but to feast.

The victory was complete. With one blow Henry was again master of his kingdom. But even in the moment of victory sorrow was great, for it had been a fight of German against German. And when among the dead, men found their fathers and brothers and best-loved friends, joy was turned into mourning.

Yet Henry rejoiced more than he sorrowed. And when a few months later the hated Hanno died he rejoiced still more. Now at length he could think without shame of that day when he had been stolen from his mother. Now at length he felt that he was King indeed.

## CHAPTER 25

# HENRY IV

HENRY was now master in his own kingdom. But almost at once he was plunged into a struggle still fiercer than that against the Saxons.

You remember that when Henry III had deposed the three rival Popes, one had come to Germany bringing with him a monk named Hildebrand. That monk had grown to great power, and in 1078 he was chosen Pope, and took the title of Gregory VII.

You remember, too, that Henry III had asserted his right as Emperor to choose the Pope, and had indeed chosen and placed on the papal throne four Popes one after the other. Henry III had done much for the Church. He had found the holy office cast down in the mud of all things evil, and had cleansed it, and set it high again.

But that the Emperor should choose the Pope seemed to Gregory VII a humiliation. This grey little man had an unbounded sense of his own greatness. He looked upon the Pope as the viceroy of God, the vicar of Christ upon earth, and therefore far above any earthly ruler, were he King or Emperor.

So in 1075 Gregory issued a decree declaring that henceforward bishops should not be chosen by the Emperor; that no longer should the ring and crozier, the badges of their office, be given them by the Emperor or by any other prince.

This giving of ring and crozier is called the investiture of bishops, and Gregory VII declared that henceforth all investitures should be in the hands of the bishops and cardinals, with the Pope at their head. He also decreed that no gifts or money should be given or taken by either side, and that if such were given or received by any bishop, then such an one was guilty of simony, and was no longer a bishop.

Now these decrees were aimed directly at the Emperor and his authority, and hit him hard. The law against simony especially hit him hard. For, when in need of money, Henry had time and again sold the office of Bishop. Now with one stroke of the pen the Pope had made these appointments unlawful. He declared these Sees to be empty, and appointed to them, not Henry's followers, but his own.

Besides this, Emperor after Emperor had tried to strengthen the clergy, in order the better to curb the nobles, and to do this Emperor after Emperor had given them land, until at length a great part of the soil of Germany was in their possession. Now if the Pope alone had the power of appointing bishops, he would appoint only such men as would do his bidding. All these lands, then, would pass into the control of the Pope, which would greatly strengthen his power, and lessen that of the Emperor.

All this Henry well knew, and he was by no means ready meekly to submit to the Pope. So he called all the German bishops together to a meeting, or Synod, at Worms, and there he deposed the Pope. He bade the bishops write and tell the Pope what he had done. And the bishops wrote, addressing their letter, not to Pope Gregory VII but to Brother Hildebrand. They wrote accusing him of many things evil, and declared that he was no true Pope. "And for that you have openly declared," they said, "that you no longer regard us as bishops, we hereby declare that none of us will henceforth look upon you as Pope."

Henry too wrote: "I, Henry," he began, "not through usurpation but through God's holy institution, King, to Hildebrand, not Pope but false Monk." Henry repeated all that the bishops had said, and added more besides. "St. Peter," he wrote, "a Pope in truth, said, 'Fear God, and honour the King.' But you, because you do not fear God, dishonour Him in me." Many hard and bitter words he wrote. At length he ended, "I, Henry, King by God's grace, cry to you with all my bishops, 'Abdicate! Abdicate!'"

The Pope's reply was both proud and unexpected. He replied by excommunicating Henry. Never before had such a weapon been used against an Emperor, and the world was startled at the Pope's daring.

Henry cared little for Gregory's anger. He remained impenitent and haughty, he flung defiance in the face of the Pope. But he did not realise how times had changed. He did not realise that in his hands the power of the Empire was far, far less than in the hands of his father. He did not realise that in the hands of Gregory VII the power of the Pope was far, far greater.

Soon, however, he learned the terrible power of the Pope. His act had set free every vassal of the Empire from his oath of fealty. No man was longer required to obey his King, he was indeed encouraged to fight against him, and all the great unruly princes joined with the Pope. Saxony, but newly subdued, rose again in rebellion; other States followed. One by one Henry's friends melted away like snow before sunshine, until once again he found himself forsaken and helpless.

Thus forsaken Henry made up his mind to submit, and to submit at once. He had learned the astonishing power of the Pope when joined to that of his own rebellious princes, and he saw that he could not fight both together. He saw that he could only break the power of the princes by making friends once more with the Pope, and he determined to go to him and humbly beg forgiveness.

It was now mid-winter. Ice and snow made the crossing of the Alps both difficult and dangerous. Yet Henry resolved to cross. He did not go as a conqueror with a great army of knights and soldiers behind him, but as a penitent with a humble following. With him went his brave wife, Queen Bertha, and his little three-year-old son.

The winter was unusually hard. The roads were almost blocked with snow, so that the Alpine villagers who guided the little party had to clear a path with great difficulty and labour.

The climb up to the top of the pass was terrible. But it was as nothing to the descent. Then the real danger began. For the frost had made the paths down the steep mountain-side as slippery as glass. It needed all the cleverness of the hardy mountaineers who acted as guides to overcome the difficulties.

The Queen and her ladies sat upon oxhides for sleighs, and were thus dragged over the snow and ice. Sometimes the men were carried on the shoulders of the sure-footed mountaineers. Sometimes they crept down on hands and knees, once and again missing their foothold and sliding and rolling for many yards. But at length they reached the plain in safety, and joyfully continued their journey.

And now no sooner did Henry appear in Lombardy than many people flocked to him. Both bishops and nobles, who were angry at the Pope's new decrees, gathered round him with their vassals and men-at-arms, until he had a great army. These nobles now urged Henry to fight the Pope, but Henry would not be turned from his purpose, and hastened on to Canossa, where the Pope awaited him.

At last the town was reached. Barefoot, clad in a hair shirt, Henry, accompanied by the bishops who had been excommunicated with him, appeared before the gates, begging for admission. But the gates remained shut. In spite of prayers and tears, in spite of frost and snow, no man took pity on the shivering penitents. All day the King waited, and still the Pope made no sign.

Again next morning Henry appeared before the gates barefoot and clad only in a hair shirt. Again he prayed in vain for admission. Again he was refused. Darkness fell and the mighty Emperor still lay under the wrath of the Pope.

A third day still Henry stood without the gates begging for grace. A third time he was refused. Worn with fasting and with tears, he went back to his lodging. He had failed, and he resolved no longer to wait on the Pope's pleasure, but to return homeward.

Then the Pope gave way. The gates were opened, and the penitent King threw himself weeping at the feet of Gregory. Loud sobs burst from the watching crowd, and even the eyes of the stern Pope were dimmed with tears.

The ban was removed. But the Empire had received a blow from which it never again recovered. In standing as a penitent before the closed gates of Canossa Henry had acknowledged the Pope's right over him, he had acknowledged that the Pope was greater than the Emperor. It was an acknowledgment which startled the world. And from that day at Canossa the glory of the Empire faded, the glory of the Pope increased. That day at Canossa is one of the turning-points in the world's history.

The ban was removed, but not the evil that it had already done to Henry. For meanwhile the discontented princes had grown more rebellious than ever, and had met together and chosen a new King. This new King was Rudolph of Swabia, Henry's own brother-in-law.

As soon as Henry heard of it he hastily left Italy, and hurried back over the Alps. This time he crossed them as a King, with a great army behind him.

The Pope demanded that the rival Kings should leave their quarrel to him to settle. But Henry, in making his submission to the Pope, had never meant to put his Empire under his control. The Pope, he said, had no right of judgment between him and his rebel subjects. So he went to war against them.

For a time the Pope took neither side, for a time victory was uncertain. It swayed now this way, now that. Many battles were fought, much blood was shed on either side, and all the land was filled with misery and wrath. Rudolph at length appealed to the Pope, and the Pope took his side. Once more the thunders of his wrath were directed against Henry, once more he was excommunicated. But this time the bolt fell harmless. Henry paid no heed to it except to call his bishops together and choose a new Pope, who was called Clement III. That same year Rudolph was killed in battle, and once more Henry triumphed.

One of Henry's most faithful followers was Frederick of Hohenstaufen. He was now married to Henry's daughter, and leaving his son-in-law to

*Barefoot, clad in a hair shirt, Henry appeared before the gates, begging for admission.*

carry on the war in Germany, Henry marched again into Italy against Gregory VII.

Entering Rome, he enthroned there his chosen Pope and received from his hands the Emperor's crown.

Gregory VII had hoped against hope that the Christian world would rise and save him from the ruthless Emperor. His hope was vain. No help came to him, save from a Norman adventurer named Robert of Guiscard. Under his protection Gregory fled from Rome, and took refuge in Salerno. And there a year later he died.

He died leaving Henry still under the curse of the Church. "Henry I will not absolve," he said, "unless he does penance as the Church demands. If he humbles himself, I will free him from the ban, for this, as the vicar of St. Peter, I have power to do."

But Henry did no penance, so there could be no reconciliation between the foes. Henry remained under the curse, and Gregory, as unyielding as his rival, died in exile. "I have loved righteousness and hated evil," he said with his last breath, "therefore I die in exile."

The death of this great Pope did not bring peace to the Empire. For meanwhile the Germans had chosen another King, and when Henry returned to Germany he had once more to fight for his crown. Once more the land was filled with civil war, until after some years the rival King was killed.

Even then Henry's troubles were not over, for his son Conrad rebelled against him, and tried to take Italy from him. When Henry heard of it his grief was so great that he wished to die.

Conrad had already been chosen to succeed his father as King. But now Henry disinherited him, and persuaded the nobles to choose and crown his younger son Henry as his successor. This they did, young Henry, with solemn oaths, swearing never to rebel against his father.

Soon after this Conrad died in Italy. It is thought by some that he was poisoned by the great Countess Mathilda, who had encouraged him to rebel against his father.

Now, having lost his eldest son, Henry turned all his love towards his younger son, Henry. But he too was led away by his father's enemies, and, forgetting his oath, rebelled against him. With sorrow in his heart Henry took up arms against his son, and once more the land was plunged in civil war.

But the Emperor was anxious for peace, and when young Henry begged for a meeting he granted it.

It was near Coblenz that father and son met. Henry threw himself at his father's feet, begging for forgiveness, and promising from henceforth to be a faithful vassal, if only his father would make peace with the Church.

The Emperor at once promised all that he asked. Henry then begged his father to go with him to Mainz. And, believing in his son's repentance, the Emperor sent away nearly all his own followers and set out with him. But young Henry's repentance was not real. It was merely a trick to get his father into his power. Yet, suspecting no evil, the Emperor followed where he led.

Then one day as they entered a strong castle the heavy iron gates clanged behind them with a fatal sound. Too late the Emperor knew himself betrayed. In vain he begged for mercy. He was flung into a dark and noisesome cell, and there he was kept without a bed to lie on, without water to wash in, without food enough to eat.

Treated thus treacherously by the son he loved, the Emperor sank into deepest despair. And when at length young Henry demanded that he should abdicate, he yielded, too utterly crushed to resist.

But by yielding the Emperor gained nothing; he was still kept a prisoner, and still treated so cruelly that he lived in daily fear of death. Yet, prisoner though he was, he was not utterly without friends, and at length with their help he escaped.

Once more the Emperor's faithful subjects gathered to him, and the war was renewed. But Henry was already old, he was worn out by all his many sufferings. Now he fell ill, and in a few days he died quietly. Before he died he confessed his sins and received the Sacrament. He also sent his forgiveness to his rebellious son, and to the Pope. To his son too he sent his sword and his ring, praying him to deal mercifully towards those who had been faithful to his father. Then, having made his peace with God and the world, he fell asleep, and after his restless life at length found rest.

Henry in dying had made his own peace with God, but even after his death the Pope's curse followed him. His coffin was refused burial in any place blessed by the Church. So without chant or prayer, or service of any kind, it was secretly buried in unhallowed ground. But even there it was not allowed to rest. It was torn from the ground again; not until five years had passed was the wrath of the Church overcome, and the bones of Henry IV laid to rest with the solemn pomp and rites of Christian burial.

CHAPTER 26

# HENRY V

AFTER the death of his father Henry V was joyfully acknowledged as King. The Pope and his party had encouraged him in his rebellion against his father, for the Pope believed that in Henry V he would find an obedient vassal. But soon he found that he had been mistaken. For Henry fought with the Pope, now Paschal II, over the right of investiture even more fiercely than his father had done. Month by month the strife between the Pope and the King grew ever bitter and more bitter, until at length Henry decided to march to Rome, there to end it, and force the Pope to crown him as Emperor.

The Italians received Henry with joy, and great preparations were made for the coronation. On the morning of February 12, 1111, all the people of Rome, with priests and soldiers, carrying flowers and green branches, banners and silken flags, went forth to greet their Emperor.

Riding on a stately war-horse, and followed by a glittering array of knights, King Henry rode towards the city while the people surged round him waving green branches, and shouting "St. Peter has chosen King Henry. St. Peter has chosen King Henry!"

At the gates of the city Henry paused to take the accustomed oath, and swear to protect the liberties of Rome. Twice he swore it, once on the drawbridge before the gate, once upon the gate itself.

But he spoke in German. Already the joyful mood was darkened. Were they to have a King who could not speak their tongue? the Roman people asked. And so great was the disappointment that some fled into the city shouting of treachery.

But still the stately procession moved onwards, until at length, amid clouds of incense, the air ringing with the shouts of the people and the chants of the priests, Henry reached the door of St. Peter's.

Here, surrounded by his red-robed cardinals, the Pope awaited him. Slowly mounting the steps Henry threw himself at the Pope's feet, humbly kissing them. The Pope raised him, took him in his arms, and kissed him. Thrice they kissed with every appearance of love and brotherhood, but in their hearts there was nought but hatred and suspicion.

Hand in hand the Pope and Henry moved through the bending

throng. But, as they slowly passed along, the Pope trembled and looked uneasily around. And well he might. For German nobles filled the great Cathedral, German soldiers surrounded it. He was encompassed by foes. Yet, knowing this, before he set the crown on Henry's head, the Pope once more demanded that he should solemnly give up the right of investiture.

In wrath Henry refused. A terrible tumult followed, some crying this, some that, all surging in anger round the Pope.

"Why so much talk?" cried one of Henry's followers at length. "Our Emperor will be crowned like Charlemagne."

But still the Pope refused. All day the strife of tongues lasted. At length, when evening fell, Paschal found himself and his cardinals prisoners of King Henry. Thus was Canossa avenged.

But the Pope's men would not thus lightly allow their master to be insulted. And for two days a terrible battle raged through the streets of Rome. Then Henry left the city, carrying his prisoner with him.

And now a prisoner, the Pope at length yielded. "For the peace and freedom of the Church," he said, "I must do that which I should never have done to save my own life." With tears and sighs he gave up the right of investiture to the King.

Then Pope and King returned to Rome. And there with all speed, almost in stealth, while the city gates were fast locked, the crown was at length set upon the Emperor's head. Then Henry marched homeward.

But the Pope was not beaten, and hardly had Henry departed when he renewed all his old claims. Even as Gregory VII had excommunicated Henry IV, Paschal II now excommunicated Henry V. He proved himself an unyielding foe, waging war with the Emperor till his death in 1118.

Henry continued the struggle, but at length, under Calixtus II, peace was made. In September 1122 a great meeting was held at Worms. This is known as the Concordat of Worms, and here, after a struggle of fifty years, the war of investiture was settled. Each side gave up something, but the Pope had the best of it. It was settled that the Pope should have the right of giving the ring and staff, but that new bishops should be chosen in presence of the Emperor and that they should do homage to him as overlord for their fiefs.

In a wide meadow near Worms, where the people were gathered in a vast throng, the Pope and Emperor kissed each other, and swore to be at peace. And at the news all Europe rejoiced.

But this peace with the Pope did not bring peace to Henry, for besides his long strife with the Pope he had many troubles in Germany. His nobles in Saxony and Thuringia time and again rebelled against him, and the whole of Northern Germany was almost always in a state of revolt. In Italy, too, he had to fight for his possessions. But with a ruthless hand he put down all rebellions.

The people had no love for him. To them he was a hard stern ruler, and when, in 1125, he died, few if any mourned his loss.

But the fear of him lived after him. The common people declared that he was not dead at all, but only hiding from the hatred of his people. Some said that he was living as a hermit in a forest near Chester, others that he was living in France. And when many years later a hermit appeared in Burgundy who declared that he was Henry V many of the common people believed that he spoke truth, and trembled lest the hated Emperor should again return to rule over them.

CHAPTER 27

# LOTHAR THE SAXON

HENRY V had married the beautiful Princess Matilda of England, the daughter of Henry I, when she was little more than a girl. She was still young and beautiful when Henry died. But as she had no children she felt that she was no longer of importance in Germany, that Germany was no longer her home, and so she went back to England. And, as you know from English history, she married Geoffrey of Anjou and fought with Stephen for the throne of England.

And now, as there was no direct heir to the throne of the Empire, the princes of the realm again met together to choose a new Emperor. It seemed likely that Duke Frederick of Hohenstaufen would be chosen as he was Henry V's nephew, besides being one of the most powerful princes of the realm. But he had a rival in Duke Lothar of Supplinburg. Duke Lothar, however, seemed to have no wish for the crown. It is even said that he threw himself on his knees before the princes, begging them with tears not to choose him.

But while the princes still hesitated, from among the waiting people there arose a cry, "Lothar shall be King! Lothar shall be King!" The choice was made, and the unwilling Duke was seized and carried shoulder high through the cheering crowd. And so almost, it seems, against his will, Lothar became King of Germany.

This choice pleased the Pope. And it was greatly owing to the advice of the priests and bishops that it had been made. Lothar had taken sides with the Church against Henry V, and the Pope believed that in him he would find a friend. The Pope was right, and under Lothar the Church gained much power.

Frederick of Hohenstaufen had been disappointed of the throne. But even so his power was greatly increased, for he had inherited all Henry V's private estates. Lothar, however, now declared that these estates belonged to the Crown, and that Frederick mus give them up. Upon this Frederick, together with his brother Conrad, rebelled against Lothar. So a long civil war began which lasted during nearly the whole of Lothar's reign. Frederick fighting against Lothar in Germany, and Conrad fighting against him in Italy. Conrad, indeed, was even chosen as a rival King, and was crowned at Milan.

In this war Lothar's greatest friend was the young Welf Duke Henry. For there was great hatred between the Hohenstaufens. He was at this time only twenty years old, but he was so powerful and splendid that people called him Henry the Proud. As a reward for his friendship Lothar married him to his only daughter Gertrude. This made Henry very powerful, and increased the hatred and jealousy of the Hohenstaufens against him.

At first the King had little success against the rebel Hohenstaufens, but as time went on fortune changed. The King won town after town, fortress after fortress, and at length Frederick, finding himself almost alone, threw himself at the King's feet begging forgiveness. A few months later Conrad also yielded. Lothar forgave both the brothers, and gave them back their lands and titles. So at length there was peace in Germany.

When this civil war was going on Lothar was also fighting for the Pope. The people of Rome had driven the Pope Innocent II out and set up an Antipope. So Innocent sought aid from Lothar. And in 1132, leaving Henry the Proud to rule in Germany, Lothar crossed the Alps to help the Pope.

But Lothar was still struggling for empire over his own people, and willing though he was to fight the Pope's battles, he had few soldiers to spare. So it was with but a very small army that he crept through the land, avoiding battle wherever it was possible. He did not go near Milan where his rival Conrad was lording it as king. He avoided the large cities where he might meet with resistance, contenting himself with forages and skirmishes in the open country. His march, indeed, was more like the raid of some adventurer than the campaign of a great king.

At length, however, with his little army Lothar reached Rome, and led the Pope into the sacred city as he had promised. But although Innocent was once more in Rome, neither he nor the King were able to drive out the Antipope. He kept possession of part of the town and of the great Cathedral of St. Peter. So Lothar was crowned Emperor in another church called the Lateran.

Almost at once after his coronation Lothar turned back to Germany, and it was not long before Innocent was once more driven out of Rome. Thus Lothar's Italian campaign seemed to have failed utterly, yet after it his might and fame increased daily. He overcame the Hohenstaufens; the Duke of Poland and King of Denmark acknowledged him as overlord, and ambassadors came from every neighbouring State to do him honour. "In all Germany," says a writer of the time, "peace and plenty ruled."

But this time of peace did not last long, for Roger of Sicily, an adventurer Norman knight, now overran the south of Italy and proclaimed himself King.

So again Lothar crossed the Alps. But this time he went with a magnificent army, and his standard-bearers were those very Hohenstaufens who had once fought so bitterly against him.

In Italy Lothar divided his army into two. The one half, under Henry the Proud, marched down the western side of the peninsula, the other, which he himself commanded, took the eastern side.

The Emperor's march was a triumphal procession. Town after town yielded, victory after victory was won, until nearly the whole of Italy was conquered. Then, having put the affairs of Italy. in order, and leaving German counts and dukes to rule the land, the Emperor once more turned homeward.

But Lothar never reached Germany. He had been over sixty when he was chosen to be King, he was now an old man, wearied with many wars, and with the hard task of governing his great and restless kingdom. Now on his homeward journey he was taken ill, and died in a poor peasant's hut among the mountains.

## CHAPTER 28
# CONRAD III

AT Würzburg the princes of the realm were gathered to welcome the grey-haired hero on his victorious return. But in place of Lothar there came to them a messenger of grief; "the Emperor is dead," he said. So instead of feasting and rejoicing the princes went in sad procession to lay their Emperor to rest.

And now once more the question arose who should be Emperor, for Lothar left no son.

Among the many powerful princes Henry the Proud was the most powerful. It seemed to himself that he had the greatest right to the throne. For he was married to Lothar's only daughter Gertrude; he had great possessions both in Italy and in Germany, for Lothar had loaded him with lands and honours, making him Marquess of Tuscany and Duke both of Saxony and of Bavaria. Besides all this he was in possession of the crown and the royal jewels, which in dying Lothar had given into his keeping. But Henry had, through his pride, made many enemies. Many feared him because of his might and his arrogance. "If he is made Emperor," they said, he will turn free Germany into a land of slaves."

Among Henry's enemies was a wily priest, Albero, Archbishop of Trier. He made up his mind that Henry should not be chosen.

Now the day upon which the election of the King should take place had been fixed for May. But early in March Albero called many of the bishops and nobles who were friendly to him together. Among them were no Saxon or Bavarian nobles, none that might be friendly to Henry. But both Frederick and Conrad of Hohenstaufen, his sworn enemies, were there.

And when these princes were gathered together Albero bade them choose a King. This they did, and Conrad of Hohenstaufen was chosen and crowned with great haste. Thus the man who for so many years had been a rebel against Lothar, and who for seven years had called himself King, was now King indeed.

But he was elected in a hole-and-corner fashion. It was not a true election, and by it Albero had shown his scorn of the rights of the nobles, and of the old customs of the realm. Conrad too, by accepting his throne in such a manner, put himself more under the power of the Church, and more into the hands of the Pope, than any German Emperor before him.

As soon as the Bavarian and other princes heard that a new King had been crowned and anointed without their knowledge or leave, they were very angry. They raised a great outcry against the election. They had been cheated of their rights, they said. It was against the law, and no true election, and Conrad was no true King.

But Albero's bold stroke of state had won the day. The anger of the princes calmed by degrees, and one after another they submitted to the new King. Only Henry the Proud refused to acknowledge him. He was very powerful. All Bavaria and Saxony were his. And well Conrad knew that there was no security for his throne so long as his enemy thus held half the Empire in fief. So Conrad commanded Henry the Proud to give up the dukedom of Saxony, as, he said, no man might hold two dukedoms.

Henry indignantly refused to give up anything that was his, so he was declared an outlaw, and Saxony was given to another great noble named Albert the Bear.

Then Henry took up arms against the King. In answer to this the King took from him his second dukedom and gave it to another noble, Leopold of Austria.

At this the wrath of Henry the Proud was terrible. "Like a lion," says a man who lived at the time, "did he fall upon Saxony, and utterly did he destroy the castles and towns of all his enemies there." So fiercely did he fight that Albert the Bear was hunted forth from his new dukedom, and Henry the Proud was once more master in Saxony.

Once master of Saxony, Henry next prepared to carry the war into Bavaria. In the midst of his preparations, however, he suddenly fell ill and died. He was only thirty-five, but he was the richest and mightiest prince in Germany, and one of the greatest soldiers of his time. He left a little son ten years old to succeed him, and before he died he begged the Saxons to accept this little boy as their Duke and fight for his rights.

Henry's widow, the Duchess Gertrude, and her mother, the Empress Richenza, were also determined to fight for their boy. So if Conrad hoped that the death of his great enemy would bring peace, he was mistaken. The Saxons accepted the little boy Henry as their Duke and refused to acknowledge Albert the Bear. The war therefore went on. In Saxony

Gertrude and Richenza fought. In Bavaria Welf, Henry's brother, led the rebel troops, and Leopold was driven forth.

At length, near the town of Weinsberg, Welf was defeated. Weinsberg had been besieged by the King's troops for many weeks. It was now mid-winter. Yet, in spite of much suffering, the town held out. For it was known that Welf was marching with a large army to relieve the town. At length he came; and on December 21 a great battle was fought.

The two armies dashed upon each other, the rebels shouting "Welf," the King's men shouting "Waiblingen." It was the first time these war-cries were used, but they came to be the names of the two great parties which for many long years divided the Empire; the Welfs siding with the Popes, the Waiblingens with the Emperors. Welf was the family name of Henry the Proud's house, Waiblingen the name of a castle belonging to the Hohenstaufens. The Italians changed the names to Guelph and Ghibelline, and we too generally use the Italian spelling.

As the battle raged the King himself did mighty deeds, for he felt that his very crown was in the balance. He must win or die. So in the thickest of the battle he was found. Fierce and long was the struggle, but Welf was beaten. His army fled in wild panic. Many were slain in the pursuit, many were drowned in the river Neckar, many more were taken prisoner. Welf himself barely escaped with his life.

Then the people of Weinsberg sent messengers to the King promising to yield on condition that the women should go free, and be allowed to take with them what they held most precious. To this the King agreed. So next morning the great gates of Weinsberg were slowly swung open, and a long line of women as slowly marched out, bending beneath the weights upon their shoulders.

Truly, thought some, these women had taken full advantage of the King's promise. There was like to be little treasure left, little booty as the soldier's reward. Slowly the long procession stumbled on. Then, as it came near, the astonished army saw that what the women carried were no bundles of treasure, but men. Each woman had come forth bearing on her shoulders her husband, or father, or brother.

Loud were the shouts of anger in the royal camp. They had been betrayed, said the men. They had been cheated of their prisoners. Duke Frederick too was angry, and he would have seized and slain the men. But King Conrad forbade it. "A King's word must neither be strained nor broken," he said. And he not only bade the men go free, but allowed the brave women to return to the town and bring forth all their treasures And because of this great deed the town was afterward called Weiberstreue or Womansfaith.

But although Welf was defeated the war was not yet at an end. At length, however, Conrad became anxious for peace, and in May 1142 he acknowledged young Henry, who soon became known as Henry the Lion, as Duke of Saxony. And to make peace quite sure the young Duke's mother, Gertrude, married the King's brother Henry. So for a time there was peace between Welf and Waiblingen. Only Count Welf, who had not been considered, was still wrathful against the King.

Meantime, while these things had been happening is Germany, St. Bernard had been preaching the Second Crusade in France. The First Crusade had already taken place in the time of Henry IV, but it had made little impression on Germany. Now, however, St. Bernard came to Germany to preach, and arouse the people to set forth upon the Holy War.

But at first Conrad had no wish to go. Germany was still torn asunder by feuds, Welf was ever ready to rebel; without and within there were enemies. It was no time for the King to forsake his post and go to fight in a far-off land.

But St. Bernard was not to be denied. He preached before the King with such stirring words that at length, with tears running down his cheeks, Conrad cried out, "I am ready to serve the Lord, for He Himself calls me to it."

As the King spoke a thundering cheer rang through the great building. Again and again it was repeated as he knelt before St. Bernard to receive from his hands the sacred banner and the cross which marked him as a leader in God's wars. Then, following Conrad, noble after noble knelt to take the sign.

Throughout Germany the enthusiasm spread. From all sides high and low, rich and poor, crowded to follow the banner of the King, to fight for the Holy Sepulchre.

Great were the preparations made. Conrad's little son Henry was chosen and anointed King, so that while his father was in Palestine he might take his place. But as he was only ten years old the real power lay in the hand of a regent named Abbot Wibald. A general peace within the land was declared. The strife between Welf and Waiblingen seemed buried for the time. All thoughts were turned to the Holy Land. At length, in

June 1147, the mighty army of a hundred thousand men left German soil and marched on its way to the East.

The huge army was made up of all kinds of men, bad and good. Some were thirsting only for blood and plunder, some sought new adventures, some were filled with holy zeal. It was a disorderly crowd rather than an army. There was little or no discipline in the ranks, and each man did as he would.

Still, without serious mishap Conrad reached Constantinople and crossed into Asia Minor. But from there onwards the difficulties of the crusaders began. They were passing now through the land of the Unbeliever. They were beset on all sides by dangers; it was difficult even to get food enough to feed so great an army. Conrad, therefore, made up his mind to divide his force. He, with the greater part, took the shortest but most dangerous route; Bishop Otto of Freising led the smaller part by the longer and safer route along the seashore.

Slowly the German host, with the King at its head, advanced through the land. The cloudless sky burned overhead, the glaring yellow sand burned underfoot. Led by Greek guides the men pressed onward, weary and thirsty. Soon food began to fail. Towns and villages shut their gates against the invaders, and would sell them nothing. Treacherous traders sold them flour mixed with chalk, so that those who ate of it died in agony. Day by day the misery of the march increased.

Then suddenly one morning the guides vanished, and the German army found themselves abandoned in a great barren desert without knowledge of the way without food or water for man or beast. Almost treeless, with neither mountain nor river to mark the way, the great plain stretched for miles and miles around. Worn out by many miseries, with famine staring them in the face, none knew what to do. Some counselled this, some that. Some wanted to advance rapidly and reach better country. Some wanted to go back.

But while they still debated far on the horizon dust-clouds arose. Nearer and nearer they came, till out of the desert haze turbaned horsemen dashed.

On all sides the Germans saw themselves surrounded. Neither in going forward or back was any safety to be found. There was nothing to do but fight, and with stolid bravery they fought. But mere bravery was of no avail. The Turks, mounted upon swift horses, armed with bows and arrows, from a safe distance poured death upon the German ranks.

They, heavily armed indeed, but without bows and arrows, and mounted upon wornout war-steeds, could do little.

It was a terrible massacre which took place beneath the burning Syrian sun. Of seventy thousand men scarce seven thousand escaped. Slowly these fought their way back, harassed at every step by a pitiless foe.

At Nicea, Conrad and his shattered army met King Louis of France. With tears running down their cheeks the two Kings kissed each other, and swore never more to part, but to march side by side to the Holy Land.

Many of the Germans, however, had no more heart to continue the fight. They returned homewards, and when they reached Germany, and told their tale of disaster and loss, the land was filled with woe and lamentation.

What was left of the German army now followed the French along the coast. But even here many difficulties and dangers had to be overcome, and at length Conrad became so ill that he turned back to Constantinople. Here the Emperor of the East treated him with all kindness, and a few months later he once more set out for Jerusalem.

When at length he reached the Holy City, Baldwin, the Christian King of Jerusalem, with nobles and priests and a great concourse of people, came forth to meet him. And with palm branches waving around him, and the sound of chanting in his ears, he rode in solemn procession into the city.

But as yet the Crusaders had done nothing to free the Holy Land from the power of the Turks. So now it was decided to besiege Damascus. And to that town both French and German armies marched.

But Damascus did not fall as it had been expected to fall. The Christians were constantly deceived and betrayed by those who promised help. There was strife and treachery in the Christian army itself. And at length, disappointed and embittered, Conrad resolved to turn homeward. He went with shame in his heart, for the Crusade had been an utter failure.

Conrad had been away two years, and he returned to find that in his absence his kingdom had been but badly ruled. Many of the lawless nobles, it is true, had taken the cross, and the land had been all the more peaceful for their absence. But many too had returned to stir up strife. Among these was Count Welf, and one of the first things King Conrad had to do was to march against him.

No sooner was Count Welf subdued than others rebelled. So at the end of his reign Conrad found himself fighting for his crown just as at the beginning. In the midst of all these troubles his son Henry died. This was a terrible blow for the King, already growing old, and worn out by his sufferings in Palestine. His spirit sank under it.

At length he became very ill. He knew that his end had come, and as he lay dying he thought with grief upon the state of the Empire. His only remaining son was but a child of eight. How was it possible for a child of eight to rule in these stormy times? Conrad knew it could not be. So, calling the nobles about him, he bade them choose for their King, not his son, but his nephew, Duke Frederick Redbeard. To him ere he died he gave the crown and the royal jewels. In his hand, too, he laid the hand of his little son and begged him to love and care for him. And so he died.

Conrad was a brave soldier, but a poor weak King. He reigned for nearly fourteen years, and he accomplished nothing, he succeeded in nothing. He left the kingdom in confusion, and the kingly power at its lowest ebb. He was little more than the Pope's vassal. Yet he never went to Italy to receive the Emperor's crown at the hands of the Pope.

CHAPTER 29

# FREDERICK I, REDBEARD

AFTER the death of Conrad III, Frederick Redbeard, or Barbarossa as the Italians called him, was at once chosen and crowned as King. He was thirty-one years old and already a famous warrior. All Germany greeted him with joy, and it was hoped that the quarrels between Welf and Waiblingen would now cease, for Frederick's mother was a Welf. And to begin with, at least, there was great friendship between Frederick and Henry the Lion, the head of the House of Welf.

Frederick wanted to make the Empire great as it had been in the times of Charles the Great and Otto the Great. He meant to be master of Italy, but first he had to bring order into Germany. This he did with a strong hand, then in 1154 he marched into Italy to help the Pope who was once more in difficulties.

In the time of Henry II the Normans had begun to settle in Italy. Ever since they had been almost constantly in a state of warfare against the Emperor. They had now possession of the south of Italy and of Sicily, which they had formed into a kingdom called the kingdom of Sicily, the King being quite independent of the Empire. In Northern Italy, too, the great trading cities had grown powerful, and during the quarrels of the Pope and Emperor they had become almost free, and formed little republics in themselves.

Barbarossa now marched against these cities, and with much sternness and not a little cruelty he forced them to submit to him. Then he marched on to Rome. The Pope was now Adrian IV, the only Englishman who ever sat upon the papal throne. He was the son of poor parents. He himself had once begged his bread from door to door, but becoming a monk he had gradually risen to greater and greater power. Now that he was Pope his pride knew no bounds.

At Sutri the Pope and Emperor met. Riding upon a beautiful horse, surrounded by his cardinals in their red robes, came the Pope. Clad in splendid armour and surrounded by his nobles and princes, the King rode towards him. The two cavalcades met. The King and Pope dismounted, and the King led the Pope into a splendid tent and set him upon a throne prepared for him. Then, as the custom was, he threw himself at the Pope's feet and kissed his toe. Barbarossa then expected the Pope to raise him, and give him the kiss of peace. But the Pope did not move. His proud face was dark with anger. When he spoke his voice trembled with rage.

"You have not paid to St. Peter that honour which is due," he said. "You have indeed dishonoured him. You have neither held my stirrup nor have you led my steed by the bridle."

"Not want of reverence, but want of knowledge is the cause of this oversight," replied the King proudly. "For truly I am not used to the holding of stirrups."

But the Pope would not be pacified. "Shall I not judge great things by little?" he cried. "If Frederick out of ignorance neglects little things, how does he suppose that he can ever succeed in great things?"

When he heard these words the King started up in anger. "It behoves me to ask you how this custom arose," he cried: "if out of pure courtesy, or out of right and duty? If out of courtesy, then the Pope has nothing to complain of. For a courtesy freely done can never have the force of law."

Hot and long was the strife which followed. At length, full of pride, the Pope left the tent, with his cardinals behind him.

Many of the princes were troubled and anxious. "A quarrel between the Church and the Empire could only bring harm," they said to Barbarossa. "If you give way, your kingly dignity will not really be hurt, and the Pope will have no excuse for unfriendly acts."

So the King gave way. Next day he rode to meet the Pope. As they met he dismounted, and in the sight of the whole army, for a stone's throw, he led the Pope's horse by the bridle, then, stooping, held his stirrup while he alighted.

Thus the pride of the Pope was satisfied; he gave the King the kiss of peace, and together they rode towards Rome.

As the King neared Rome the people sent ambassadors to meet him, offering to acknowledge him as Emperor if he would pay a certain sum of money. But Barbarossa refused to buy his crown. "Am I your prisoner? Do I lie bound in your hands that I should free myself with gold?" he asked in anger.

In anger, too, the ambassadors departed, and it was plain that it would only be against the will of the Romans that Frederick would receive the crown.

But the consent of the Romans was not asked. Early one July morning St. Peter's Church was surrounded by German soldiers, the gate leading to it was closed, and then in secret, but with all rightful pomp and ceremony, the Emperor's crown was placed upon Barbarossa's head.

As soon as it became known that the Emperor was crowned, the Romans rose in wild revolt. They fell upon the Germans in fury, and a fierce battle raged in the streets of Rome from morning until the sun was near setting. Then at length the Romans gave way.

But although the Romans yielded for the time they were not really subdued. The King of Sicily too still held firm sway over Southern Italy. Yet, in spite of the Pope's entreaties, Barbarossa turned homeward. For his army was dwindling fast. Beneath the burning sun of Italy his northern soldiers drooped and died, and it was with sadly thinned ranks that he once more crossed into Germany.

Now for two years Barbarossa ruled his own land wisely and well. He quelled the lawless nobles who filled the land with bloodshed and strife. He punished robbers and evil-doers, he cared for trade, and in many ways sought the good of the country.

But after two years the Emperor resolved once more to march into Italy. For the Lombard cities, especially Milan, were still in a state of rebellion, besides which a quarrel had arisen with the Pope.

This quarrel was brought about once more by the Pope's pride. For he wrote a letter to the Emperor in which he seemed to want to make the Emperor understand that the Empire was the Pope's gift, and that the Emperor was merely his (the Pope's) vassal. This letter was read aloud to Frederick and his nobles who were gathered in the chapel of his palace. When the reading was finished the nobles were very angry. Such insolence was not to be borne, they cried. The Empire a fief of the Pope indeed! Where would his arrogance end? they asked.

"And from whom then does the Emperor receive the Empire, if not from the Pope?" insolently demanded his messenger.

"By heaven," cried Frederick in wrath, "if we were not in a church you would feel how sharp is a German sword for these words."

Even as he spoke one of the nobles sprang forward with drawn sword. Church or no church the insolent priest should pay for his words. But the Emperor held him back. With his own hands he protected the Pope's messenger, and presently the uproar ceased.

But although Barbarossa had saved the life of the Pope's messenger he had no mind to let his insolence go unpunished. So, burning with wrath, he crossed the Alps once more, determined to prove to all his might and right as Emperor.

Barbarossa besieged and took Milan, then he gathered the nobles and knights together. He called the learned professors from the Italian universities, and bade them search through all the old dusty records to prove from them that he was the rightful successor to the Roman Emperors, and that the Pope's great claims were without foundation.

The Pope now threatened to excommunicate the Emperor, but he died before he could carry out his threat. His death, however, only seemed to make the quarrel blaze more furiously. For immediately two Popes were elected, the Emperor's party choosing Victor IV, the Pope's party, Alexander III. The greater number of cardinals voted for Alexander III, and he is looked upon as the true Pope. But both were at once enthroned, and each at once excommunicated his rival. Barbarossa too was excommunicated because he had ruled, said Alexander III, not as an Emperor, but as a tyrant.

Meanwhile, Milan had again revolted. Again Frederick besieged the city, which for months held out, though famine and plague stalked through the streets, while a pitiless sun blazed overhead and a pitiless Emperor watched at the gates. Around the walls, too, fierce warfare raged. Fair vineyards and oliveyards were wasted, and fertile fields became a desert waste.

Barbarossa had vowed to crush the people of Milan, who had so often rebelled against him. And in order to strike terror into their already sinking hearts he treated the prisoners he took with horrible cruelty. Blinded and maimed he sent them back to the city as a warning to their fellows. Yet summer passed and winter came, and still the city held out. But ever deeper and deeper it sank into gloom and misery, such misery as at length could not be borne, and the city yielded.

With bare feet, with ashes on their heads, crosses in their hands, and their swords tied about their necks, the chief men of Milan threw themselves at the Emperor's feet, praying for mercy.

To him they delivered up their naked swords, the keys of all the gates, and the banners of the city. Last of all, the great standard was delivered up. It floated from a huge pole set upon a chariot with trumpeters on either side. As the chariot was drawn before the Emperor the trumpeters sounded their trumpets for the last time, and as the notes died away they laid their trumpets at the Emperor's feet. The standard was lowered, and amid the tears and groans of the people the pole was hewn in pieces.

Tears stood in the eyes of the princes as they saw the broken humbled men pass before them. Only the Emperor's face remained cold and hard, only the Emperor's heart remained unmoved. There was no pity in it for the rebels, no mercy for Milan.

"Milan," he said, "has been the centre of all the rebellion. So long as it remains peace and order will never return. For the sake of peace and order the punishment must be hard."

So the terrible command went forth, "Milan shall be a desert and empty, and the plough shall pass where its palaces have stood."

Hardly had the order gone forth when the destruction began, and in a week's time the splendid city of churches and palaces was but a mass of ruins.

In terror at this ruthless deed the other cities of Lombardy yielded. At length Italy seemed to be subdued and Frederick turned home again to Germany.

But Italy was not subdued, and again and yet again Frederick marched against the rebels. And in order the better to subdue them he placed German rulers over the Italian cities and provinces. These German rulers ground the people down with pitiless taxes. So heavy were these taxes that the people called the book in which they were written the "book of pain and mourning."

Such tyranny could not be borne, and soon the most powerful cities of Lombardy joined together in a league against the Emperor. In spite of his stern commands they rebuilt Milan. They built a new town too, which they called Alessandria, after the Pope Alexander, who was the Emperor's enemy. They did everything they could to weaken the Emperor's power or overthrow it altogether.

Yet although so much of Barbarossa's time was taken up in fighting in Italy he did not forget his own country. He kept peace in the land and ruled sternly. But although he ruled sternly he did not rule as a tyrant, for on all great questions he called the nobles together and asked their advice.

Many of these princes were very powerful. But there was one prince who was greater than all the others, and whose pride and possessions almost equalled those of the emperor. This was Henry the Lion. He was both Duke of Saxony and of Bavaria. He had married Matilda, the daughter of King Henry II of England. He had fought against the peoples whose countries bordered on his possessions, and added much of their land to his dukedoms. "From the Elbe to the Rhine, from the North Sea to the Hartz is mine!" he used to say, and he became so powerful and so proud that many of the lesser nobles took up arms against him. These, however, he subdued even without the Emperor's help. And proud and powerful though Henry became, he remained true to the Emperor, who was so busy trying to subdue Italy that he never tried to curb the pride of his great vassal.

Now at length in 1174 Barbarossa made another expedition into Italy. At first things went well for the Emperor, but suddenly they took an evil turn, and he found himself face to face with an enemy far stronger than himself. Without more help from Germany he knew that he must be defeated. So he sent urgent messages to the great nobles begging them to come to his aid. Chiefly he sent to Henry the Lion.

But although in the early days Henry had willingly followed his Emperor, he was now so taken up with trying to extend his own power that he had little desire to gather an army and march away to fight in Italy. So he refused to go. When the Emperor heard that Henry refused to come to his aid, he hurried to him to implore his help in person.

"You are the greatest prince in Germany," he said, "and you ought to be the example for all. Remember that I have never denied you anything, but ever increased your might. And now you lag behind when German honour, your Emperor's fame, aye, the prize of my whole life stands in the balance."

Still Henry remained unmoved.

"I do not remind you of the oath of fealty which you have taken to me as Emperor," cried Barbarossa. "I will only remind you of the sacred bond of blood which unites us. Now in this hour of need help me, my friend and cousin, and I promise I shall repay it to you fifty-fold, right willingly."

Still the Duke remained stubborn.

Then in despair the Emperor threw himself at his vassal's feet, and on his knees implored his help.

Abashed and alarmed at seeing his Emperor on his knees before him, the Duke tried to raise him up. But his lord high steward was pleased, "Let be, my lord Duke," he said, "the crown which you now see at your feet will one day be upon your head."

These were the words of a traitor, and a troubled stillness fell upon all who heard.

Then in the stillness the Empress came forward. "Rise, my dear lord," she said. "God will help you when you remember this day and this arrogance."

The Emperor rose; with wrath and grief struggling in his breast he turned from the place, and the Duke, mounting upon his horse, rode hastily away.

CHAPTER 30

# FREDERICK I, REDBEARD

THUS once again there was wrath and bitterness between the houses of Welf and Waiblingen. But meantime the Emperor could but nurse his wrath, and he returned to fight his Italian foes with such troops as he could muster.

On May 29, 1176, the battle of Legnano was fought. And although the gallant little army did great deeds of valour, the Germans were utterly defeated. The Emperor himself was in the thickest of the fight. His standard-bearer was killed, and he himself struck from his horse, and the fighting host swept over him. As the Emperor was no more to be seen, the terrible news that he was killed spread through all the host, and in mad panic the Germans fled.

The generals tried to rally the men. But it was in vain. Each man thought only of saving himself, and fled in wild panic towards Pavia.

There the sad remnant of the army gathered to mourn their lost leader. The Empress wept and put on mourning garments. But in vain they sought his dead body among the slain. Then, greatly to the joy of all, after three days Barbarossa suddenly appeared before the gates of Pavia.

Although wounded and bruised and left for dead Frederick had not been killed. He had recovered himself, and in the darkness of the night had crept to a place of safety, and there he had remained until it was safe for him to join his friends.

The battle of Legnano was a turning-point in Barbarossa's reign. He saw that it was useless to fight longer against the spirit of freedom which had grown up among the great Italian cities. So he made up his mind to make peace with them. He acknowledged their right to govern themselves and choose their own magistrates, keeping over them only a vague title of Emperor. He also gave up the cause of the rival Pope, and made friends with Alexander III, who removed the ban of excommunication from him.

Having thus made peace in Italy, Barbarossa returned to Germany. He had been away four years, and he found that many of the great nobles had quarrelled among themselves, disturbing the peace of the land. Above all, he found Henry the Lion at war with many of the lesser

*In vain they sought his dead body among the slain.*

nobles. Many of these nobles now came before the Emperor to complain of the oppression of the great Duke.

Barbarossa too had somewhat against the Lion; he had not forgotten the day upon which he had knelt in vain, and he commanded the Duke to appear before him to answer for his misdeeds. Henry did not come.

Four times he was commanded to come. Four times he refused. Then the Emperor declared Henry the Lion to be an outlaw. All his lands and possessions were taken from him, his vassals were freed of their oaths to him, and his life was at the mercy of any who chose to take it.

Undismayed at the Emperor's wrath, Henry prepared for war. So once more the smouldering hate between Welf and Waiblingen leapt up in flames. Many battles had Barbarossa fought in Italy. But against his own people his sword had scarce been drawn. Now he made ready to draw it, not only against his own people but against his own cousin and life-long friend.

Soon through all the land the noise of war spread; armies marched to and fro, battles were fought, towns and castles were taken and retaken.

Henry was so powerful that it seemed at first doubtful which side would win. But in the days of his greatness Henry's pride had made for him many enemies. Now one by one many left his side and joined that of the Emperor. Others who had promised help did not send it. Loss after loss fell upon him. At length, unable to hold out longer, he yielded, and throwing himself at the Emperor's feet, begged forgiveness.

With tears in his eyes the Emperor raised him. "You are the creator of your own misfortune," he said, and kissed him.

But even though Barbarossa forgave Henry he could not raise him to his former power. For the nobles were against him. So, although some land was still left to him, both his dukedoms were taken from him, and he was banished for three years.

With his wife and children he went to England to the court of his father-in-law, Henry II. And it is interesting to remember that in England his son William was born. It is from this son that our own King George V is descended.

Since the destruction of Milan Frederick had won no such victory as he had now won over his greatest vassal. All the power he had lost in Italy he had more than regained in Germany.

Now there followed a time of peace and splendour. Barbarossa made another journey to Italy, but this time he went, not intent on war, but on peace. Both by the cities and by the Pope he was greeted in friendly fashion. Even with the King of Sicily there was peace, and Barbarossa's son Henry was married to the Princess Constance of Sicily.

But now from the East there came terrible news. The Holy Land was once more in the hands of the Turks. The Christian kingdom of Jerusalem lay in ruins.

Once more a crusade was preached. In England Richard Coeur de Lion, in France Philip Augustus, took the Cross. Frederick Redbeard, old man though he was, followed their example; and leaving his son to rule, he set out for the Holy Land with a great army.

Through many dangers, hardships, and disappointments, the great army fought its way onward. But Barbarossa never saw Jerusalem. In Asia Minor the army had to cross a river swollen by the rain. There was only one bridge, and the Emperor, becoming impatient at the slow passage, urged his horse into the river and tried to swim across. But the stream was too strong, he was swept away by it and was drowned. His knights and nobles tried to save him, but in vain, and it was only a dead body that they drew at length from the swirling waters.

Sorrowfully the army now went forward, carrying the dead body of their Emperor, and led by his young son, also called Frederick. But young Frederick too died before Palestine was reached. Already many of the great host had perished on the way, far more by famine and plague than by the sword. Now many more, utterly disheartened, returned homeward; only a few reached the Promised Land, and joined the English and French at the siege of Acre.

Somewhere in the wastes of Asia Minor the bones of the great Emperor were laid to rest. But no one knows certainly where they were laid. And as he died so far away, and was buried no man knew where, the German people refused to believe that he was really dead. So there arose a legend that he was only resting, weary of his great labours, and that one day he would come again.

In a cave within the hill of Kyffhausen, it is said, he sits upon an ivory chair asleep, his head pillowed upon a great marble table, through which his beard has grown. Peacefully he sleeps, but when danger threatens the Fatherland he stirs uneasily. Then those who listen may hear the clash and clang of armour. Sometimes, too, the sound of chant and psalm, the roll of organ music, may be heard to come from that magic cave.

And ever round the summit of the hill black ravens fly. Day by day in silent mysterious circles they sweep. But when they cease their circling flight, it is said, Barbarossa will awake. Forth from his cave he will stride, and hang his great shield upon the blasted tree which stands in the valley. Then once again the tree will become green and flourishing, once again Barbarossa will lead the Empire to new and brighter glory. Until that day he sleeps. But sometimes he stirs and half awakes. Opening his eyes, still heavy with sleep, he calls a dwarf to him.

"Go," he says, "look if the ravens still fly around the hill, for if it be so, I must yet sleep another hundred years."

Such was the old legend. Some say that Barbarossa still sleeps within his mysterious cave. Some say that he awoke when, in 1871, after long years of degradation and disunion, Germany once more formed a strong, united Empire.

Barbarossa is one of the great heroes of the German nation. He was a stern ruler, pitilessly cruel to his enemies, but with all his strength he laboured to make Germany free and great. He was not always victorious; he was beaten by the free cities of Italy and by the Pope. But he knew how to yield, and so win victory out of defeat.

## CHAPTER 31

# HENRY VI

THE great Barbarossa was succeeded by his son Henry. He was twenty-five years old, and had already been chosen and crowned King in his father's lifetime. In many ways he was like his father, but he lacked his large-heartedness; he was hard and cruel, and the people did not love him as they had loved Barbarossa.

Frederick had ruled so firmly that rebellion against the Emperor had almost ceased in Germany. But after his death it soon burst out again. Henry the Lion returned, and, encouraged by his friend Richard the Lion-heart of England, became once more the centre of rebellions. Sicily too, which Henry claimed through his wife Constance, also rebelled. Here too the rebels were encouraged by Richard. They refused to look upon either Constance or Henry as their ruler, and chose a prince named Tancred for their King.

In order to be free to fight the Sicilians, Henry made a truce with the Lion, and hurried southward to be crowned Emperor and conquer Sicily. But it was with difficulty that Henry persuaded the Pope to crown him, for now that the Emperor claimed not only the north of Italy but the south, the Pope began to be more than ever afraid of his might. He feared for his own possessions if they could be attacked both on the north and on the south by the Emperor.

Henry did at length, however, receive the crown. Then he marched onward to conquer Sicily. Through the land he passed triumphantly, town after town, castle after castle, yielding to him, until he reached Naples. Here his triumphant march was stopped, for Naples would not yield. For three months it held out against the conqueror. Besieged and besiegers both fought bravely. But at length a terrible plague broke out in the German army. The men died in hundreds. Even the Emperor himself fell ill. There was no choice left to him. If he would save even a remnant of his army, he must leave the plague-stricken spot.

So Henry turned northward. Then, to add to his misfortunes, the news came to him that the Empress was a prisoner. For greater safety she had left the camp before Naples and gone to Salerno. Now the people of

Salerno had betrayed her into the hands of Tancred. Dressed in all the splendour of an Empress she was led before him.

"Why can you not be content with the glory of half the world?" he asked. "Why do you come to rob me of my land? See how a just God has punished both you and your husband for your greed."

Very proudly Constance answered, "Now, indeed, our star sinks, but soon yours too will sink. Not after a strange land have I sought, but after my own kingdom, which you have wantonly torn from me."

But Tancred cared little for the proud words of the Empress. He cared as little for Henry's persuasions and threats. He kept the Empress a prisoner, and a beaten man, leaving his wife in captivity, Henry returned homewards. His conquests were wiped out, and all that remained to him from his Italian expedition was the Imperial crown.

He returned to find Germany too in a state of rebellion. For the peace he had made with Henry the Lion had been but a false peace. And now, from all sides, troubles seemed to crowd upon the Emperor. But at length a piece of good fortune befell him.

Richard Coeur de Lion, returning from the Holy Land, was taken prisoner by Leopold of Austria.

When the Emperor heard the news he was delighted. It was worth more to him than gold and gems, he said; for Richard was his great enemy, the friend of both Henry the Lion and Tancred. So he sent a messenger to the Duke of Austria, saying that no mere duke might keep a King prisoner, and commanding that Richard should be given over to him as Emperor.

Henry resolved to use Richard as a hostage to force his enemies to make peace, and not to set him free until he had paid an enormous ransom. Seeing their mighty friend thus a prisoner, many of the revolted nobles made peace with the Emperor, and at length Richard, having paid an enormous ransom and taken an oath of fealty to Henry, was set free.

With the money which Henry received from the English, he was able to raise another army in order to conquer Sicily. He was able, too, to leave Germany with no fear of rebellion. For that great rebel, Henry the Lion, had grown weary of strife, and he now troubled Germany no more. He went away to his own castle, and lived there quietly until he died.

So Henry once again marched into Italy to take possession of the kingdom of Sicily. Meanwhile Tancred had died, and this time Henry was successful. And when he had subdued the people he took a horrible and cruel vengeance on all those who had withstood him. Many of the nobles were beheaded, others were blinded, tortured, and cruelly ill-treated.

Even Tancred's little four-year-old son did not escape. He was blinded and sent a prisoner to Germany with his mother and sisters. There he soon died.

Henry now was more greedy of power than ever. He had dreams of a world-wide German Empire over which the Hohenstaufens should rule. So now he tried to persuade the nobles to make the crown hereditary in his family. He offered them many privileges if they would consent. Many of the princes were willing to agree to this, but the Saxons held out against it, and Henry could do no more than persuade them to choose his son as his successor, as many Emperors before him had done.

Still Henry clung to his dreams of a world-wide Empire. He claimed the King of England as his vassal; he called himself overlord of France; he cast longing eyes on Spain. He claimed large parts of the Eastern Empire, and was about to set out to conquer Constantinople, when he suddenly died at Messina in 1197.

CHAPTER 32

# PHILIP OF SWABIA

HENRY'S son Frederick was only three years old when his father died. He had been chosen as King, but he had not been crowned. And now the nobles were very unwilling to accept a little child as their ruler, and they resolved to choose another King. But they could not agree as to who that other should be. Some chose and crowned a Hohenstaufen, Philip, Henry's brother. Others chose and crowned a Welf, Otto, the son of Henry the Lion. So there were two Kings in Germany, and once again strife between Welf and Waiblingen.

The Pope now claimed the right to decide between the rival Kings, and he decided for Otto and excommunicated Philip. But Philip would not give up his crown at the bidding of the Pope, so once again there was civil war. It was chiefly in Saxony that Otto found followers, but throughout Philip's reign the whole land was filled with bloodshed, and rang with the rival cries of Welf and Waiblingen.

The state of the country became truly terrible. As the Pope himself wrote: "Goodness and truth vanish, wicked men flourish. The seed rots in the field, and famine lays its hand upon all. Day by day misery increases. Robbery and murder stalk unashamed through the land, so that no street, no house is safe."

At length Philip and Otto met together to try to come to some agreement. But the meeting was without result, for neither would give way in the least. Philip offered his rival a royal princess for his wife, a dukedom, and many lands, and honours besides, if he would but give up his claim to the crown. Otto, however, would have none of them. "Death alone shall make me give up the crown," he said.

But Philip was a brave and kindly man, and his people grew to love him. So one by one Otto's friends fell away from him, until at length it became plain that his cause was lost. Even the Pope forsook him, and made peace with Philip. The end of the strife seemed near.

Then one day, as King Philip lay resting in his palace at Bamberg, a loud knock was heard at the door. Immediately after it was thrown rudely open, and Count Otto of Wittelsbach strode into the room, drawn sword in hand.

Otto of Wittelsbach was a wild young noble, famed for his lawless and insolent deeds. He was for ever at strife with his neighbours, and he rode about the country with a rope at his girdle ready to hang any one who roused his wrath. Once in a weak moment Philip had promised him his daughter in marriage, but finding him so wild and passionate he had withdrawn his promise. For that Otto had never forgiven the King.

Now as Philip saw this fiery young Count stride into the room with drawn sword in hand, he raised himself on his elbow. "Put up your sword," he said sternly; "this is no place to use it."

Passionately the Count sprang forward. "It is the place to punish your treachery," he cried. And with a quick lunge of the sword he pierced the King in the throat. With a cry Philip rose, staggered forward a few steps, and fell lifeless to the ground.

Only two men were with the King, a bishop and his chamberlain. The bishop fled in terror, the chamberlain, drawn sword in hand, sprang upon the murderer; but, with a second sword-stroke, Otto wounded him also, so that he fell helpless to the ground. Then he fled from the room, sprang upon his horse, and galloped madly away.

Thus by the hand of a murderer died the kindliest of all the Hohenstaufen rulers. He was brave and strong, his people loved him, and even his enemies praised him. His whole reign, indeed, had been spent in warfare, and he had been able to do little for his kingdom. Now, just as peace seemed sure, he was struck down.

For some time the murderer wandered about, fleeing from place to place, hunted and hounded by all. No town would receive him; in neither castle nor cottage could he find refuge, and at length, after months of hunted misery, he was slain. His castle was razed to the ground, and, in order in some way to atone for his ruthless deed, a church was built upon the spot.

CHAPTER 33

# OTTO IV

FREDERICK, the little son of Henry VI, was now a boy of thirteen. The Pope had taken him under his care and crowned him King of Sicily. But no one thought making him King of Germany. So upon Philip's death the rival King Otto was accepted by all as ruler. Once more the land had peace, and Otto journeyed to Rome to receive the imperial crown.

He was crowned at Rome with all the usual ceremony, but almost at once a quarrel with the Pope began. For Otto did not mean to give up any of his rights over Italy, and he determined to reconquer young Frederick's kingdom of Sicily.

At this the Pope was full of wrath, and he excommunicated Otto. He also incited the nobles to depose him, and elect Frederick as Emperor.

But Otto cared not a whit for the Pope and his ban. His conquering armies swept through Italy, carrying all before them. He was already on the shore preparing to sail over to Sicily to give the finishing stroke to the last of the Hohenstaufens; young Frederick was ready flee to Africa, when the news came from Germany that many of the nobles had risen in revolt against Otto. They would no more acknowledge him as King, they said, and they chose Frederick the Hohenstaufen in his stead.

When he heard the news Otto determined to give up the conquest of Sicily, for the meantime. And in all haste he turned back to Germany to put down the rebellion.

Frederick too hastened towards Germany to put himself at the head of the rebel princes. But for him the journey was one of danger and adventure. For Italy was still full of Otto's friends, and Frederick had no army and hardly any money. Now in secret he hurried through an unfriendly city, again he lingered in one that was friendly. From one he slipped away in danger of his life, in another he was joyfully received. The town of Genoa lent him money, which Frederick promised to repay when he became Emperor. And the people of Genoa, knowing well that it was doubtful if they would ever see him or their money more, yet wished him Godspeed.

At length, after many dangers, Frederick reached the Alps, and crossed over into Germany. And there, before the magic of his name, beneath the sunshine of his smile, Otto's power seemed to melt away. More and more the princes forsook the gloomy, selfish Emperor, and flocked to the side of the handsome, pleasure-loving pretender, until, almost without a battle, Frederick became master of the whole of Southern Germany.

Foreign countries too took part in the quarrel. John, King of England, sent his nephew Otto help. And as France and England were deadly enemies, of course Philip of France took the opposite side and helped Frederick.

The Kings of France and England had quarrels of their own to settle. John of England at this time made up his mind to fight for his French possessions. And Otto, who, hated Philip of France, was well pleased to join with John against him. "It is the King of France alone," he said, "who destroys my power. Therefore, before all, Philip Augustus must die."

Otto's hatred of Philip was no new thing. It dated from the days when, as a new-made knight, he had followed in the train of Richard Coeur de Lion. In these days Richard and Philip had been fast friends.

"What think you of our noble cousin Otto?" asked Richard one day.

"Oh! I like him well enough," replied Philip carelessly.

The tone of this reply seemed to Richard so disdainful and scornful that he added quickly, "Ah, but one day Otto will be Roman Emperor."

Philip laughed mockingly. "If he," he cried, "ever becomes Roman Emperor, I will give him Chartres, Orleans, and Paris."

Quickly Richard turned to Otto. "Get up, nephew," he cried; "bow before the King for such great gifts."

Otto rose and bowed, and Philip thought no more of his scornful words. But as soon as Otto became Emperor he sent messengers to Philip reminding him of them, and bidding him fulfil his promise.

At first Philip laughed. He knew nothing of such folly, he said. But at length, the time and the place being recalled to him, he remembered. Then he laughed still more. "Tell your master," he said, "that I did not mean these three towns, but three young hounds who bore their names. If Emperor Otto liketh to have them they are at his service."

Because of this insult Otto had nursed wrath against Philip for many a long day. Now he meant to have his revenge. So, gathering all the men he could, he marched against the French.

The Germans with their English allies so greatly out-numbered the French that some of the French nobles, fearing defeat, begged the King not to fight, but to leave the battle to them.

"That would be most unkingly," replied Philip. "Far be it from me to flee so long as I have strength to fight. Shall I leave my people in the lurch, my people who are ready to die with me and for me? I shall remain to the last on the field, and either fall honourably or win gloriously. Who is most worthy," he added, "to carry the Oriflamme?"

"I know a poor, but brave and warlike knight," replied the Duke of Burgundy. "In order to fight for you he has sold all he had, that he might buy a horse. Give him the standard."

So the knight was called.

"Friend," said Philip, "I give the honour of France into your keeping."

"My lord King," cried he, astonished, "who am I that I should have so great an honour?"

"You are," said Philip, smiling, "a man who dares fear nothing, and who shall be richly rewarded so soon as we are victorious."

"What man can do, that will I do," replied the knight, taking the standard. "Well do I see," he cried, looking up at it, "that this Oriflamme is bloodthirsty. I will quench its thirst in the blood of the foe."

Then, having entered into a chapel near by to pray shortly, Philip mounted upon his war-horse and dashed into the fight.

Long and fiercely the battle raged, and long the victory seemed doubtful. Once the French King lay upon the ground, the sword of death at his throat, but his trusty armour and the swords of his faithful followers saved him. Once and again Otto's horse was slain under him. Then, seeing that the day went ill for him, he fled from the field.

The battle was lost; and in losing the battle of Bouvines Otto lost the last vestige of his power. He rode from the field a fallen Emperor.

The following year Frederick was crowned at Aachen. Otto still fought feebly for his crown, but with ill success. He had few followers left to him, and their rebellions scarcely disturbed the peace of the Empire. At length, in 1218, he died. With him died also the great struggle between Welf and Waiblingen which had torn Germany asunder for so many years.

CHAPTER 34

# FREDERICK II, THE WORLD'S WONDER

UNTIL Frederick II came to Germany to fight for the crown he had lived all his life in Italy, and he was far more Italian than German. He was brilliant and clever, a scholar and a poet, as well as a soldier and statesman. He could speak six languages, and was learned in all the learning of his time, as well as in all knightly arts, so that he was called the World's Wonder.

So long as Otto lived Frederick dared not leave Germany. But after he died he began to think once more of Italy, and in 1220 he journeyed to Rome, to receive the imperial crown.

The Pope had helped Frederick greatly in his struggle for the throne. But he had made him promise him many things in return, one being that he should go on a Crusade. But now Frederick did not seem inclined to keep his word, and for this and other reasons the Pope soon began to quarrel with him. Yet again and again he prayed him to set forth on his promised Crusade. Again and again Frederick found some excuse. At length, however, he married the daughter of the exiled King of Jerusalem, and calling himself King of Jerusalem he set out upon a Crusade. But before he had been three days at sea, much sickness broke out among the army, and he himself became so ill that he turned back again to Italy.

When the Pope, now Gregory IX, heard of this return he hardly knew what to do for grief and anger. He believed that this illness was merely a pretence. He believed that this was merely the last and worst of Frederick's many excuses. So once more the thunders of the Church were launched against a German Emperor, and Frederick was excommunicated.

The next year, however, Frederick set forth again. But this only made the Pope more angry. That an excommunicated man should dare to lead a crusade was an insult to the holy places, a mockery of God. So this crusade was followed not by the Pope's blessing, but by his curse. And while Frederick marched to free the Holy Land, the Pope proclaimed a crusade against him and sent soldiers to invade Sicily.

Still, dismayed neither by the Pope's soldiers nor by his threats and curses, Frederick continued on his journey. He reached the Holy Land, but he fought no battles. For he won from the Sultan by treaty far more than all the crusaders before him had won by the sword.

He met the Turks with smiles and soft words, instead of spears and blows, and he won from them a ten years' peace, and the possession of Jerusalem, Bethlehem, and Nazareth, as well as a strip of land leading from the coast to these towns. So henceforth without fear, pilgrims could pass through the land, to visit the holy places. Thus it was that a man under the curse of the Church won possession of the Holy Land for Christians, for the last time. Fifteen years later it was lost once more, and since then has never again been in the possession of Christians.

Greatly rejoicing at their quick and easy success, the crusaders now marched on to Jerusalem. But even here the anger of the Pope followed the Emperor, and because of him, the Holy City was laid under an interdict. No priest dared offer up a prayer of thanksgiving, or chant a hymn of victory. For he who had delivered the Holy Sepulchre was one accursed. No bishop dared set the crown upon his head, and anoint him King of Jerusalem. So it was through a silent church that Frederick walked in his kingly robes. He reached the altar where lay the crown. Lifting it, he placed it upon his head, and in silence as he had come, he returned with no holy oil upon his brow, with no blessing in his ear.

Less than a month later Frederick, having appointed a regent, left Palestine, and sailed back to Italy. Here he at once set himself to fight the Pope and drive his soldiers out of Sicily. This was soon done. Then, generously, Frederick tried again to make friends with the Pope. The Pope yielded; he removed the ban, and there was peace once more.

Now followed a quiet and prosperous time, during which Frederick ruled Sicily well, and with a statesmanship and wisdom far beyond that of any other ruler of his day. But he neglected Germany. The Emperor's young son Henry indeed ruled as regent, but he was a mere boy, and little regarded. Meanwhile, the great princes of Germany were pleased enough to be left to themselves, for they could do much as they liked. The great trading towns too grew more and more powerful. To protect their trade, they banded themselves together into leagues, the most powerful being the Hansa League.

This League became so important that all the trade of the Baltic and much of the trade of the North Sea, came into its hands. Much of the trade even of England was carried on by the merchants of the Hansa League. It had many soldiers in its pay, and great fleets of ships, so that

*He reached the altar where the crown lay;
lifting it, he placed it upon his head.*

not only the Emperor, but proud foreign kings like the King of England, or of France, were forced to respect its power.

Now between the strength of the nobles and the strength of the towns Frederick's power in Germany sank to little more than a name. And at length, when his power seemed at its lowest ebb, his son Henry headed a rebellion against him. Then, after fifteen years' absence, Frederick came back to Germany. Before his approach the rebellion melted away. He forgave his rebel son, but Henry would show neither sorrow nor repentance. So he was sent to prison in the south of Italy. There, still proud and unrepentant, he died a few years later, greatly to his father's grief. "I am not the first or the last," he said, "who, having suffered from a child's disobedience, must yet weep over his grave."

Frederick remained but a short time in Germany. Then he returned once more to Italy, and although he reigned thirteen years longer, he visited Germany no more.

Soon after Frederick's return to Italy he quarrelled once more with the Pope, and all his last years were filled with this struggle. The Pope once more excommunicated the Emperor and solemnly declared that he was deposed; but Frederick in his turn flung defiance at the Pope, and waged a war against him and his curses such as never King before him had dared to do.

The two heads of the Christian world fought with bitter hate, heaping scorn and insult upon each other. The Emperor called the Pope a mad priest, the Pope called the Emperor a pestilential King. The Pope then turned king-maker, and chose Henry Raspe as King. But he never had any power. Frederick's son Conrad, who now ruled Germany, defeated him near Ulm, and in a short time he died. The Pope then chose another King, William of Holland. But neither did he have any power. The whole country was, however, torn asunder by wars.

At length, in the midst of his struggle and defiance, Frederick fell suddenly ill and died in December 1250. "Let the heavens rejoice, and let the earth be glad," said the Pope when he heard of it.

CHAPTER 35

# CONRAD IV AND THE GREAT INTERREGNUM

DEATH did not put an end to the quarrel between Pope end Emperor, for the Pope at once turned his anger against Conrad IV, who succeeded his father.

Conrad IV was excommunicated; his kingdom was full of revolt and bloodshed. William of Holland disputed the throne with him, and he could hardly be said to rule, and after four years he died. He was the last of the Hohenstaufens to rule in Germany. After Conrad's death in 1254 began what is known as the Great Interregnum. Interregnum means, as you know, "between reigns," and for nineteen years there was no real emperor, although there were many who claimed the throne.

The first was William of Holland. Now that his rival was dead, he felt sure of the crown. He spent huge sums of money to win the great trading cities to his side, he bribed and flattered the princes. But he was too much a Pope's man, his power in Germany was small, and in 1256 he died in battle.

The great princes would now have been pleased to have the throne empty, and have no Emperor, so that they themselves might do as they liked. But the lesser nobles, and the cities, knowing the tyranny of the great princes, demanded an Emperor. The great princes were therefore forced to choose a new ruler. But they were determined that he should be a King only in name, so instead of choosing one from among themselves, they decided to choose a foreign prince, who would not be likely to live in Germany.

The choice fell upon two. One was Richard, Duke of Cornwall, the brother of our own Henry III. The other was King Alfonso of Castile. Both were anxious for the crown, and both scattered money broadcast among the people, and so it came about that both were chosen. But of the seven princes who now alone held the right of choosing, four voted for Richard, and three for Alfonso.

When at length messengers came to Richard telling him that he was chosen Emperor of Germany, he pretended at first to be unwilling to go to take possession of the throne. But after a little persuasion he yielded, and, bursting into tears, he swore to rule the kingdom well and justly.

Then in great state he set out with his wife and children and many followers for his new kingdom. Across the North Sea they sailed in fifty great ships, richly laden with gifts and money.

On May 17, 1257, Richard of Cornwall was crowned at Aachen, with the splendid new crown which he had brought with him from England. Then for nearly two years Richard stayed in Germany. He travelled here and there, scattering money and promises wherever he went, until all the Rhineland owned his sway, and many of the cities of Italy acknowledged him. But he won obedience only by his gold, and at length he had no more to give, and speedily many who had promised to support him fell away from him.

Richard wanted very much to go to Rome to be crowned, but that too required money. So he decided to return to England in order to get more.

But Richard found it impossible to get all the money he wanted, and after this he only paid short visits to his kingdom, and in April 1272 he died. He was the only Englishman who ever tried to rule the Holy Roman Empire.

As to Alfonso, the rival King, he had never visited his kingdom at all. So when Richard died the people became anxious to have a real Emperor once more. The great nobles, it is true, did not want one, for now they did much as they liked. They obeyed no will but their own; the only right in the land was might. The great castles were little more than the dens of thieves, and bands of robbers haunted the highways, a terror to the peaceful and law-abiding.

But the Pope had found that while Germany was in such a state of disorder, he got little money from the people there. He therefore sternly told the electors that they must choose an Emperor, for if they did not, he would choose one for them. So at length Count Rudolph of Hapsburg was chosen.

CHAPTER 36

# RUDOLPH OF HAPSBURG

RUDOLPH was already an elderly man of fifty-four when he was chosen as King. But he was a brave soldier, kindly and simple, yet full of wisdom. All the princes gave their votes for him except Ottocar, King of Bohemia. He had hoped to be chosen himself, for he was a mighty King, ruling not only over Bohemia, but over many lands around, which by one means or another he had brought under his sway. A great King himself, he was angry that a mere Count had been chosen, and he refused to acknowledge him.

Rudolph was crowned at Aachen with great and solemn ceremony. But when after the coronation the princes came, as was the custom, to touch the tip of the sceptre, and take the oath of allegiance to the new King, the sceptre could not be found. In the troubles of the Interregnum it had been lost.

At once there arose an angry tumult. Without the sceptre, said some, the ceremony could not be held binding, and both King and vassals might deny their oath. "How could we be sure," some asked, "that the land we do fealty for is certainly ours if the ceremony be not properly performed?"

Hotter and hotter the tumult waxed, then in the midst of it Rudolph went quietly to the altar, and took from it a crucifix. "See," he cried as he held it aloft, "behold the sign by which we and the whole world are saved. It opens all heaven to us; surely it may serve to ensure our little bits of earth." Then reverently he kissed the crucifix, and, turning, again took his place upon the throne, ready to receive the homage of his nobles.

The tumult was stilled at once. All were pleased at Rudolph's ready wit, and the ceremony ended peacefully. Then, as the people crowded about the King, cheering and rejoicing, he cried aloud, "To-day I forgive every one who has done me ill. All prisoners who languish in my prisons shall go free, and I swear from this day forward to be a protector of the country's peace."

When the people heard these words they were right glad, and it seemed to them that with their new King a new and better time was coming for them.

Already, it was said, swords began to rust, the peasants once more brought out their ploughs, and the merchant passed through the land no longer in fear of robbers.

But the new King had one bitter enemy. This was Ottocar, King of Bohemia. He would not acknowledge Rudolph. Three times he was called upon to do homage. Three times with many scornful words he refused to bend the knee to this "miserable count."

Rudolph then resolved to fight against his rebel vassal. He had scarcely any army, it is true, and all his kingly treasure was five bad shillings. But he was a brave soldier, and had no fear of defeat.

And as Rudolph marched through the land, soldiers from every town and village flocked to his banner. Many of the rebel lords who had joined with Ottocar yielded to him, and everywhere the common people welcomed him as a deliverer.

With ever-growing fear, proud Ottocar saw the great army which had gathered about the despised count, and when at length Rudolph reached the Danube, and made ready to cross it, Ottocar yielded.

Upon a meadow by the Danube Rudolph and his vassal met. The King, clad in a plain grey robe, sat upon a three-legged stool to receive his homage. Ottocar, proud and splendidly handsome, came dressed in glittering robes, sparkling with gems and gold. Behind him followed a great train of knights and vassals almost as gorgeous as their master.

When the Germans saw this glittering procession approach, they begged Rudolph to array himself in his kingly robes, so that he should not be outdone in magnificence by the King of Bohemia. But Rudolph only laughed.

"The King of Bohemia has scoffed often enough at my grey robe," he said. "Now my grey robe shall scoff at him. German fame is won by good armour, not by clothes."

The November sky was dark, and creeping mists spread over the plain as slowly the glittering procession approached. It paused, and the King, in his resplendent robes, bent his knee before the tall lean figure in the shabby grey coat. It was so strange a sight that shouts of rude laughter burst from the crowd of onlookers.

Ottocar's face flushed red at the insult. Yet he curbed his anger for the moment, and knelt to give back to this grey-clad man all his mighty possessions, Austria, Syria, Corinthia, Carniola, Moravia, and Bohemia. Rudolph received them all, giving back only Moravia and Bohemia to be held as fiefs of the Empire. Then, the better to bind Ottocar to the

Empire, he commanded that the young prince, his son, should be married to Ottocar's daughter.

But Ottocar rose from his knees with hatred and wrath burning in his heart. The scornful laughter of Rudolph's followers still rang in his ears, and he turned from his King, no humble vassal, but a rebel more bitter than before.

Ottocar determined that his daughter should not marry the King's son, and to prevent her doing so he sent her to a convent, and once more he declared war against his liege lord.

On August 26, 1278, a great battle was fought at Marchfeld, near Vienna. It was a glorious sunny morning, and the Germans dashed to battle crying "Rome and Christ! Rome and Christ!"

A knight in Ottocar's army had sworn to kill Rudolph, and as the battle raged he galloped wildly towards the King. He aimed a mighty blow at him. It missed the King but struck his horse, which stumbled and threw its rider into a river which flowed near by. Quickly the King recovered himself. With one hand he grasped the branches of an overhanging tree so that he might not be swept away. With the other he defended himself, dealing mighty blows to right and left. The King was in great danger of his life until a young knight, seeing his evil plight, fought his way to him, drew him out of the stream, and set him upon a fresh horse.

Still the battle raged, swaying now this way, now that. At length, from the German side arose the cry, "They flee! They flee!"

It was true. Yet, though all about him fled, surrounded by a faithful few Ottocar still fought on. Great deeds he did, mighty blows he dealt, and man after man went down before him.

But he was worn out by the heat of the day, and by the long fighting. At length he could make a stand no longer, and, well-nigh dazed, he too turned and fled.

After him dashed his foes. One by one his few remaining followers were struck to the ground. At last he too fell, sorely wounded. Helpless, swooning, all but dead, he lay upon the ground. Then his enemies, forgetting all knightly courtesy, killed him where he lay. One thrust a sword through his heart, another a dagger at his throat. Then they rode quickly away, leaving him dead. And there some camp-followers, seeking for plunder, found the once proud and splendid King. They robbed him of his rich armour and clothing, and left his body all naked and blood-stained upon the field.

Soon it was known through all the camp that Ottocar was slain, and many who had trembled before him in life gathered round to scoff at his dead body. But Rudolph looked upon his fallen foe with sorrowful eyes. He commanded that the dead King should be clad in robes of befitting splendour and be reverently buried.

Thus Rudolph of Hapsburg conquered. Ottocar's son, Wenceslas, made peace with him, and married one of his daughters. But Wenceslas was shorn of much of his land, for Rudolph took the dukedom of Austria and gave it to his own son Albert. It is interesting to remember that the house of Hapsburg still rules in Austria.

And now Rudolph, having conquered his great enemy at home, might have turned his thoughts to Italy. But instead of trying to extend his sway over Italy, as so many rulers of Germany before him had done, he gave up all his time to bringing peace and order into disordered Germany. "Italy," he said, "is for Germany but the den of the sick lion. I see many footsteps leading into it, but none leading out from it." So Rudolph left Italy alone, thereby avoiding fierce and useless warfare with the Pope, and the loss of many brave soldiers and much money. He did not even go to Italy to be crowned.

Having no wars with Italy, Rudolph had all the more time to give to ruling Germany. He rooted out the robber nobles. "No man who lives by robbery and dishonesty," he said, "is fit to be a knight." And in one year he hanged twenty-nine of these free-booting lords, and razed sixty-six of their castles to the ground.

Rudolph was very stern to these unruly nobles, but he was very kindly to the poor, and no poor man ever sought his help in vain. "In God's name," he cried once, when his courtiers would have driven away a poor man, "let every one come to me. I did not become a King to be shut up in a cage. Nay, but that all who need my help might come to me unhindered."

Rudolph's soldiers had to suffer many hardships, for at the beginning of his reign the King was very poor, and both he and they were often in want of food. But the King shared all the hardships with his men. Once it is said, when every one was crying aloud for bread, Rudolph went to a field of turnips. Pulling one up he peeled and ate it. "As long as we have these," he said, "we can do without bread."

Another time, as they were besieging a city, a captain came to him asking what he was to do for food, for his men had nothing to eat. "If we take the town," replied Rudolph calmly, "we shall find food enough within it. If we are killed we shall have no more need of food. If we are taken prisoner our captives will feed us. Take your choice."

The King's men took the town, and as Rudolph had promised, they found plenty of food within it.

Rudolph loved a jest too, and many stories are told of him. Once when he lay encamped near Mainz the weather became very cold and he could not get warm, in his tent. So in the early morning he went to a baker's oven to warm himself. He was dressed, as usual, in his old grey cloak, and the baker's wife was angry when she saw this loafer hanging around, looking out for a chance to steal anything he could lay hands on, as it seemed to her. So in an angry voice she bade him be off.

"Don't be so angry, good wife," replied the King. "I am an honest soldier, and if I'm poor, why that's because King Rudolph is poor too."

"Be off with you to your Beggar-King, "answered the woman. "You deserve all you get, coming into our land, and stealing the bread out of poor folks' mouths."

"What has the poor King done that is so very bad?" asked Rudolph.

"Done!" cried the woman; "is it not enough that all the bakers have become beggars through him and his war? Done! indeed! be off with you, or I will send you packing a way you won't like."

But the King was very comfortable by the warm fire. He was amused, too, at the old woman, and he refused to go, in spite of all her scolding. So, as nothing would make him move, she suddenly seized a pail of cold water and flung it over him. Dripping wet, the King at length turned and fled.

At mid-day, when the King sat at dinner, he called a page to him and commanded him to take a dish with all the choicest meats, together with a bottle of good wine, and carry it to the old dame. "Say to her," he said, "that it is from the old soldier, with his best thanks for the cold bath she gave him this morning."

As soon as the messenger had gone, the King, with much laughter, told the assembled company of his adventure of the morning.

But when the baker's wife heard that it was the King she had railed at, and drenched with water, she was filled with fear. With a heavy heart, knowing not what would become of her, she went at once to him where he sat at table, and throwing herself on her knees, begged forgiveness.

"Nay, my good dame," said the King, with a laugh, I will not forgive you unless you repeat all the words you said to me this morning."

The poor woman trembled on her knees; fear robbed her of speech. Dumb with terror, she looked at the King. Then she saw the merry twinkle in his eye, and taking heart she rose to her feet. And there, before all the knights and nobles, amid roars of laughter, she poured forth a torrent of abuse upon the King, even as she had done in the morning.

From such stories we learn that there was little of the splendour of the Hohenstaufens about Rudolph. But he was brave and kindly, and in an evil time he ruled well, he wrought order out of disorder, he crushed the lawless great, and befriended the poor. So the people loved him.

To the end he faced life as a soldier should. At the age of seventy-four he fell ill. And when his doctors told him that he had little longer to live, he did not blench. "Up then to Spires," he cried, "where my kingly forbears lie. No man shall carry me thither. I shall myself ride to them." And thus Rudolph set out for the last resting-place of the Emperors, and all the way was lined with sorrowing people who came to snatch one last look at their King.

He had his last wish indeed, and reached Spires, but only as a dying man, and there, on July 15, 1291, he died.

CHAPTER 37

# ADOLPHUS I OF NASSAU

DURING his lifetime Rudolph had tried to make the nobles choose and crown his son Albert as his successor. But he had tried in vain. For Albert was a gloomy, unlovable man, and the nobles feared him. Therefore, upon Rudolph's death, they rejected Albert and chose Adolphus, Count of Nassau, as King.

Adolphus was a poor Count, poorer even than Rudolph had been when he came to the throne, and he won the crown by the help of the clergy, chiefly by that of the Archbishop of Mainz. But he won it, too, by giving many and great promises to the Church—promises he never meant to keep.

But however Adolphus had won the crown, he showed himself to be a bold, stern king. He kept peace within the land, and even the dark-browed Albert bent the knee to him and acknowledged him as overlord.

Edward I of England was at war with France, so he made friends with Adolphus. And, to win his help against the King of France, Edward gave Adolphus a large sum of money. Adolphus took the money right willingly, but he never struck one blow in Edward's cause.

Instead of raising an army to fight for England he spent part of the money in buying Thuringia from Albert the Worthless. But Albert's sons, Frederick of the Bitten Cheek, and Diezmann, rebelled at being thus defrauded of their heritage. Then there was war between them and Adolphus.

Meanwhile the Archbishop of Mainz had been growing ever more and more angry because Adolphus had not kept his promises to make the Church more powerful. The King, whom he had hoped to find a mere tool in his hands, had grown self-willed. So the Archbishop began to urge the princes of the realm to depose Adolphus and make Albert, Duke of Austria, the son of Rudolph of Hapsburg, King instead.

Albert was very willing to be King. He had always hated Adolphus, and although he had done homage to him he had ever thwarted him, and done him all the mischief he could.

So King Adolphus was deposed and Albert chosen to succeed him.

But Adolphus would not lightly give up his crown, and he gathered his army to fight for it.

Albert also gathered his army, and the foes met on the field of Gollheim near Worms. On both sides fluttered the same royal standard—the white cross on a red ground. Both kings wore the same golden armour, with the black eagle embroidered on their surcoats.

It was July. The heat was terrific, and many fell dead, struck down, not by their foes, but by the sun. Stifled by the heat the Duke's standard-bearer died in the saddle. But dead, he still sat upon his horse, his stiffened hand still clung to the standard, while the maddened steed galloped wildly up and down the ranks, a sight terrible to behold.

Hotly the battle raged, and fiercely the sun beat upon the struggling men. The King was thrown from his horse. Shaken and stunned he was led out of the press. But as soon as he recovered himself he leaped upon another horse. His head however was so hurt that he could not wear a helmet. Glad of the relief, unmindful of the danger, he dashed bareheaded once more into the fray. In the midst of the clash and clang of battle the rival kings met. They were clad alike, save that the head of Adolphus was bare.

"Here shall you yield me the Empire," cried Adolphus, as he dashed upon the foe.

"That lies in the hand of God," answered Albert, and his heavy sword descended upon the King's bare head. Quickly knights rushed between them. The King was surrounded, and fought with desperate courage, but at length he fell wounded to death.

As the news of Adolphus's death spread over the field fighting ceased. Albert was now undisputed King, and there was no more reason for fighting.

CHAPTER 38

# ALBERT THE ONE-EYED

ALBERT had already been chosen as King; the battle of Gollheim and the death of Adolphus had left him without a rival. But he was not willing to seem to have won the throne by force. So a second election was held. Albert was again chosen King, and crowned with great ceremony at Aachen.

As King Albert, holding high state, sat upon his throne with his Queen beside him, a beautiful lady, clad in mourning robes, came slowly towards them. It was Queen Imogen, King Adolphus's widow. She threw herself at the Queen's feet, begging that her son who had been taken prisoner at Gollheim might be set free.

Cold and unmoved Albert looked down upon the strained white face; with a scornful smile he listened to the pleading voice. With scornful words he refused to set the young prince free.

Sobbing bitterly, Queen Imogen rose from her knees. She flung back her veil, and as the tears streamed from her eyes a bright spot burned on her pale cheeks. It was at the Queen's feet she had knelt. It was the Queen's mercy she implored, and the Queen had been silent. Young, beautiful, and serene, she looked unmoved upon the sorrow of the uncrowned Queen.

"May God reward you," cried Imogen. "One day may your heart know the sorrow that is mine." And so she turned and left the Court.

Less than ten years later there came a day when Queen Elizabeth remembered these words in bitterness of heart.

The princes and nobles now found that the one-eyed Albert was a far more powerful and stern ruler than ever the despised Count of Nassau had been.

He was cold and stern, but wise, and he set himself at once to bring peace into the land, to curb the power of the nobles, and strengthen the power of the King.

Meanwhile, however, the Pope would not acknowledge him. For, said the Pope, Albert was no better than a rebel who had murdered his liege lord. But Albert declared that the Pope had nothing to do with it, and that it was enough that the German princes had chosen him as King. And the better to strengthen himself against the Pope, Albert made friends with

Germany's old enemy, Philip the Handsome, King of France. For Philip, too, was at this time quarrelling with the Pope.

It was agreed that Albert's son Rudolph should marry Philip's sister, and should succeed him as King France.

But this dallying with France made the princes of Germany very angry. Encouraged by the Pope, some of them plotted to depose Albert, even as they had deposed Adolphus. They bound themselves together against "Albert, Duke of Austria, who is now called King of Germany." And they declared him no longer King, because he had rebelled against Adolphus and murdered him. Albert, however, marched against the rebel princes with an army, and soon subdued the revolt.

Albert's victory over the rebels was brilliant and complete. Never, since the days of Henry VI, had King ruled more absolutely in Germany. But in his heart Albert well knew that his seat upon the throne of Germany was most uncertain. The hearts of the people were not with him. So now he resolved to make friends with the Pope, in order that he might receive from him the Imperial crown, and thus strengthen his position in Germany.

And the Pope, who lived in daily fear of the French King's ever-growing power and hate, was glad to make friends with the King of Germany.

All the same, in return for his friendship, the Pope made Albert take the oath of fealty to him as to his overlord. He made Albert acknowledge that it was from the Pope that the princes of the Empire received the right to choose their King. Thus did Albert lightly give up much that those before him had fought for fiercely.

It was a heavy price to pay for the Pope's friendship, and in return he got little of the expected help from the Pope. For Philip the Handsome, as you will read in French history, took the Pope prisoner. A month later he died, and the new Pope was little more than a tool in the hands of the French King.

Albert now turned his attention to making his own family and house rich and great. That had for long been his chief desire, and he tried continually to bring more and more lands under the direct rule of the Hapsburgs.

Like Adolphus, he tried to force Frederick of the Bitten Cheek and his brother to give up Thuringia. He declared Bohemia to be his fief, and gave it to his son Rudolph. He tried to usurp the countship of Holland, and to make the free Cantons of Switzerland into a Hapsburg possession. But in all these schemes he failed, and added but little to his own lands. His struggle, however, to subdue Switzerland into a mere family possession, has become world-famous.

## ALBERT THE ONE-EYED

In Germany Albert was a stern ruler; towards Switzerland, it is said, he showed himself a very tyrant, and out of this tyranny rose the free republic of Switzerland.

Up to this time the country, which we now call Switzerland, as a country did not exist. It was divided into Cantons, one of which was called Schwyz, and this one Canton being always foremost in the fight for freedom, in time gave its name to the whole country. All these cantons formed part of the Empire, and the struggle for freedom was at first not a revolt against the Empire, but against the tyranny of the Hapsburgs.

Already upon the death of Rudolph, three of these cantons had joined together in what is called the Everlasting League. Soon others joined, for the tyranny and the insolence of the Hapsburgs grew daily greater.

It was now that Hermann Gessler was sent as ruler of the Cantons of Schwyz and Uri. He, in his pride and insolence, one day set up his cap, upon a pole, in the market-place of Altdorf, and bade the people bow to it.

The story hardly belongs to the History of Germany, so you must read elsewhere how William Tell refused to obey, how Gessler, in his wrath, forced him to shoot an apple from his son's head, and how in revenge Tell slew Gessler.

Tell came to be looked upon as the national hero of Switzerland, and his wonderful shot the beginning of the Swiss struggle for freedom. Wise people, however, say that Tell never lived, and that the stories of Albert's tyranny are not true.

That may be so. But it is now, at least, that the Swiss fight for freedom truly began. It was a long, hard struggle, and two hundred years passed before Switzerland was really free.

Meanwhile, whether Albert was a tyrant or not, he strove to make the Swiss Cantons fiefs of the house of Austria. But all his strivings came to a sudden end.

Albert had a nephew, Duke John of Swabia. His father had died when he was a tiny boy, and his uncle had become his guardian, ruling his lands. But now that Duke John had grown to manhood, Albert, in his greed for land and power, still kept possession of the lands belonging to his nephew. Again and again Duke John had prayed his uncle to give him back his possession. Again and again Albert refused with scorn.

So bitter hatred against his uncle grew up in Duke John's heart, and at length, with three other nobles, he plotted to murder the King.

On the first day of May, as Duke John sat at dinner with his uncle, once more he begged to be given his inheritance. Once more Albert refused, putting him off with promises.

At this moment a page entered, bringing in wreaths of flowers. To each of his guests Albert gave one, with some jesting word. The most beautiful he gave to his nephew. "You shall be a May King," he said with a laugh, as he placed the flowery wreath upon Duke John's head.

But with tears of anger in his eyes Duke John tore off the wreath, and tossed it upon the table. And while the other guests drank and feasted, he and his companions sat sullenly refusing either to eat or drink.

As soon as the feast was over the King rose, and, mounting his horse, set forth to meet his Queen who was journeying towards him. As his custom was he wore no armour and carried no weapon, and was accompanied only by a few followers.

On the way the river Reuss had to be crossed by a narrow ford. Here Duke John succeeded in separating Albert from his followers, and upon the other side of the river the unsuspecting King found himself alone with the conspirators.

As they rode along one of the conspirators suddenly exclaimed, "How long shall we let this knave ride?" Then Duke John's servant sprang forward and seized the King's bridle. Before he could cry out for help, Duke John had thrust him through the heart. The others, too, sprang upon him, and Albert sank to the ground, wounded in neck and breast and face.

The murderers fled, leaving the dying King upon the ground. There a poor woman who passed that way found him. She did what she could for him, but that was little, and when his followers arrived they found their King, who scarce an hour ago they had seen riding forward full of life, dying, his head pillowed on the lap of a beggar woman.

The Queen was filled with unutterable grief at the death of her husband, and she pursued his murderers with bitter hatred. Yet most of them escaped. One, indeed, was brought to death in terrible fashion. But with that the Queen's vengeance was by no means satisfied, and many innocent men and women suffered death and torture ere it was stilled.

Duke John escaped. But he found no man to pity or shelter him. All turned from him in horror, and he is known in history as John the Parricide. For many months he wandered about in misery. At length he found refuge in a monastery, where he died.

CHAPTER 39

# HENRY VII OF LUXEMBURG

EXCEPT his wife and children, who loved him dearly, few, if any, mourned for Albert's death. He had been a stern and harsh ruler, yet he was wise with a wisdom beyond his times. He had ruled Germany with more of the spirit of modern times than any King before him. He had protected the cities and their trade, and he had curbed the pride of the unruly nobles. Therefore the nobles hated him, and now they determined to choose a King who would have little power and no desire to make his family great.

But Philip of France now cast a greedy eye upon the Empire. He had made himself master of the Pope, and had forced him to leave Rome and come to live in France. He now hoped to be master of the Empire too, and he did all he could to make the electors choose his brother, Charles of Valois.

Philip forced the Pope also to appear to wish Charles to be chosen. But in his heart the Pope was against such a choice, and while openly he encouraged it, in secret he urged the electors to choose another King.

In spite of all Philip's persuasions and scheming, the electors rejected Charles of Valois, and to be ruler of Germany they chose once again a poor Count. This was Henry, Count of Luxemburg. He seemed rather a Frenchman than a German. For French was his mother-tongue and the language spoken at his little court, his countship being on the borders of France and Germany.

It was a wild and lonely district. Yet he ruled so well that no spot in all the Empire was more peaceful or more safe. Far and near he was known as a peace-loving, wise, and brave man.

As soon as he was crowned Henry did all he could to bring peace to the land. He made friends with Albert's proud sons, Leopold and Frederick, and in one way or another worked for the good of the country.

Then having made peace in Germany, Henry resolved to cross the Alps and receive the Imperial crown. Not for fifty years had a German King claimed rule over Italy, not since Frederick II had any German King borne the title of Emperor, and German power over Italy was really at an end. But for centuries the German kings had, in name at least, been rulers of the world. They were loth to give up that proud title, and so the nobles gladly accompanied their King over the Alps.

Italy was at this time in a state of wildest confusion. The whole country was divided into factions, the rival parties still calling themselves Guelph and Ghibelline. although the old meaning of the name had long since died out. At first Henry was received as a herald of peace, both parties greeting him with joy. The great poet Dante came forth to meet him, praising him as the saviour of Italy. Even the city of Milan, the bitterest enemy of German rule, opened its gates to the King who came in peace, and with rejoicing on all sides the iron crown of Lombardy was placed upon his brow.

But all this peace and joy was short-lived. Party hate was not dead, it did not even slumber. Soon it burst forth in fury, and it was with his sword that Henry had to cut his way to Rome and the long-desired Imperial crown.

Rome was reached, but only after two months' fighting. Even then part of the city, with the great church of St. Peter, in which the Emperors had always been crowned, was still held by the enemy. Weeks, even months, might pass ere they could be forced to yield. So rather than delay longer, Henry caused himself to be crowned in the Church of the Lateran.

Then once more he set forth to fight. It seemed now as if he might be victorious. Frederick of Sicily made peace with him. Pisa and Genoa opened their gates. Venice promised him ships, a great army was hurrying from Germany to his aid. Then suddenly, on the threshold of his success, when all Italy trembled before him, Henry died at Buonconvento, near Siena.

The noblest men of Italy mourned his loss. With him their hopes of a united, peaceful country sank into the grave. In Germany, too, although he had spent little time there, his loss was mourned. Since the time of the great King Charlemagne there had been none greater, it was said. But while his friends mourned his death his enemies shouted aloud for joy. Towns were illuminated, bonfires were lit, religious processions were held in thanksgiving. "I send you the most joyful news," wrote one Italian, "that terrible tyrant Henry, Count of Luxemburg, whom the rebels call King of the Romans and Emperor of Germany, is dead."

With the death of the Emperor all his conquests vanished, and the Germans turned quickly home again, leaving their dead Emperor in Pisa. Soon the stone above his grave was the only sign left of his conquering march, and in Italy the might of the Emperor was no more than the light of a blown-out candle.

CHAPTER 40

# LEWIS IV OF BAVARIA AND FREDERICK THE HANDSOME

UPON the death of Henry VII the electors could not agree among themselves as to who should be the next king. In the end two were chosen. The one was Frederick the Handsome, the son of Albert I. The other was Lewis, Duke of Bavaria. They had both been born in the same year; they had been brought up together as loving comrades. Now suddenly, both desiring to be Emperor, they became bitter enemies.

Each party was determined to have its chosen King and none other, and so soon all Germany was divided into two hostile camps, and a great army was gathered on either side.

Lewis gained possession of Aachen. Frederick, finding his rival master of the royal city, hastened to Bonn and was crowned there the day before Lewis was crowned at Aachen.

Now Germany was filled with war and bloodshed, every prince taking one side or another, but for some time no decisive battle was fought. Each side seemed to want to ruin the cause of the other by plundering expeditions rather than face a great battle.

In this quarrel the Swiss sided with Lewis. So Frederick's brother, Leopold, marched against them, full of anger and insolently sure of victory.

Leopold's army was large. It was full of the greatest knights and nobles of the land, and the men were well armed and well drilled. When the Swiss heard of the coming of this mighty host they were greatly troubled, and they sought if they might by any means make peace. But Leopold of Austria was sure of victory, and he refused to listen to any terms.

The Swiss then made their preparations, determined to die rather than yield. They took possession of the height above the narrow pass through which the Austrian army must come. There both day and night they kept watch.

At length, one November morning, the Austrian army came riding down the pass in all its pride and splendour. The heavily-armoured knights rode first in careless array, for they were full of contempt for the peasants against whom they came, and were certain of an easy victory. Behind them pressed the foot soldiers, rank on rank.

But suddenly from the heights above them great boulders came thundering down, heavy tree trunks and showers of stones crashed upon them. Men and horses were crushed beneath the falling masses, the whole army was thrown into mad confusion. Then with wild shouts the mountaineers rushed down the slopes. Shod with spiked boots, which gave them safe foothold on the steep descent, they moved quickly and surely, dealing deadly blows with their terrible spiked clubs called Morning-stars.

It was scarce a battle; it was a massacre. The Austrian knights, caught like wild animals in a trap, hemmed in between the mountain and lake, were at the mercy of the Swiss peasants. They fell by thousands, while of the Swiss but twenty were killed.

Those who escaped from the narrow pass of death fled in all directions. But even in flight there was little safety, and many perished among the snows of the pathless mountain valleys.

Leopold himself escaped, however, and after many trials, reached home half dead with shame and sorrow.

Lewis rejoiced greatly over this victory. And although it was not important enough to end the quarrel between the two kings, it helped to encourage the Swiss in their struggle for freedom.

For ten years the war of succession continued, and at last was brought to an end by the terrible battle at Muhldorf.

Clad in splendid armour with a golden crown upon his helmet, and the royal eagle as his crest, so that all might know him for the King, Frederick dashed into the fray. Where the fight waxed fiercest, there was his golden crowned helmet to be seen, and with his own hand, it is said, he slew fifty knights.

Lewis, on his side, took little part in the fighting, but left the leadership to an old knight, Siegfried of Schweppermann.

Clad in a blue surcoat marked with a white cross, and surrounded by eleven other knights dressed like him, Lewis watched the battle as it raged before him. Victory seemed uncertain. Now one side gained an advantage, now another. At length a new army of soldiers was seen approaching.

At first the Austrians thought that it was Duke Leopold come to aid his brother. But soon they saw their mistake. The new soldiers had come to help Lewis. The battle was won and the Austrians fled before the onslaught of these fresh soldiers.

Many prisoners were taken, among them King Frederick. He fought while he could, but his horse being killed beneath him he at last yielded to a noble and was led before King Lewis.

Standing under the spreading branches of a great tree Lewis received his prisoner. "Cousin," he said, "I was never more glad to see you."

"And I," said Frederick, a dark frown on his beautiful face, "was never more sorry to see you."

Lewis, it is said, was right grateful to the brave old knight who had won the victory for him. When evening came, and the tired troops sat down to a well-earned meal, there was little to eat. For the country round had been plundered, and laid bare. All that could be got was an egg for each man, and two for the King. But the King would not have it so. "Nay," he said, "every man of us shall have an egg, but the ever blessed Schweppermann shall have two."

Frederick was now shut up in the castle of Trausnitz, and there for nearly three years he remained, while his beautiful wife wept herself blind for him, and his brother Leopold still fought for him.

Leopold made friends with the Pope and with the King of France, with any or everybody who would help him against Lewis. For he loved his brother passionately and longed to set him free and see him King. But all that Leopold could do was of no avail, and Frederick still remained a prisoner.

It was Lewis himself who at length sought to make friends once more. He went to Frederick in his prison and promised to set him free if he would give up all claim to the throne.

The long imprisonment had broken Frederick's spirit. He no longer wished to fight, he longed only for freedom. So willingly he gave up his claim to the throne, Together the two enemies knelt at the altar, and received the Holy Sacrament, then with tears in their eyes they kissed each other and swore to be friends once more.

After this, Frederick set out to find his brother and pursuade him to lay down his arms, and make his peace with Lewis. Before he went he promised that, should he not succeed, he would return again to his prison. When he reached home his nobles and vassals received him with joy. But they hardly knew him, for his shining golden hair had grown grey, and his beard which, as a sign of grief he had never cut during all the time of his imprisonment, was long and white as that of an old man. But his changed appearance mattered little to his wife. His voice she heard and knew; trembling with joy, she felt his arms once more about her. She could not see the face she loved so well, for her grief had made her blind.

CHAPTER 41

# LEWIS IV OF BAVARIA AND FREDERICK THE HANDSOME

FREDERICK could not persuade his brother Leopold to yield to Lewis, and so after a short time he bade a sad farewell to his family, and once more returned to prison. But now Lewis received him as a friend. Touched to the heart by his enemy's knightly deed, he threw his arms about him, and swore that henceforth they should be as brothers. And henceforth it was so. They sat together at table, they shared one bed, and at length Lewis decided that they should share the throne.

So to all the Empire he sent forth the decree that they two should be looked upon as one Emperor. "We, Lewis and Frederick," ran the decree, "by the grace of God, Kings of the Romans, do hereby declare and make known that we are united and bound together for ever more; that we having both been chosen and consecrated shall as one person have, and possess, guide and rule, the Holy Roman Empire. Equal honour shall we have in street, and in church, and in every place."

And now at length, seeing his brother on the throne, Leopold yielded and made peace with Lewis. Soon afterwards he died, to the great grief of Frederick. "Why have you left me thus lonely?" he cried in despair. "Of what good is life to me without you?"

Frederick grieved for the loss of his brother, but Lewis well knew that, by his death, peace was made more secure. So now he prepared to march into Italy, to receive the Imperial crown. For it had been agreed that although Frederick should share the title of King, Lewis alone should receive that of Emperor.

Lewis had already quarrelled with the Pope, who denied his right to the throne and excommunicated him. But Lewis determined to set the claims of the Pope at nought, and be crowned Emperor in spite of him.

The Ghibellines of Milan received him with joy, and set upon his head the iron crown of Lombardy. From Milan he marched southward to Rome. Here too, the people received him gladly. But there was no Pope to crown him either willingly or unwillingly. For the Pope, still under the power of the French King, was more than half a prisoner at Avignon.

But in spite of the Pope's absence and anger, the coronation took place. A bishop was found to anoint Lewis, and a noble placed the crown upon his head.

Then, when the Pope preached a crusade against Lewis, and thundered against him all the curses of the Church, Lewis declared him deposed and set up a Pope of his own choosing. And by this Pope, Nicholas V, Lewis was for the second time crowned Emperor.

But the fickle Italians soon began to tire of their new Emperor. Many of them took the real Pope's part against him. And when in 1330, on the news of Frederick's death, Lewis returned to Germany, Italy was already lost to him. His anti-pope was driven from the throne. By his expedition to Italy, he had gained nothing but a life-long and very bitter enemy in Pope John XXII.

Frederick having died, Lewis was now sole ruler of Germany, and after a time he tried to make friends with the Pope, but he tried in vain. But the Pope had no longer the tremendous power he used to have. The people and the Emperor of Germany no longer cowered beneath his ban, and the princes of the realm were not afraid to take the part of their Emperor against him. In 1338 the Electors all met together and solemnly declared that the Emperor took his rank and crown, not from the Pope but from them.

The princes thus showed themselves boldly to be on the side of their King. And had Lewis been wise, he might have become one of the most powerful Emperors Germany had ever known. But Lewis was not wise. Instead of thinking of the Empire, he thought merely of his own house, and tried to make that great. In many ways he added land upon land to his private possessions until at length he and his son became so rich that the jealousy and anger of the princes was aroused.

Tyrol belonged to a lady named Margaret Maultasch, and Lewis thought he would like that land too for his son, and resolved that he should marry the Lady Margaret. The Lady Margaret was already married, but she was very unhappy, so Lewis took upon himself to divorce her from her husband, and allow her to marry his son. In doing this he usurped the power of the Pope, for he alone had power to unmake a marriage. So once more the sleeping wrath of the Pope was roused against the Emperor. Once more the thunders of Rome shook the Imperial throne, and the Pope called upon the princes to depose the King and choose another. This time the princes were ready to listen to the Pope. They declared

Lewis deposed, and chose Charles, the son of the blind King John of Bohemia, and grandson of Henry VII, as the next Emperor. This was in July. In August, the battle of Crecy was fought between the French and English, and both King John and his son the new chosen Emperor, fought on the side of the French. John, you remember, met his death in the thick of the fight, while his son fled from the field.

After Crecy, Charles returned to Germany. But although he had been chosen King the people of Germany now refused to acknowledge him. Both the royal cities of Aachen and Cologne shut their gates against him, so he had to content himself with being crowned in Bonn, as Frederick the Handsome had been.

But, crowned or not, the people would still not acknowledge him. "A priest's king," they called him in scorn. And at length, disguised as a peasant, the would-be Emperor had to steal through the land until he reached Bohemia. There in his own country he began to gather an army to fight for the crown.

Lewis too, began to gather his army. But one morning, not feeling well, and hoping that the fresh air would do him good, he set out upon a boar hunt in the forest near Munich. Suddenly, as he rode along, he swayed in the saddle and, almost without warning, he fell to the ground.

Anxiously his attendants crowded round him. But there was little to be done, for the hand of death was upon him. "Sweet Queen, our Lady," he murmured, "be with me at my passing." Then he lay still.

CHAPTER 42

# CHARLES IV—THE STEP-FATHER OF THE EMPIRE

ALTHOUGH their leader was now dead, Lewis's friends and followers still refused to acknowledge Charles as ruler. So they elected first Edward III of England, and then Frederick, Marquess of Meissen, to be king. But both refused. Then they chose Gunther, Count of Schwarzburg, who accepted the crown. He was a brave knight and splendid soldier, and for some months he held his own gallantly against Charles. He was a dangerous rival and Charles knew it. So he fought him in every way, not alone with the sword and spear, but with gold.

He scattered broadcast gold and promises, titles and honours, so that many forsook Gunther. But in spite of these desertions Gunther kept a brave front. Then he fell ill. Poison, some say, was at work. He could fight no longer. Sick in mind and body, he gave up the struggle and renounced his right to the throne for the sum of 20,000 francs. But he was a dying man, and neither gold nor kingdom could avail him more. And so only a few months after his election he died.

Charles had indeed bought the kingdom rather than conquered it, but after Gunther's death he reigned without a rival.

And now, no sooner had the country escaped the miseries of civil war, than it had to suffer a still more terrible evil. This was the Black Death, a dreadful plague which had been brought from the East in trading vessels. It swept Europe from end to end; for three years Germany was made desolate by it. Whole families, whole villages, whole towns were wiped out.

At the first sign of the dreaded disease the rich fled. But often they carried with them the seeds of the evil from which they tried to escape. They died even as they fled, often from sheer terror. Many a strong castle stood silent and empty, with no knight to guard its walls, no knave to serve in hall, no page in bower. For all lay dead of the fearful plague, leaving no last survivor to tell the awful tale of the miseries endured. No spot on land was safe. Even upon the sea fugitives found no safety, and many a richly laden vessel tossed here and there upon the waves, with not a living soul on board to guide its course, all being stricken down by the fell disease.

In this dreadful time all bonds of love seemed broken, and both men and women fled from their nearest and dearest, leaving them to die alone and untended. Some who escaped the plague went mad with horror and terror. Fear and greed stalked through the land, hand in hand with death. Some in their greed for gold would consent for great sums of money to watch by the sick. But many a time they would take the money and leave the plague-stricken folk to die untended.

They died by hundreds and by thousands. The graveyards were all too narrow to hold them, and so great trenches were dug outside the city walls, and into these dreadful graves, in haste and fear, the dead were cast. Grass grew in the streets; flocks wandered shepherdless; unreaped, the harvest rotted in the fields.

The doctors of the time were few and ignorant, and they were powerless to stay the plague. But there were many rogues who pretended to have found cures, and who sold worthless medicines for great sums of money. Many thus grew rich, only themselves to be seized suddenly by the dread disease, and be forced to leave their ill-gotten gains and gold.

Many looked upon the Black Death as a punishment from God. Haggard and gaunt they wandered through the land calling upon men to repent of their sins, and humble themselves before the Almighty.

Thus arose the strange order of the Flagellants or whippers. Every man of the order carried at his girdle a terrible little scourge with iron-pointed ends, and twice daily, having worked themselves into a religious fury, they scourged themselves until the blood ran and their bodies were covered with wounds. Half mad with zeal to turn aside God's wrath, from town to town they marched in a piteous procession. In front lighted candles and splendid banners of silk and gold were carried. Behind came the grim procession. Barefoot, with garments marked with a red cross and stained with their own blood, they marched two by two, chanting mournful hymns.

Like vexed spirits they passed through all the land in restless haste, for their vows bound them never to spend more than one night in any town. So from one infected place to another they flitted, often spreading the disease which by their frenzied penance they hoped to stay.

The Flagellants punished themselves. They rejoiced in their own martyrdoms. But the fury of the plague was not stayed; it yielded to neither prayers nor penance, but continued through winter frosts and summer suns. The wrath of God, it seemed, was not thus to be appeased.

Then dreadful doubts laid hold upon the people. Perhaps, after all, said some, this thing had not been caused by God, but by a foe. So the people, filled with terror and unrest as they were, sought some new cause for their agony. Soon they found a scapegoat on which to wreak their fury. It was noised abroad that the Jews had caused the plague. They, it was said, had joined in a general plot to kill the Christians, and had poisoned all the springs and wells.

In this time of tumult and frenzy, when terror had robbed men of all sense of justice, such a lie was only too readily believed. And so a terrible persecution of the Jews began. They were robbed of their goods and lands, their houses were sacked and burned, they themselves were put to death by hundreds and by thousands. They were tortured, they were cut in pieces, they were burned alive, and no man pitied them. So terrible were their sufferings that many put themselves to death, with their wives and children. "It is better to fall into the hands of God," they said, "than into the hands of the Christians."

This persecution of the Jews is one of the most cruel the world has ever seen. And it was not only the mad belief that they had caused the plague which roused men against them. It was greed too, for men were jealous of their wealth. "Their money was the poison which slew the Jews," said a writer of the time. "Had the Jews been poor," said another, "and had the nobles owed them nothing, they would have never been burned."

But at length, so horrible did the persecution become, that the nobles themselves were moved to pity, and even the Pope took the part of the poor Jews. But there were few left alive in Germany when the fury of hatred had worn itself out.

The plague, too, wore itself out. "And then," says an old writer, "the world began again to be merry, and men made unto themselves new garments and sang new songs."

Charles IV, like so many kings before him, journeyed to Rome and was there crowned by the Pope. But he had no dreams of Empire. The old Roman Empire was dead, he said, and would never again be brought to life.

He was cunning and selfish, and he also loved money. He had no wish to waste it in a useless attempt to govern Italy. So for gold he sold all that was left of the rights of Empire to the cities and Italian nobles, and as soon as possible he left Italy, and hurried back to Germany, followed by the scorn of many noble Italians. "You carry back with you both the iron and the golden crown," cried the great poet Petrarch, "but the title of Emperor is empty. You, Emperor of the Romans, will be known only as the King of Bohemia."

After his return from Italy, Charles issued the decree for which his name is best remembered. This was called the Golden Bull. It received this name from the colour of its great seal, and it was almost as important for the German Empire as the Great Charter was for us. For it formed the groundwork of the laws for more than 400 years. One of its chief aims was to put an end to the strife over the election of the Emperor, and to make the law so plain and clear that the choosing of rival Emperors would be impossible.

And one very surprising thing is that in all the Golden Bull there is not a word about the Pope or his claims. Indeed there is no mention of Italy at all. This shows two things; that German rule over Italy was really at to end, and that the Pope's power over Germany was growing very weak.

Yet towards the end of his life Charles himself broke the rules of his own Golden Bull, and yielded in all sorts of ways to the Pope's demands in order to win the crown for his son Wenceslaus. He at last succeeded; and before Charles died, his son Wenceslaus was chosen to succeed him.

As has been said, Charles was greedy of money and of land, and he spent his last years adding to his own possessions. He cared little for the welfare of the Empire and of his subjects at large, but he loved his own special kingdom of Bohemia. He made the capital, Prague, both strong and beautiful, and founded there the first German university. Indeed he did so much for Bohemia that a later Emperor (Maximilian I) called him "The Father of Bohemia and the Stepfather of the Empire." "Germany," said the same Emperor, "never suffered from a more pestilent plague than the reign of Charles IV."

CHAPTER 43

# WENCESLAUS OF BOHEMIA AND RUPERT THE MILD

CHARLES IV died in 1878, and was succeeded by his son Wenceslaus. He was only seventeen when he came to the throne, and he proved to be neither a good King of Bohemia nor a good Emperor. Perhaps no one less noble has ever sat upon the throne of Germany.

Wenceslaus cared nothing for his people; he thought only of low, mean pleasures. So besotted was he that it is said he could hardly be induced to attend to any business at all. What little he did attend to had to be done in the morning, lest later in the day he should be too drunk.

Charles IV had utterly neglected Germany, and the country was in wild confusion. The land was full of robber knights and barons who fought against the cities. The cities banded themselves together in Leagues. The nobles formed new confederations or societies, calling themselves knights of St. William or St. George, of the Falcon or the Lion, or what not. And while the land was wasted with their wars, Wenceslaus sat at ease, drinking and carousing in Prague.

Little cared he that the fair fields and vineyards were trampled and destroyed, that towns and villages lay in ruins. And when his courtiers urged him to mount his horse, to set his lance in rest and ride forth, as a King should, to quell the tumult, he replied indolently, "Every one knows where I live. If any one wishes to see me, let him come to Prague."

But as well as being slothful and drunken, Wenceslaus was passionate and cruel. His favourite companion was the hangman. He went about with him ever at his heels, together with a pack of savage hounds. Scant mercy was shown to any who aroused the wrath of Wenceslaus; and many are the stories told of his cruelty.

It was under this slothful and savage King that the Swiss made another great fight for freedom. Ever since the victory of Morgarten they had continued the struggle. Now once again a Leopold of Austria (nephew of that Leopold who was defeated at Morgarten) marched against them. Once again the peasants of Switzerland gathered to defy him.

The army which Leopold led into Switzerland was very great. In it were all the best and bravest knights and nobles of Austria. Clad in glittering armour, with banners fluttering in the wind, with trumpets blowing, they rode gaily along. Near the little town of Sempach hey met the rough-clad mountaineers.

The ground was uneven, it was almost impossible to charge on horseback, so most of the knights dismounted. Sending their horses to the rear, they stood shoulder to shoulder, a solid wall of steel bristling with lances.

On a slope above the Austrian army stood the Swiss, in the shadow of dark pine woods which stretched far behind them. Their weapons were poor and old-fashioned. Many of them, indeed, carried the clubs with which their forefathers had fought at Morgarten; many instead of shields carried a small board on their left arms. But their hearts were full of courage, and ere the battle began they fell upon their knees, as their custom was, to pray. "Oh, dear God in Heaven," they cried, "through Thy bitter death help us poor sinners in this hour of anguish and need." Then springing to their feet, and uttering a ringing war-cry, they charged.

But against the glittering mass of the Austrian nobles the Swiss threw themselves again and again in vain. The knights stood in firm unbroken order, while many a mountaineer fell dead, pierced by their long lances.

Already the hearts of the Swiss began to sink. Then a brave man, Arnold of Winkelried, resolved to die for his country, and force a way through that grim barrier.

"Comrades," he cried, "to your care I leave my wife and child. I will make a way for you."

Then stretching out his arms he ran upon the bristling fence of spears, gathering as many as he could in his embrace.

"Make way for Liberty," he cried as, pierced by many wounds, he fell, bearing to the ground with him all the knights whose spears he had gathered to his heart.

The wall of steel was broken, a breach was made, and over Arnold of Winkelried's dead body his comrades swept like a torrent. The nobles of Austria were now an easy prey to the lightly armed, agile Swiss. Hampered by their heavy armour, they fell and were unable to rise again. The day, too, was one of fearful heat, and many died, not from the blows of the Swiss, but from the heat of the sun.

The Swiss victory was complete. Duke Leopold himself was among the slain, and there was scarcely a castle in all Austria in which the sound of mourning was not heard.

For Austria the battle of Sempach was a crushing blow. But for the Swiss Sempach and the battle of Nafels, fought two years later, meant Liberty, and for many a long day they were left to enjoy it undisturbed.

Meanwhile, in Germany itself, the desolating war between princes and cities went on. Trade was at a standstill, the country for miles round every town was a barren waste, the roads were overgrown with weeds and nettles.

And the King cared little about it. He hunted and drank and idled his time away, "Like a pig in his sty," it was said. So at length the people grew weary of him and in 1400 the electors met together and declared that Wenceslaus was not worthy to be king. The next day they chose Rupert the Count Palatine to succeed him.

When Wenceslaus heard the news he burst into a terrible passion. "I will avenge this insult or die of it," he cried. "Rupert shall be cast down as far as he is now raised high." But Wenceslaus was not the man to fight valiantly for his crown, so the war against Rupert was long and undecisive.

Rupert was brave, and well fitted to be a king, yet he could not win the love or obedience of the people. He was king in little more than name. Seeing that he could do little in Germany, he turned his thoughts to Italy, and made up his mind to go there to try to win back some of the power which had been lost.

But the expedition to Italy was a pitiful failure. Defeated and beggared both in fame and in fortune, Rupert fled back over the Alps, followed by the scorn and laughter of his foes.

Rupert fled from Italy a beaten man, he returned to Germany to find the country in confusion, and himself of little importance. His reign was one long struggle for power, and just as it seemed as if he were about to succeed, he died.

Rupert was brave and kindly, and he received the name of the "Mild." For ten years he was, in name, ruler of Germany. But he was not strong enough really to rule in those turbulent times.

CHAPTER 44

# SIGMUND

THE death of Rupert left the Empire in confusion. Wenceslaus was still alive, and once more tried to claim the throne. But he tried in vain, for the electors were all agreed that whatever king was chosen, it should not be Wenceslaus. But although the electors were agreed not to have Wenceslaus, they were divided as to who they should have. So two Emperors were chosen.

One was Jobst, Margrave of Moravia, a greedy, ambitious old man. "He passed for a great man," said an old writer, "but there was nothing great about him but his beard." The other was Sigmund, Wenceslaus' younger brother. Both young and handsome, he was well versed in every knightly art, and in all the learning of the times. He was already very powerful, being King of Hungary and Elector of Brandenburg. He was arrogant too, and being one of the electors he voted for himself. "No prince in the Empire surpasses me in power," he said, "or in the art of ruling. Therefore I, as elector of Brandenburg, give Sigmund, King of Hungary, my vote, and herewith elect myself Emperor." But although Sigmund thus elected himself, others of the Electors chose Jobst. And besides this, Wenceslaus was ready to fight them both.

With three princes thus claiming the crown, a great a fight around it seemed certain. But Jobst died suddenly, it may be by poison, Wenceslaus came to an agreement with his haughty younger brother, contenting himself henceforth with being only King of Bohemia. Thus, at length, Sigmund was allowed to take the throne of Germany in peace.

But it was not in Germany alone that there was strife. For while three Emperors had been fighting over the Empire, three Popes had been fighting for the headship of the Church. It was a sad time for those who looked up to the Pope as their guide and leader in all things holy. For the three Popes hated each other bitterly. They quarrelled amongst themselves, they excommunicated each other, and as all of them had need of money, they stooped to many evil ways in order to get it. Church livings and sacred offices were sold to the highest bidder, and forgiveness of sins was sold to any who would pay. These things made earnest people very sorrowful, they could not but see that such things were wrong, and many good men began to preach against the evils that had grown up in the Church. Among these was John Huss, a teacher in the University of Prague.

That there should be three Popes at one time all wrangling together, was a scandal and grief to the whole Christian world. Sigmund wished to put an end to this discord and wickedness, and he called together a great council at Constance. It was a Parliament of the whole Christian world, and all the pomp and splendour of the earth seemed gathered together.

It is true only one of the three Popes came, but, about him crowded many cardinals in their red robes, bishops in splendid array, abbots and learned doctors, there were knights and nobles too in silver and cloth of gold, in blue and crimson, and the streets of Constance were a very rainbow of colours. Magnificent in crimson and cloth of gold, wearing his great glittering crown upon his head, Sigmund himself opened the Council.

As he read his grand Latin speech he made a mistake, calling schism feminine.

"Your Majesty?" said a cardinal quietly, "schism is neuter."

Sigmund looked at him in disdain. "I," he answered proudly, "am King of the Romans, and above grammar."

So amid a babel of tongues, with the sound of trumpets and of bells, the Council of Constance set to work to cleanse the evils of the Church. By its decrees the three Popes were all deposed and a new Pope chosen. But the Council of Constance did little lasting good, and the act for which it is most remembered is a dark blot on Sigmund's name.

You remember that a man named John Huss had begun to preach against some of the teaching of the Roman Church. He was a friend and follower of our reformer Wycliffe, and he did much to spread Wycliffe's writings among the people of Bohemia. The great men of the Church looked upon him, therefore, with jealousy and mistrust.

So John Huss was summoned to appear before the Council to answer for his misdeeds. Once already Huss had been summoned to Rome. But, well knowing that he could expect scant justice from a godless Pope, he had refused to obey the summons. Now he obeyed, for King Sigmund granted him a safe-conduct both going and coming. "To all princes as well spiritual as worldly, and to all our other subjects, greeting," he wrote. "We affectionately recommend to you all, the honourable Master John Huss, M.A. and B.D., the bearer of these presents, going from Bohemia to the Council of Constance, whom we have taken into our protection and safeguard. We desire you when he comes among you, to receive him well, and entertain him kindly, furnishing him with all that is needful for his safety, whether he goes by land or by water, and to let him freely and securely pass, sojourn, stop and repass."

Armed with this safe-conduct, trusting in the sacredness of a King's word, Huss went to Constance without fear. But in spite of the King's safe-conduct, as soon as he arrived in Constance he was seized and thrown into prison. There, suffering many cruelties, being chained both hand and foot, he lay in darkness and pain until he was brought forth to be tried.

As Huss stood before his accusers his courage did not fail him. "Of my own accord I came to this Council," he said, "under the public faith of the Emperor present." So saying he looked earnestly at Sigmund.

The hot blood rushed to the Emperor's face. He had broken his kingly word, and he blushed for very shame, but he kept silence. Then seeing that he could expect no help from the King, Huss tried to defend himself, but all in vain. Before ever he had left Bohemia his fate had been sealed. So "having the fear of God before their eyes "the Council of Constance declared John Huss a heretic and an outcast. For he had spread abroad the teaching of John Wycliffe of accursed memory, and done much that was evil.

After this the Church had done with him, and with fearful curses they gave his body to the Evil one.

"And I," said Huss quietly, "give it into the hand of my Lord Jesus Christ."

Thus was John Huss, a good and holy man, cast forth from the Church. He might no longer preach or teach; he might no longer wear the robes of a priest. So now his judges surrounded him.

They took from him his vestments, one after the other, uttering over him at the taking of each some dreadful curse. Upon his head in mockery they placed a paper cap a yard high, like a fool's cap, and thereon were painted three horrible demons and the word "Arch-heretic." And in the robe of a penitent, with the hateful paper cap upon his head, he was led forth to the stake to die the death of a martyr. He went with a brave heart and smiling face, "as if," says an old writer, "he were being led forth to a banquet."

He walked unbound with two of the city serjeants in front of him and two behind, and a great crowd of well-armed soldiers following. About them pressed the people, filled with wonder, fear, and pity.

Singing hymns of praise to God, John Huss reached the stake. And as the cruel flames rose about him he cried aloud, "Father, into Thy hands I commend my spirit." Then he bowed his head and died. He died upon his birthday, July 6, 1415.

The leaders in the Church hoped that after the death of Huss no more would be heard of his new religion. But they were mistaken. Never yet have the fires of persecution burned up the flame of reform. John Huss indeed was dead, others too followed him to the stake, but his work lived on.

To the Bohemians he was a hero, and they were now filled with anger and bitterness against Sigmund, who, by giving him a false safe-conduct, had delivered their hero to death. So when in 1419 Wenceslaus died, leaving no child to succeed him, and Sigmund claimed the throne of Bohemia, the Bohemians rose in rebellion against him. They would have none of him, and what is called the Hussite War now began and lasted for more than fifteen years.

The Bohemians were led by a soldier named Ziska. He was a ferocious-looking man, not very tall, but very strong, with broad shoulders and a large head. His face was tanned and brown, and his big black beard and shaggy black eyebrows made his face look fierce and stern. He was blind of one eye, too, which made him look still more terrible.

Ziska was a born leader of men; he made war ruthlessly and fiercely, and in some ways was not unlike our own Oliver Cromwell. Out of the mob of peasants who crowded to his standard he made one of the finest armies the world has ever seen. He was the first man in the German Empire to form a well-drilled army of foot soldiers. He was among the first to make much use of guns and cannon, which were then but newly invented.

Ziska's soldiers became almost unconquerable. Now here, now there, across the plains of Bohemia he led them, winning victory after victory.

At length, while storming a town, Ziska was hit in the eye—his one remaining eye—by an arrow. Great was the sorrow among his soldiers, for their beloved leader was now quite blind. And not only that, he became so ill that they thought he would die.

But Ziska did not die, and blind though he was, he would not give up his leadership. "I have still my blood to shed," he said. So he continued to lead his army. He rode in a carriage near the standard, and his knowledge both of the country and of his men was so sure that he still led them to victory.

*"Father, into Thy hands I commend my spirit," cried Huss.*

And blind though he was, he was still as stern as ever; he still made war as ruthlessly as before. Once he made his array march both night and day till the weary men began to grumble. "It is all very well for you," they said, "for both day and night are alike to you. But we, we cannot see at night."

"What!" cried Ziska fiercely, "you cannot see? Well, set fire to a couple of villages; that will give you light."

But at length, at the age of seventy, this fierce old soldier, still fighting, was seized with plague and died. His spirit, however, seemed to descend on his followers. They took the name of "orphans," for they had lost their father in their leader, and still fought on as fiercely as before.

At length in 1436 Sigmund, weary of the war, made many promises and concessions to the Bohemians, and so won peace.

In July he entered Prague in state, as the acknowledged King of Bohemia. But he did not live long to enjoy this new-won peace, for the next year he died.

Sigmund had always loved pomp and splendour, and even in death this love did not leave him. When he was told that he was soon to die, he bade his attendants dress him in his royal robes, place the crown on his head, and the sceptre in his hand. And thus, seated upon his throne, in all the magnificence of earthly pride, he awaited the last call which even kings and emperors must obey.

And ere he died he bade his servants draw the shroud over his splendid raiment, and leave him sitting dead upon the throne for two or three days, "so that all the people may know," he said, "that the lord of the world is dead."

CHAPTER 45

# ALBERT II

A hundred and thirty years had come and gone since a Hapsburg, Albert I, sat upon the throne. Now, with Albert II, once more the crown came to the House of Hapsburg.

Albert, Duke of Austria, had married Sigmund's only daughter, Elizabeth. In dying, Sigmund left to his son-in-law the crowns of Hungary and of Bohemia, and the hope that he should receive also that of the Empire. And as Albert was the most powerful of all the German princes, he was chosen as Emperor.

But many of the Bohemians were unwilling to accept Albert either as their King or as Emperor. He was a stranger, and he could not even understand the language which most of them spoke. They refused to agree to the choice of the Electors, and some of them chose a rival King.

But with the help of some of the German nobles, and chiefly with that of Albert, Marquess of Brandenburg, called Achilles because of his strength, Albert succeeded in driving the rival King out of the land. Then in order to win them over to his side, he granted the Bohemians several things they asked, and was at length received by the most of them as King.

But before the trouble with Bohemia was really at an end, Albert was called away by a still greater danger.

For some years the Turks had been attacking the borders of the Empire in Hungary and elsewhere. In the summer of 1438 they made a sudden descent. They wasted the land, burned the villages, killed the people, and carried away many into captivity.

Albert made up his mind now to gather an army and march against these infidel foes. But such was the Hungarian hatred of Germany that very few Hungarians joined his banner. It seemed as if they chose rather to be overwhelmed by the Turks than saved by the Germans. So with an army far too small, Albert marched against the Turks.

The campaign was an utter failure. Plague broke out in the Imperial army, and disappointed and crushed Albert turned homeward. On the way he fell ill. Still he hurried homeward. For he believed that if he could only reach Vienna he would be well. But in spite of all his great longing and his haste, he died before he reached the city.

He had reigned scarcely eighteen months, and he had never been crowned. His death was a great loss to the Empire, for he was wise and brave, and during his short rule he had done all he could for the happiness of his people. He was a big handsome man, but very grave and stern; and his large bright eyes were so fierce that many feared to look upon him. He could not gain the love of his people, but he gained their respect. "In spite of being a German," said an old Bohemian writer, "he was good, brave, and kindly."

CHAPTER 46

# FREDERICK III

THE Electors chose Frederick of Austria, the son of Ernst the Lion, to succeed to Albert II. He reigned longer than any other German Emperor, and never was there a more lazy and unkingly ruler.

He cared nothing for the Empire, and he did nothing for it. "He was a useless Emperor," said an old writer, "and the people, during his long reign, forgot that they had a King." He cared so little about his people that he would fall asleep in Parliament, and once when something very important was being discussed, he got up and went away to look after some plants, and see that they were protected from the frost. For Frederick was a very keen gardener, and cared more about his garden than his Empire. He was also fond of astrology and alchemy, and spent much time trying to find a way to turn common metals into gold.

But although Frederick was a slothful Emperor, he was a great believer in the greatness of the House of Austria. And he took for his motto the letters A.E.LO.U., which stand for the Latin words, Austriae Vest imperare orbi universo, meaning, "The whole earth is subject to Austria."

Amidst all his shiftlessness and idleness, Frederick thought he would try to win back Switzerland, which by this time had almost become free. But he had neither money nor soldiers enough, so he made friends with Charles VII of France and asked him for help.

Charles gave the help for which he was asked, and sent Frederick some troops called the Armagnacs, They were so called from their leader the Count Armagnac. This French army was little more than a mob of hungry adventurers, eager for plunder, and drawn from the very lowest of the people. The Germans called them not Armagnacs, but "Arme Gecken," which means "poor fools."

The Dauphin of France led this rabble army, and a terrible fight took place between a few of the Swiss and the whole French force at St. Jacob, not far from Basle.

The Swiss were far outnumbered by the foe, but from early morning till six in the evening they fought like heroes. They fought on foot, the French on horseback, and there were four Frenchmen to one Swiss.

Man after man the Swiss fell. As the day wore on fewer and fewer were left, and they at length took refuge in the Monastery of St. Jacob. The French at once set fire to the building, and of all the fifteen hundred who took part in the fight only one escaped alive.

But the French too had lost many men, and the Dauphin had no mind to fight such a desperate foe a second time. So he marched into Germany, his wild soldiers wasting the land and slaughtering the people by the way. This was by no means to the liking of the Germans, and at length, by bribes and threats, these dangerous friends were forced once more across the border.

Although the Swiss lost the battle of St. Jacob, it was such a noble defeat that it counted to them almost more than a victory. For them it was one more step towards liberty. But thirty years later Charles the Bold, Duke of Burgundy, having made friends with the Emperor Frederick, thought to conquer them. Like one man they rose against him, and he was defeated in two great battles, one at Granson, and one at Morat. The following year Charles himself was killed in a battle near Nancy.

After this the Swiss were really free. So that is something at least to remember in the reign of this slothful Emperor.

From this time Switzerland can no longer be looked upon as forming a part of the Empire. But it was not until the Peace of Westphalia in 1648 that it was really acknowledged by law to be a free country.

Meantime a far greater danger than the loss of Switzerland was threatening the Empire. For many years, as you have read, the Turks had been growing a greater and greater danger to the Empire and to Europe. Albert II had fought against them with but ill success. And although up to this time they had no real foothold in Europe, they had begun to grow more and more bold. At length, in 1453, they took Constantinople.

This was a great blow to the whole Christian world, for Constantinople had been, for many hundreds of years, the Christian barrier against the Turks. Now it had fallen, and the Turks spread unhindered westward. They attacked Hungary, they attacked Poland. At length they crossed the borders of Austria and threatened, not only the Empire, but the Emperor's own land.

But still Frederick did nothing. Parliament after Parliament was called, and the Emperor did not even appear at them. He contented himself with ordering a bell to be rung at midday throughout all the kingdom, which for long was called the Turk's bell.

The great nobles were fighting among themselves, and had grown to care for little but their own interests, and so it was left to the Hungarians and the Poles to protect themselves and the rest of Christian Europe from the infidel Turks as best they could.

Frederick's slothfulness was so great that he was often in danger of being chased from the throne by the angry Electors. He was, indeed, hunted out of his own land of Austria. And for long years the man who was in name the most powerful ruler in the world wandered about poor and helpless, glad to accept charity from any who would give it.

In the end, however, he recovered all his possessions. From beggary he returned to the splendour of his palaces. But he was as idle as ever, and during the last years of his life he left everything to his son Maximilian. He himself lived shut up in his castle of Linz, star-gazing, dreaming, and trying to make gold.

He died at length in August 1493. He was an old man, and ill, it is true, but he caused his death, it was said, by eating eight melons and drinking a lot of cold water one fast day.

Frederick III was the last Emperor to go to Rome to be crowned. He had reigned, if reigning it could be called, for fifty-three years.

CHAPTER 47

# MAXIMILIAN I

DURING his father's lifetime Maximilian had already been chosen King of the Romans, and he now succeeded to the Empire without any trouble. Long before this, in 1477, he had married Mary, the beautiful Duchess of Burgundy. She was the daughter of that turbulent Duke of Burgundy who had been defeated by the Swiss, and she had married Maximilian to free herself from the greedy clutches of Louis XI of France.

Mary brought to her husband fair and broad lands, both in the Netherlands and in Burgundy. But she did not live long, and when she died Maximilian had great trouble with both these provinces, for the peoples refused to acknowledge him as their ruler. And when he became Emperor he was glad to give up the government of the Netherlands to his son Philip.

This Philip married Joanna, the daughter of the King of Spain, and thus the Netherlands and Spain were united. It is rather important to remember this, for later on we will hear a great deal about the sons of Philip and Joanna.

Maximilian I was, in his own time, one of the best-loved of all the German Emperors. Yet he never did one thing for the Empire. He was gallant and brave and daring to rashness. He loved knightly sports and games, and he has been called the last of all the Knights. He would often take part in tournaments, sometime in disguise. And when, having defeated all those knights who came against him, he raised his visor, he would be greeted with thunders of applause.

But even more than tournaments Maximilian loved hunting, and many stories are told of his daring and skill. Once when attacked by a she-bear he choked her with his bare hands. Another time when attacked by a wild boar, which bit his horse's leg in two, Maximilian sprang from his horse, and with his hunting spear he pierced the boar through the body, running great risk of himself being killed.

He loved all sorts of sport. But best of all he loved to hunt the chamois, and he would follow his game high upon the Alps, among the ice and snow, fearlessly jumping over wide clefts, and scrambling among boulders. Once, it is told, he followed a chamois from rock to rock, higher and higher, in the heat and eagerness of the chase caring little where he went. But at length he found himself in a spot from which he could neither go forward nor back. Beneath him was a sheer precipice, before him a great rock jutted out.

Far below in the valley his people watched. But none knew how to reach him. For two days they tried in vain. They could not even succeed in throwing him a rope. All thought the King was lost, and headed by the village priest they marched around the church in solemn procession, praying for his safety. And Maximilian, having eaten all the food that he had with him, resigned himself to die of hunger.

Then suddenly, as he lay waiting for death, he heard something rustle beside him. Turning his head cautiously he saw a peasant huntsman not far off upon the mountain side. "Hallo!" cried the peasant in astonishment, "What are you doing there?"

"I am waiting," replied Maximilian quietly,—waiting for death, he meant.

At once the peasant began to creep slowly towards the Emperor. Hardly daring to hope that help had really come to him, he lay still and watched the peasant creeping slowly and cautiously along. At length he reached the spot where the Emperor lay. Quickly he bound climbing irons to his hands and feet, and at length Maximilian was able to climb down from that giddy height where he had lain for two long days.

Some people say that the peasant vanished as soon as the King was in safety, and that he was no mortal man, but an angel sent to his aid. Others say that he was a chamois hunter named Oswald Zips, and that as a reward Maximilian made him a noble.

But although Maximilian loved jousting and hunting, he was also a learned man and a lover of art. He could speak several languages, he himself wrote several books, and he loved poetry and painting and music. He was, indeed, called "The father of the learned," and one of the greatest of German painters, Albert Durer, was his friend.

Yet much as he loved all peaceful arts, Maximilian was almost constantly at war. And in spite of his bravery and fearlessness he was nearly always defeated. He fought against the Swiss and against the Turks; he fought in Bavaria, he fought in the Netherlands. But his chief wars were in Italy, and against the French. Long before Maximilian became Emperor, his little daughter Margaret had been betrothed to the Dauphin of France, and as she was only a tiny child she had been sent to live at the

*Once when attacked by a she-bear he choked her with his bare hands.*

*Maximilian would often take part in tournaments.*

French Court until she should be old enough to be married. But when the Dauphin became King, instead of marrying Margaret he sent her home to her father, and married the Duchess Anne of Brittany.

This was a double insult to Maximilian. Not only had his daughter been insulted, but he himself had been robbed of his own bride. For he was betrothed, and indeed already married by proxy to Anne of Brittany. Maximilian was furiously angry, but after a time he comforted himself for his lost bride by marrying a rich Italian heiress, the grand-daughter of a poor peasant who had risen to fame.

Charles VIII of France had now splendid dreams of conquering Italy, and Maximilian, who hated him and who also was a dreamer, wanted to drive him out. He wanted with one blow to avenge his private hate, and at the same time once more make the power of the Empire supreme in Italy.

But Maximilian was poor. He was always open-handed and careless with money, and he never had enough for his splendid schemes. How poor he was is shown by a letter from his advisers begging him to send money at once. For, say they, "for our gracious lady the Queen and her ladies, we have only enough to last them a few days longer. And if money does not come by that time even our food will be at an end." He was so poor that he actually sold his sword, and fought for pay as many poor nobles did in those days. At the battle of Guinegate he fought on the side of England for 100 marks a day.

So now that Maximilian wanted to go to war against Charles VIII in Italy, he called the princes of the Empire together to ask them to help him with money. But the princes and nobles refused to give him any money, or help him with his foreign wars until peace within the Empire was made sure.

Maximilian stormed and raged. He did not wish to barter and bargain, or give up one jot of his kingly power. He wished to command, and be obeyed. He would not be tied and bound, he declared, he would not be dictated to. Would they force him, he asked, to throw his crown down among their feet and scramble for the pieces?

But all Maximilian's anger was of no avail. The nobles stood firm, so he yielded. Peace within the Empire was proclaimed. It was not to last only for a certain number of years. It was to be for ever, and private warfare between princes within the realm was forbidden. A court called the Imperial Chamber was set up, and to this court nobles were commanded to bring their quarrels to be decided, instead of fighting them out between themselves. A tax called the common penny was also instituted to pay for this court. And although the King was president of this court it took a great deal of power out of his hands.

Maximilian, having at length received help and money, set out for Italy, but he did little good in his wars there. He tried to march to Rome, to be crowned there by the Pope. But the people of Venice refused to let him pass through their land. So he contented himself with naming himself King of Germany and "Emperor Elect." Before this the title of King of Germany had never been used, and after this the Kings of Germany took the title of Emperor without waiting to be crowned by the Pope.

Maximilian was always full of great schemes. He was always beginning things, and never finishing them. He was for ever making plans and unmaking them. "He says one thing at night, and changes his mind before morning," said Charles VIII, and so he never succeeded in doing anything great. He made the wildest, maddest plans. At one time he thought of making himself Pope as well as Emperor. He wrote to his daughter telling her that after his death she would have to look upon him as a saint to be adored, and signing himself, "Your good father the future Pope."

Yet with all his wild schemes, with all his folly and vain-gloriousness, Maximilian loved Germany. He was far more German at heart than many of the Emperors who had gone before him, some of whom were willing to sacrifice all that was German for a little empty glory in Italy. "My honour is German honour," said Maximilian, "and German honour is my honour!"

Maximilian began at length to feel that his life was nearly at an end. For some years, whenever he travelled he carried his coffin with him. In 1518 he held a last Diet in Augsburg. He left it a weary and disappointed man. His son Philip had died, and he had tried to make the Electors choose his grandson Charles, the son of Philip and Joanna of Spain, as his successor. They refused. He had tried to rouse them to go upon a crusade against the Turks. They refused. All his life to crush the Turks had been one of his dearest hopes. But no one would follow him, and to the last Maximilian was doomed to failure and disappointment.

On his way home from this profitless Diet, Maximilian died. "It is time to make your peace with God," said the priest, as he bent over the dying Emperor.

"I have done that long ago," he replied wearily, "else now it would be too late."

CHAPTER 48

# CHARLES V

MAXIMILIAN had not been able to make the Electors choose his grandson as his successor during his lifetime. Now after his death there was a hot competition for the throne. The three greatest rulers in Europe appeared as rivals for the honour. These were Henry VIII, King of England, Francis I, King of France, and Charles I, King of Castile and Aragon, sovereign of the Netherlands and King of Sicily, and lord of many scattered realms besides. Indeed he was ruler of so many lands, that if he gained the Empire no fewer than twenty-five crowns would be his.

Henry of England had little chance of being chosen, and the real struggle lay between Francis and Charles. Both flattered and bribed the Electors, both poured out gold in lavish streams, and for a time the choice was uncertain.

But after all Charles was a Hapsburg; he was the grandson of Maximilian, who had been beloved by the people in spite of all his failings. Francis, on the other hand, was a stranger, he was a despot in his own country, and the Germans had no mind to place a despot over themselves. So in the end Charles was chosen. But even in choosing him the Electors feared his power. And before they elected him they made him sign a deed in which he promised to protect and respect the separate rights of each state in the Empire. He promised too that German or Latin should be the language of state, and that no German subject should be tried before any but a German court. Then with great splendour Charles I of Spain, who as German Emperor is known as Charles V, was crowned at Aachen.

Above all things Charles was a Catholic. When he was crowned he lay prone before the altar, and spreading forth his arms in the form of a cross, he promised to defend the Church and to obey the Pope in everything. But Charles was soon to come face to face with one of the Pope's greatest enemies. This was the monk Martin Luther.

Martin Luther was the son of a poor workman. But poor though he was, Martin's father managed to send his son to school, and afterwards to the University of Erfurt. After a time, however, Luther gave up his studies and became a monk.

From the time when he had been quite a boy Luther had been religious. Now he had given up all his life to religion, and ought to have been happy. But Luther was not happy. He was attacked by terrible doubts. It seemed to him that many wicked things were being done by the Church, and by the Pope whom he had been taught to look upon as holy. One of these wicked things was the selling of pardons, the granting of forgiveness of sins, both done and to be done, for money. Whenever the Pope wanted money for anything he sent messengers from Rome to carry into all the countries round about his letters giving them power to sell pardons.

With incense and lighted candles, with banners flying and trumpets blowing, and the papal letter or bull carried on a crimson cushion, these messengers moved from place to place. Thus they would enter a town, and, to the sound of chanting and ringing of bells, march to the church. And there, before the altar, in the shadow of the crucifix, they would set up their tables and spread forth their wares, and all who chose might come to buy.

Now at this time a monk named Tetzel came to Germany with pardons to sell. He was vulgar and blasphemous, and his ways of selling pardons shocked many people who had found no evil in it before. They filled Luther's heart with sorrow and indignation and he began to preach against the indulgences, as they were called.

At first Luther preached with some doubt and hesitation; then ever more and more boldly. For as he preached his doubts vanished, and it became more and more clear to himself that to sell God's forgiveness for money was wrong. At length one day Luther wrote out ninety-five reasons against these indulgences, and nailed them to the door of the church in Wittenberg. The chief reason was "that by true sorrow and penance alone, and not by payment of money, forgiveness can be won."

Luther himself little knew what a great deed he did when he nailed his paper to the door of the church at Wittenberg. For long years many people had been discontented with the Church as it was, but they dared not speak. Luther's hammer broke the spell of silence which was upon them, and the Reformation was begun.

The excitement was tremendous. In a month's time Luther's Theses, as they are called, were spread through all the length and breadth of the Empire. Many people rejoiced, but the Pope was angry. Luther was therefore commanded to appear at Augsburg before the Pope's messenger, Cardinal Cajetanus, and there answer for his heresy.

To Augsburg Luther went, although many of his friends feared for his safety. Then for three days the cardinal and the monk disputed with each other. The Cardinal would gladly have bribed Luther to silence. But Luther would accept no bribe. Then the cardinal grew angry. "Recant and see your error," he said. "The Pope wills it thus, whether you like it or no."

But Luther stood firm. He talked and argued till he made the Cardinal fear him. "I will talk no longer with this monster," said he at last, "for he has deep eyes and marvellous ideas in his brain"; and he sought means to imprison him.

Then, hearing that the Cardinal was about to have him taken prisoner and thrown into jail, Luther fled in the night. Friends opened a little gate in the city wall, and, clad only in his monk's robe, and mounted on a swift little horse, Luther galloped away and reached his home in safety. There he began again to teach and preach as boldly as before.

But the Pope was determined to silence Luther, and excommunicated him. Sixty days were given him in which to repent, and if within that time he did not confess his errors, then he was to be cast out of the Church. In whatever town he should be no bell might call the people together for prayer, no child might be baptized, no couple wedded, even the dead must be laid to rest without chant or prayer.

This was the Pope's decree, and he sent his messenger to publish it to the people of Germany. But the Pope little knew the state of Germany. Instead of receiving the bull with trembling fear the people received it with scorn and anger. It was torn in pieces, it was trampled in the mud, and by Luther himself it was publicly burned. "Because thou dost trouble the Holy One of the Lord, may everlasting fire consume thee," he cried, as he cast it into the leaping flames.

All these things happened just as Maximilian died and Charles V came to the throne. Now Charles called his first Diet at Worms, and to it Luther was summoned.

So with a safe-conduct from the Emperor Luther set forth upon what both he and his friends well knew was perilous journey. Some would have had him refuse to go. But Luther would not hear them. "Nay," he cried, "I am lawfully called to appear in that city. And thither will I go in the name of the Lord. Yea, though there were as many devils in Worms as there are tiles on the houses, I would still go on."

When Luther arrived in Worms the people came out to greet him in thousands, they thronged in the street, they followed him to his lodging, calling upon God to bless him, happy if they might touch his hand or even his clothes.

When at length Luther appeared before the Emperor, the Great Council Hall was thronged from end to end. Seldom had so many princes and nobles been gathered together. The Emperor, in his splendid robes, sat upon his throne beneath a canopy of cloth of gold. On one side of him were the cardinals, on the other the Electors, and all around them sat and stood a glittering throng of knights and nobles. They were all come to judge the case of one poor monk.

As Luther in his dark robe made his way through the brilliant crowd, a friendly knight patted him on the shoulder. "Little monk, little monk," he said in tones of admiration, "you go your way to make a stand such as I, and many a commander beside, even in our fiercest fight have never taken. Are you of good intent and certain of your affair, so go in God's name and be comforted. God will not forsake you."

The sitting was long; dusk fell, and the great hall was lit up by countless candles. In the dim and flickering light the young monk stood alone, a dusky figure amid the surrounding splendour. His face was pale, his eyes bright and shining. From first to last he refused to retract his heresies. "Here I stand," he said, "I can do no other. So help me, God. Amen."

It was his last word, and Charles bade him begone for a rebel and a heretic. But there were some there who would not thus lightly have let him go. He was in their power; why not have done with him? Why should he not die, as Huss had died? they asked.

"Nay," answered Charles, "he has my safe-conduct. I would not have cause to blush as Sigmund blushed."

So Luther was allowed to depart in safety. But hard upon his heels followed the Edict of Worms. By this Luther was declared to be under the ban of the Empire; that is, he was an outlaw. He had lost all the rights of man, and was but as a hunted animal on the face of the earth. No man might give him shelter or food, but was commanded to deliver him up to the powers of justice.

But Luther had many friends. Among them was Frederick the Wise, Duke of Saxony. While the anger of the Pope's party was so strong against Luther, Frederick feared for his safety. He determined, therefore, that Luther should disappear from friend and foe alike, until the storm was calmed.

So one day as Luther's carriage drove along on his way homeward, a band of masked and armed warriors suddenly dashed from the forest. The carriage was surrounded, Luther's servants were scattered, and he himself was seized and carried off, none knew whither.

Great was the anger of his foes, great the grief of his friends, when Luther thus suddenly and mysteriously disappeared. His followers mourned for him as dead; and for a time they were as sheep without a shepherd But at length they were comforted, for letters came to them from their leader. Yet they knew not whence they came, for Luther dated them "from my Patmos." This was in memory of the Isle of Patmos to which the apostle John had been banished.

Luther, meanwhile, was a prisoner in kindly hands, For he was hidden in the Duke Frederick's strong castle of Wartburg. For better concealment he was dressed like a knight, and rode forth with a golden chain about his neck, and a sword by his side. He was called the Chevalier George, and none knew who he really was save his friendly jailer. But Luther was soon weary of his life of ease, weary of splendid clothes and rich food. He spent much of his time translating the Bible into German. But still he felt that he was living in idleness.

At length, after nearly a year of this pleasant imprisonment, Luther left the Wartburg. In his absence many of his followers had become over-zealous, and were doing deeds of violence against the old religion which made Luther sorry. He felt that he must do something to stop these deeds. So he returned to Wittenberg, and once more began to teach and preach. He bade his followers to be kindly and tolerant, and at length succeeded in quieting their excesses.

For the next few years Luther was busy translating the Bible into German, and building up a new Church out of the ruins of the old. He grew farther and farther away from the Romish Church, and in 1525 he married a nun named Catherine Bora. Many other priests and clergy followed his example, and so the division between the old Catholic Church and the new Protestant Church grew wider and wider.

CHAPTER 49

# CHARLES V

MEANWHILE Germany was being torn asunder by one of the most terrible struggles ever known in Europe.

For hundreds of years the peasants of Germany had been ground down by their masters with unthinking cruelty. They were looked upon as little better than beasts of burden, created to toil and sweat, to live in pain and poverty, so that their lords might enjoy ease and comfort. In many places they were little better than slaves. From the day of their birth to the day of their death they were the bondmen of their lord. They might not move away to another town, they might not change their trade unless they paid heavy fines. They were taxed almost beyond endurance; they had to pay their dues in money, in labour, and in the produce of their farms. Often too, at the very busiest times, when the fields were waiting to be sown, or the corn ripe for harvest, they would be called away to catch frogs so that their croaking might not disturb her ladyship, or to gather snails that she might wind her homespun wool upon the shells.

Still, patiently the peasants bore all their hardships. It was the custom, it had always been the custom, and they knew nothing better. But at length they grew restless beneath their misery. They began to form leagues amongst themselves, and taking a common shoe for their badge, they rose in rebellion, once and again. But these rebellions were always put down with great sternness, and the position of the peasants grew no better, but rather worse.

Then came Luther. He rebelled against the tyranny of the Church, he preached freedom. Nowhere in all Germany did he get a more ready hearing than among the peasants. They hoped that this new freedom in religion would bring with it another sort of freedom too. The protestant religion taught that rich and poor alike were the children of one great and merciful Father, and that Christ had shed his blood for all alike; therefore, said the peasant, all must be alike free, and soon on every side they rose in wild rebellion.

Banner after banner was raised. Now it was a golden sun with the words, "Whoso would be free, let him come out into the sunshine"; now it was a flag of black, white, and red.

One of the leaders was called Hans Muller. With a red cap upon his head and a red cloak about his shoulders, he journeyed throughout the country rousing the people to rebellion. A herald went before him, and a cart decorated with wreaths and ribbons, and carrying the war-standard of black, white, and red, followed him. So through all the land the peasants passed, forcing and persuading others to join them. If any man refused, they drove a stake into the ground in front of his house as a sign that he was a traitor and that he might be despoiled of all his possessions.

Soon the peasant army grew great, but it was a wild, undisciplined mob. Many indeed were honest men driven by cruelty at last to rebel. But many too were thieves and murderers, the riff-raff of the towns, who joined the army for the love of bloodshed, and in the hope of plunder.

The peasants demanded twelve things, and they became known as the Twelve Articles. Among them were the rights of hunting and fishing, and of hewing wood, and the right of choosing their own clergy. These demands do not seem very outrageous, but they were sternly refused. Then the peasants turned upon their masters with awful fury. They vowed to put to death every man who wore spurs, that is every knight and noble. There should be neither towns nor castles now, they swore, but only villages and farmhouses. For the castles and the great towns were the dwellings of the hated nobles. Castles, churches, monasteries were sacked and burned. Many of the nobles and clergy were reduced to misery and utter poverty, and all the land was filled with blood and ruin.

Noble after noble was forced to yield to the peasants' demands, or die. At the castle of Weinsberg, the Count Lewis of Helfenstein made a brave stand against them. This is the town which, you remember, won the name of "Women's Faithfulness" in the reign of Conrad III.

Eight thousand maddened peasants now stormed without its walls. Within, Count Lewis and his handful of knights prepared manfully to defend it. Gathering all his men together into the market-place the Count spoke brave words to them. But the hearts of the citizens were with the foe without, not with their lord within the castle.

So one of the city gates was opened and the wild mob rushed in. They swarmed up the castle walls like mountain cats; they wrecked and plundered it from dungeon to turret, and laid it in ruins.

In the church the Count and his knights made a last stand, but here too the rabble followed them, and every man of them was slain or taken prisoner. It was a terrible scene of fury and rage.

Count Lewis and a few of his followers were taken alive, and the peasants resolved to put them to death in cruel fashion. They were led out to a meadow before the town. There, armed with spears, the peasants formed themselves into two long lines. Down this lane of bristling steel, the Count was ordered to march.

With her little two-year-old boy in her arms, the countess threw herself on her knees before the peasant leader, and implored him to have mercy on her husband. But all her tears and prayers were in vain. The rough peasants pushed her back, one of them wounding the little boy with his dagger.

The Count too tried to buy his freedom, and offered the peasants a great sum of gold. But they scornfully refused it. "If you offered us two tons of gold, it would make no difference; you would still have to die," they said.

So, seeing that there was no escape, Count Lewis marched bravely to his death. His piper went before him playing a mocking tune. Upon his head was the Count's plumed hat, which he had snatched from his master. "You have worn it long enough," he said; "it is now my turn to be count. Often enough have I piped for your dancing, but now I shall pipe you a right good tune, and you shall dance to my piping."

With bare head held proudly erect, the Count followed his mocking leader, and scarce three strides had he taken down that glittering, bristling lane, when two hundred spears were buried in his heart.

The poor Countess thus left alone among her foes was insulted, and wounded, and robbed of her jewels. She was placed in a common refuse cart, and driven to the nearest town, while the mob howled and raged around her. "You are used to a chariot of gold," they jeered; "now you have a refuse cart."

The news of the taking of Weinsberg spread through the land, striking terror to the hearts of many. And still the slaughter and destruction went on. Two brother counts, Count George and Count Albert of Hohenlohe, were forced on their bended knees to yield to the peasants. "Come here, brother George, and brother Albert," called a peasant to them; "come here and promise the peasants that you will henceforth look upon them as brothers, for you are no longer lords, but peasants."

"Dear brothers," said another of the peasant leaders, fearing that the prayers of the nobles might touch his followers' hearts, "do not let your hearts be softened because Esau speaks you fair. Have no pity for the godless. Do not let the blood grow cold upon your sword, and smite a merry cling-clang on the anvil of these hunters. Throw down their strong towers while yet there is day."

The peasant leaders boasted that they would reform the whole Empire, and that now a new and happy time was about to begin. But the peasants were after all but a mob without discipline. Their leaders were neither statesmen nor soldiers. When at length the nobles really banded against them, it was soon seen how powerless they were. They were badly armed, they knew no discipline; they had guns without powder, cannon without shot. They trusted in miracles rather than in armies.

Weaponless, they dashed against the foe, singing psalms and hymns.

Now, in battle after battle they were defeated, with terrible slaughter, until a hundred thousand peasants were slain. Many too were taken prisoner, and these, to strike terror to the hearts of others, were treated with frightful cruelty. Their eyes were put out, their hands cut off, and thus they were sent to their homes as a lesson to others.

At length the revolt was utterly crushed. Thousands of peasants had died, and those who remained were more wretched than before, and they sank back into a state of sullen misery, cursing alike their old masters and the new religion.

For Luther, himself a peasant's son, had sided against the peasants. To begin with, his writing and preaching had helped to give them courage to rise. But when they rebelled, he wrote and preached against them. At first he tried to preach peace, and quell the storm he had helped to raise. But when he saw that was useless, he took the side of the nobles, and preached and thundered against the revolt with all his might. This seemed to many in days to come like a great betrayal, a black blot on the kindly character of Luther. Yet he believed himself to be right. "Their blood is upon my head," he said, long years afterwards, "but I lay it all on God, who bade me so to speak."

The peasants, however, felt themselves betrayed and deceived, and for a time the name of Luther and his new religion were hated by them with a bitter hatred.

CHAPTER 50

# CHARLES V

MEANWHILE the Emperor Charles V remained far away. He had sworn to crush Luther and his heresy, and had by no means given up the idea. But for the time being his hands were full. Almost at once, after the Diet of Worms, he had left Germany, and he did not return for nine years. During a great part of that time he was fighting Francis I of France in Italy, in the hope of once more gaining that country for the Empire.

At length, in 1529, the Peace of Cambray was signed, and the following year Charles was crowned Emperor by the Pope at Bologna. Frederick III, you remember, was the last Emperor to be crowned at Rome. Charles V was the last Emperor of Germany ever to be crowned by the Pope at all.

Charles had now time to think a little about Germany and German heresy. In 1529, the Diet, or Parliament, met at Spires, and there a decree was passed forbidding any more changes of religion, and commanding that Mass should be said in all churches. The nobles and people who had followed Luther protested against this, and from that all those who broke away from the Church of Rome have received the name of Protestants.

The following year, after nine years' absence, Charles returned to Germany. He called together the Diet at Augsburg, and hoped very quickly to make short work of the Protestants. But he was mistaken. Luther was still under the ban of the Empire, and was forbidden to come to Augsburg, so Melanchthon, another but much milder reformer, appeared as leader of the Protestants. They drew up a statement of their beliefs, which was read before the Diet. This was afterwards called the Augsburg Confession, and was accepted as a Confession of Faith by all the Lutheran Churches.

The Catholics too drew up a statement, and there was a great deal of argument on both sides. Neither side would give way. So Charles forbade further talk. He ordered all Protestants to return to the old religion, and threatened all those who disobeyed with the ban of the Empire.

The Protestant nobles then banded together in what is known as the Schmalkald League, so called from the town of Schmalkald, and made ready to fight for freedom of conscience.

Charles was eager enough to fight these insolent Protestants. But another enemy, too, appeared. The Turks for a long time had been a danger to the Empire. Now the proud Sultan Solyman made ready to invade Germany with a mighty army. He came in pride and insolence, regarding the Emperor as a mere upstart, and refusing him any title but King of Spain. Himself he called "the Sultan of sultans, the King of kings, the Dispenser of Crowns to the monarchs on the face of the globe, the Shadow of God upon the earth."

"Be it known to you," he wrote, "that by the grace of God, and of the Prophet, I have set forth with all my nobles, slaves, and with a numberless host to seek the King of Spain. By the grace of God, I march against him. If he be of a high courage let him await me on the field of battle, and that which shall be, shall be. If he will not so await me, let him pay tribute to my majesty."

So he set forth, swearing never to return to Constantinople till he had laid waste the whole of Germany with fire and sword, and till he had conquered Italy. "Night and day," he said, "we are girt with our sword; our horse is ready saddled."

And now Charles V looked this way and that in vain for help against this mighty foe, Both England and France were in league with the Protestant princes against him. For Francis I, in spite of his treaties and his signed peace, was ever an enemy, and jealous of the Imperial crown, which he had hoped to win for himself. Secretly he was indeed in league with the Turks. Henry of England too was an enemy, and at this very time he was treating the Emperor's aunt, Catherine of Aragon, very cruelly, and seeking to divorce her. From abroad then there was little hope of help. At home there was as little. And Charles begged in vain for men and money to check the advance of the terrible Turks. The Protestant princes would grant him nothing until the Decree of Augsburg was recalled.

So at length Charles yielded, and the first religious truce, known as the Peace of Nuremburg, was signed in 1532. By this, Protestants were granted full freedom to worship God as they would, until a General Council should be called to discuss and settle these matters.

The Protestant nobles then gave the help which the Emperor asked, and a great army marched against the Turks. The Turks were defeated, and Solyman and his followers quickly marched back to their own land. And with that Charles was content. He let the Sultan go, making no effort to pursue him, greatly to the disgust of his army. "We fight," said a great general who lived in those days, "as this Emperor has always fought, like so many oxen in a rich meadow. When he has had enough, he lies down and chews the cud; so soon as hunger pricks him, he sets off again in search of fresh pasture."

Satisfied with what he had done against the Turks, Charles once more left Germany, and was soon again fighting with Francis I of France. But it would be impossible in this book to follow all the journeys and the wars of Charles. For the history of Charles is almost the history of Europe, and many of his wars and expeditions had to do with other of his many possessions, and not with the Empire.

As long as Charles wanted help for his wars, he kept the truce with the Protestants. So they were left in peace to grow strong and prosperous. The new religion spread rapidly until the whole of North Germany and a large part of South Germany had become Protestant. But Charles never lost the desire of crushing them one day, when it should be convenient to himself.

At length it seemed to him the time had come, and in 1545 a General Council was called by the Pope and met at Trent. But the Protestants refused to recognise this Council, and both sides made ready to fight. Before the war began, Luther died. He had done his best to keep the peace, but at the end his power had been but small.

At first the Emperor had only a small army, while that of the Schmalkaldic League was large. Had they attacked at once, all might have been well with them. But they hesitated, they were not united, orders were given and recalled, the troops marched now here, now there, without accomplishing anything.

Charles, on the other hand, fought with skill. One by one the cities fell away from the League. One by one the princes yielded. The last battle of the war was fought at Muhlberg in Saxony. Yet it could hardly be called a battle, it was rather a headlong flight and pursuit.

"I came, I saw, and God conquered," said Charles proudly.

The Emperor lost scarcely fifty men, the Protestants nearly three thousand, besides banners and baggage waggons, cannon and ammunition. The Elector of Saxony also was among the prisoners.

Battle-stained and dusty, the blood trickling down his face from a wound in the head, the Elector was led before Charles. Humbled, with bare head, he bowed before his master begging forgiveness. "Most gracious Emperor," he began. But Charles interrupted him. "Hah," he cried, "so I am now a gracious Emperor. Had you not fared better by finding that out sooner?"

John Frederick of Saxony was, however, as proud as the Emperor. He would not endure insults.

Quickly he drew himself up. He crammed his hat again upon his head, "I am your prisoner," he cried. "Do with me as you will."

"Be assured," answered Charles, "we shall treat you as you deserve."

The Elector was condemned to death, but the sentence was not carried out. He was, however, obliged to give up his title, and nearly all his land, and remain a prisoner at the court of Charles.

Charles was now at the height of his power. The German Protestants were crushed, he had made a long truce with the Turks, and last but not least, his two great rivals, Henry of England, and Francis of France, were dead. With no one left who dared defy him, his pride knew no bounds.

Charles now held a Diet at Augsburg. At this Diet he brought forward what is known as the Interim. This was a plan drawn up to settle all religious differences. It really took from the Protestants almost everything for which they had fought. After twenty-five years of freedom they were to be once more bound to the Romish Church. But although the princes and the cities were forced to seem to accept the Interim, it never was really accepted. The people laughed it to scorn.

Soon once more war broke out. Charles had made Duke Maurice Elector of Saxony, in place of the imprisoned John Frederick. For a time Duke Maurice seemed to be the Emperor's friend. Then he rebelled against him. He found an ally in Henry II of France, who hated the Emperor with a deep and bitter hatred.

And now there began a more dreadful war than had ever before been fought on German soil. Not even in the terrible Peasants' War had there been such bloodshed and cruelty. And yet the war was fought in the name of German liberty, and for the love of "the pure Word of God." Germans fought against Germans, Catholic against Protestant, with a cruelty more horrible than even the Turks had used. They destroyed churches and monasteries, in the name of Christ, more wantonly than any Saracen host had ever done.

Henry II of France, who persecuted the Protestants in his own land, now entered Germany to fight for German Protestants. At the same time Duke Maurice marched southward to attack Charles in Innsbruck.

The Emperor was quite unprepared. Broken down and ill, he fled from the city, and was carried in a litter across the mountains, to the town of Villach in Carinthia.

The Catholics were in despair, the Protestants triumphant. Three days after Duke Maurice entered Innsbruck, a truce was signed, and this was followed by the Treaty of Passau. By this Treaty Charles gave the Protestants full freedom to follow their own religion until a Diet should be called to settle the matter. He promised, too, that if the Diet failed to find a way of agreement between the two parties, that the Protestants should be left in peace. But this promise was wrung from him with difficulty, for he hoped still to crush out the heresy.

Peace having at length been restored, Charles turned to fight "that Protector of German liberties" Henry II. But for months his cannon thundered in vain against the walls of Metz, which was held against him by the Duke of Guise. At length, sick at heart, Charles turned away from the hopeless struggle. "Fortune is but a fickle jade," he said, "I well see, she prefers a young king to an old Emperor." He had fought his last battle. Never again did he mount his war-horse or lay his lance in rest.

In 1555 the promised Diet was called to settle the question of religion. And after much talk, the so-called Religious Peace of Augsburg was signed. It did not give freedom of conscience to every man. The princes, so it was decreed, might be of what religion they chose, and the people must obey their prince. If he chose he could leave them free; if he chose he could force them to follow his religion. "To whom the land belongs, to him belongs the religion of the land," was the groundwork of the law. It put an end to all real freedom of conscience, and it was the cause of terrible misery for Germany in days to come.

But now the Emperor was spent and old. He longed for peace. Of late all his plans had failed, he was ill and weary of the weight of his many crowns, so one day he laid them down. To his son Philip he gave the Netherlands and Spain with solemn ceremony. He tried also, as he had tried many times before, to have him chosen King of the Romans and Emperor. But he tried in vain. So at length he yielded the rule of Germany to his brother Ferdinand. Then he said farewell to royal state, and went away to spend his last days in the monastery of San Yuste in Spain. There he gave himself up to working with mechanical things, making models and mechanical toys, digging in the garden, and other simple pleasures. He spent much time, it is said, trying to make two clocks keep time with each other, and could not do it. At length, in despair, he cried out, "I cannot even make two clocks keep time together, and yet I set myself to force a million souls to conform to one belief."

Charles was a strange mixture and full of contradictions. He was timid and he was brave, he would tremble at a mouse and walk unmoved amid the roar and crash of cannon. At times he was painfully irresolute, at others obstinate as a mule. And he knew it.

"I am by nature obstinate," he said once to a cardinal. "To cling to good opinions, Sire," replied the cardinal, "is not to be obstinate, but to be firm."

"Ah, but," answered Charles, "sometimes I cling to bad ones."

Charles was the greatest ruler of his century, half the known world was under his sway. He died in 1558.

CHAPTER 51

# FERDINAND I AND MAXIMILIAN II

CHARLES'S younger brother Ferdinand succeeded him as Emperor. He was already King of Austria. During his brother's reign too he had been chosen King of the Romans, and had acted as Regent in the Emperor's long absence from Germany.

Ferdinand was lively and kindly, and altogether very different from his cold and scheming brother. Yet he too was a Spaniard, born and brought up in Spain. But after Ferdinand came to live in Austria he began to lose his Spanish ways. He took a real interest in the people he had to rule over. He learned to speak German, and began to live as a German noble. And so he won the love of the German people.

Like Charles, Ferdinand was a firm Catholic. But to begin with he had a fierce quarrel with the Pope. The Pope declared that Charles V had no right to give up the crown without first asking his leave, and that Ferdinand had no right to take it. So the Pope declared that he would only acknowledge Ferdinand as Emperor if he would refuse to keep the Treaty of Augsburg. Ferdinand, however, knew the strength of the Protestants. So he would do nothing to make them angry, but tried his best to make peace between the two parties.

Ferdinand's reign was not a long one, and it was of no great importance in German history. He died in 1564, and his son Maximilian was at once chosen Emperor. Maximilian looked so kindly upon the Protestant religion, that many people expected that he would himself turn Protestant. But he did not. He left the German Protestants quite free to worship God their own way, but he did not raise a finger to help other Protestants who were fighting for a like freedom.

And at this time a bitter warfare was going on in a land which had but lately been part of the Empire.

When Charles V abdicated you remember that gave the Netherlands to his son Philip. He is known as Philip II of Spain, and was both a tyrant and a bigoted Catholic. It was quite unnatural that the Netherlands should belong to Spain. The country really belonged to the Empire. And Germany's longest river, the Rhine, flowed to the sea through the Netherlands. But the Emperor's power was so great that one dared question his deed. The Netherlands were Protestant, but Philip was determined that there should be no Protestants in his kingdom. The Dutch were just as determined never to give up their religion, so there began in Holland one of the most bitter persecutions, and one of the most gallant struggles for liberty in all history.

And while Holland was splendidly struggling for freedom, Protestant Germany, under an Emperor who was himself almost a Protestant, looked on. Again and again the Dutch asked the Emperor for aid, again and again it was refused. At length, after years of fighting, Holland won its liberty. It became a free state, independent alike of Spain or of the Empire. To Germany this was a great loss. For Holland was a rich country, its people were industrious, its trade and manufactures flourished, its ships were famous upon every sea. All that was now lost to the Empire, and Germany's great river now reaches the sea by way of a foreign land.

Although Maximilian was himself almost a Protestant he had married his cousin Maria, the daughter of Charles V. She was a firm Catholic, and she brought up her children also as Catholics, and two of her daughters married the fiercest persecutors of the heretics. For one married Philip II of Spain, another Charles IX of France. It was under Charles IX that the terrible massacre of St. Bartholomew took place, of which you will read in French history. When Maximilian heard of it he was filled with grief. "Would God," he said, "that my son-in-law had asked my advice. I should have advised him faithfully as a father, so that he should never have been persuaded to this shameful deed."

But Maximilian took no care to save his own people from a like fate. He gave them freedom while he lived, but made no laws to protect them after his death. He died in 1576. With him all freedom of conscience in Germany was buried for many a long day.

CHAPTER 52
# RUDOLPH II

MAXIMILIAN was succeeded by his son Rudolph. He had been brought up in Spain by the Jesuits, so was a staunch Catholic. He was only twenty-four when he came to the throne, and was far more learned than any prince of his time. But he was weak and changeable, uncertain of himself and suspicious of others, and little fitted to rule. The business of state wearied him. He loved alchemy and astrology. He loved fine horses too, and he spent the happiest hours visiting his stables, or in his laboratory trying to find out how to make gold, or seeking to read the secrets of the stars.

Yet at first Rudolph seemed to take some interest in the Empire. He opened the Diets in person, and he made laws against the Protestants, which, however, he never had strength of will to enforce, and which only led to revolts. Indeed he was so weak and irresolute over everything that by degrees the country drifted into confusion. Meanwhile the Emperor yielded more and more to sullen and passionate moods which almost amounted to madness. He shut himself up in his palace among the treasures of art, the paintings and sculptures which he had gathered there, and refused to see any one. His bedroom windows were barred like those of a prison, he ate his meals alone, being waited on by two servants only. He never laughed, and became so furious at the slightest noise that servants and courtiers approached him in fear of their lives.

Yet Rudolph would give up to others nothing of his kingly power. For weeks his table would be piled with papers waiting for his royal signature, for months ambassadors from foreign countries would beg an audience in vain. The affairs of the Empire were at length so neglected, that Rudolph's brother, Matthias, called a council together to decide what should be done.

It was decided that Rudolph was no longer fit to rule, and that Matthias must henceforth be looked upon as head of the House of Hapsburg.

Yet half crazy though Rudolph was, he would not yield quietly. So Matthias gathered his army, and marching against his brother soon forced him to yield. Rudolph, indeed, still kept the title of Emperor, but he gave up all his own lands, Austria, Hungary, and Moravia, to his brother. Bohemia alone was left to him.

Meanwhile the Protestants throughout the Empire had grown very much alarmed at Rudolph's efforts to crush them. So to protect themselves, they formed a league known as the Protestant Union. At once the Catholics became uneasy, and they on their side formed another league, which was called the Catholic League, and was meant to be a check upon the Protestant League. Thus both sides watched each other with fear and suspicion, each ready to fight for their rights.

The Protestant nobles of Austria had helped Matthias in his war against Rudolph, and now as a reward he gave them freedom of worship. Upon this the people of Bohemia also demanded a like freedom from Rudolph. Seeing no help for it, he granted them what is known as the Letter of Majesty, which gave to all freedom to worship God as they thought right.

But Rudolph had no sooner granted this liberty than he regretted it. He allowed his cousin, the Bishop of Passau, to enter Bohemia with an army, and waste it with fire and sword. The Bohemians then sent to Matthias for help. He came, and Rudolph soon found himself a prisoner in his own castle of Prague, and forced to yield the last of his possessions to his brother. With great pomp and ceremony Matthias was crowned King of Bohemia. But while the crown was placed upon his head, and while the people shouted, and the church bells clanged forth joyfully, the wretched Rudolph hid himself deep in the furthest corner of his palace, stopping his ears lest he should catch the slightest sound of the rejoicings.

But still another bitter humiliation was in store for him. He was forced to sign his abdication. He submitted, but his passion was so great that he could scarcely hold the pen, and his signature looked more like a blot than a name. And when he had finished it he tore the pen to pieces with his teeth in mad rage.

Rudolph was now little better than a beggar in his own kingdom. He was ill and broken-hearted, and in a few months he died.

CHAPTER 53

# MATTHIAS

RUDOLPH II had never married. He left no children who might succeed him, and at his death his brother Matthias was chosen as Emperor. Matthias, as you know, had already made himself King of Austria, Bohemia, and all the other Austrian states. But he proved himself no better an Emperor than his brother Rudolph. He was already growing old (he was fifty-seven when he became Emperor) and he found himself quite unable to rule. Difficulties and dangers were daily growing thicker around him, bitterness and suspicion were daily increasing between the two parties, and the Emperor felt himself too weak to cope with them or bring peace between them.

Matthias, therefore, left the government to his chief minister Bishop Klesl, and to his nephew Ferdinand. Then after a time Ferdinand was proclaimed King of Bohemia. At this the Protestants were much dismayed, for Ferdinand was a Catholic, already well known as the pitiless foe of all Protestants. Ferdinand was greatly influenced in all that he did by the Jesuits, who had lately risen to great power in Germany. Led by them he did all he could to hamper the Protestants and make the Letter of Majesty granted to them by Rudolph of no avail. He shut up the Protestant churches, burned the Bibles and hymn-books, and forced people in every way he could to attend Mass once more. "Better a desert," he was wont to say, "than a land full of heretics."

So the anger and unrest grew deeper and deeper, and at length it burst out into wild rebellion.

In Bohemia the Protestants had built two churches. One was on land belonging to a bishop, the other on land belonging to an abbot. The Catholics said that the Protestants had no right to build these churches, and the abbot closed the one, and the Archbishop forced the Protestants to pull down the other.

At this the Protestants were very angry. They declared that the Letter of Majesty gave them the right to build these churches, and they appealed to the Emperor.

The Emperor received their petition coldly. He would not help them, but approved rather of what had been done by the Archbishop and the Abbot.

This made the people of Bohemia furiously angry, but they did not blame the Emperor. They did not believe that he had sent the answer to their petition, but that it had been made up by two men, Slawata and Martinitz, in whose hands the government really was. Slawata had once been a Protestant, but having now turned against them persecuted them cruelly. Martinitz too hated the Protestants.

Headed by Count Thurn the nobles gathered to Prague, and followed by a great mob of people they marched to the Council Chambers. There they demanded an answer to their question as to whether the Emperor had ever seen their petition or not.

Martinitz and Slawata refused to answer. Then a fearful tumult arose. Swords were drawn, hoarse cries and threats rang through the hall. With flashing eyes and flushed faces the insurgents crowded round the two hated regents. They were traitors to their country, cried the mob, and must die.

Rough hands were laid upon them, and they were dragged towards the windows. In vain they struggled, in vain they besought for mercy. "Let us at least first confess our sins," cried Martinitz.

"Commend your soul to God," was the stern reply, "we will have no Jesuit rascals here."

Then, amid the shouting and confusion, the windows were thrown wide, and the two men were flung out. "Jesus! Maria!" wailed Martinitz as he fell.

"Let us see whether his Mary will help him," laughed some one coarsely as he leaned from the window to watch.

"By heaven!" he cried a moment later in an awed tone, "she has helped him."

The Council Chamber was high, and the wretched men had been thrown from a height of eighty feet or more into the moat of the castle. It was filled with old papers and all sorts of litter and rubbish. And to the astonishment of all, the two men fell upon it almost unhurt.

A secretary was flung down after his masters. He too was almost unhurt. Long afterwards he was given the title of Hohenfall or Highfall in memory of his wonderful escape. Now, however, his first feeling was not of thankfulness for his escape, but one of anger against the rioters.

"What have I done to them," he asked tearfully, "that they should throw me out?"

"This is no time to ask questions, sir," replied Martinitz. "You had better get up and help us."

Of the three Slawata was the most hurt. He was indeed terribly bruised and shaken, but with the help of the others he began to crawl away. In angry astonishment the rioters looked down upon the three from the windows above. Then shots were fired. One struck Martinitz's collar, a second his coat, and a third just grazed his arm. "Great God," he cried in wonder, "hast Thou made me invulnerable and immortal!"

By this time some of the Regent's servants came hurrying to help their masters, and with their aid they reached a place of safety. The secretary, however, fled away hatless and coatless as he was, and was the first to bring the news of the revolt to the Emperor.

This riot, although none knew it at the time, was the beginning of a most dreadful war which was to last for thirty years, and lay Germany waste from end to end.

Having thus thrown the Regents forth, the Protestants took possession of the castle. They chose leaders from their own number, and prepared for war.

The Emperor was old and ill, and he very gladly would have made peace. But his nephew Ferdinand would have none of it. He blamed the Emperor's adviser Bishop Klesl for wishing to make peace, and so one day as the Bishop came to see Matthias, he was stopped in the anteroom. Here he was ordered to change his Bishop's robes for those of an ordinary priest. At first he refused. But at length, terrified by dreadful threats, he yielded.

Klesl was then hurried to a carriage and driven away. On and on he went, far into the mountains. When the roads became too steep and narrow for a carriage, he was ordered to descend. Then, in a Sedan chair, he was carried still upward, until the Castle of Ambas, not far from Innsbruck, was reached. Here he was shut up in prison.

The poor Emperor was at first very angry when he heard what had been done. But soon he sank into sadness and gloom. He had lost his best friend, and most faithful adviser. He felt himself surrounded only by enemies. His spirit was utterly broken, and in a few months he died.

CHAPTER 54

# FERDINAND II

FERDINAND, the nephew of Matthias, was now chosen and crowned as Emperor. But the Bohemians refused to acknowledge him as King. Instead they chose the young Elector Palatine known as Frederick V. He was weak and easily led, but he seemed to be more powerful than he really was, for he had married the Princess Elizabeth of England, and it was hoped that James I would help him. Our George I, it may interest you to remember, was the grandson of this Frederick V.

In November Frederick was crowned at Prague with great splendour, a great deal of money being spent on the ceremony, in spite of the fact that the army was in need, and the soldiers forced to plunder in order to find food.

But all his splendour notwithstanding, those on the Emperor's side thought little of King Frederick. "He is but a winter king," they said, sure that before the summer came his grandeur would have melted away.

Ferdinand was resolved to conquer his rival, and at the same time crush out Protestantism, not only in Bohemia, but in all Germany. So he set out to fight the Winter King. In 1620 a great battle was fought at Weissenberg, or White Hill, near Prague. The leader on the Emperor's side was a great general named Tilly. Tilly was a little lean man of very strange appearance. Great gloomy eyes looked forth from his brown and wrinkled face. His beard was pointed, and his grey moustache bristled fiercely. Upon his shock of rough grey hair he wore a little green cap with a tall red feather, and he generally dressed himself in a green satin coat.

On Frederick's side the Prince Christian of Anhalt led. The King himself took no part in the battle. He left his ragged soldiers to fight for his crown while he entertained two British ambassadors at dinner.

The numbers on either side were nearly equal. But Ferdinand's soldiers were well fed and well drilled. Frederick's were hungry, ragged, and undisciplined. The fight was not long. It began about 12 o'clock on a dull November Sunday, and little more than an hour later the Bohemians were fleeing madly from the field.

Frederick rose from dinner, a king without a country. He had done nothing to win the love of his people, much to make them hate him and his foreign wife. The day after the defeat of the White Hill they fled, followed by the curses of their subjects.

With the flight of the King, Bohemian resistance was at an end. The Imperial troops entered Prague, and Bohemia yielded to the Emperor. The news of the victory was brought to him at Vienna. There, too, he received much treasure which had been captured. Among it was the Letter of Majesty, Bohemia's charter of freedom. When he saw it, Ferdinand, with great joy, tore the royal seal from off it, and cut the parchment in two.

Ferdinand now took bitter vengeance on Bohemia for its revolt. Some of the Protestant leaders were put to death, thousands were sent into exile. The Protestant clergy were banished, and none but the Catholic religion was allowed. The people were fined and taxed, and robbed of their lands and money, until, instead of being a wealthy and prosperous land, Bohemia became a poor and miserable land. Instead of having four million inhabitants, it had barely one.

Meanwhile, the war which had begun as a quarrel between Bohemia and the Emperor spread until almost every country in Europe was drawn into it. For some it was a religious war, a fight for freedom of conscience. For others it was merely a war of politics, a fight against the every-increasing might of the Hapsburgs. Britain, Holland, Denmark, and Sweden took sides against the Emperor. France too fought against him. For although Richelieu was at this time cruelly crushing out the Protestants in France, he was willing enough to help them in Germany, for through them he hoped to weaken the power of the Emperor.

So in spite of many successes, Ferdinand's position was by no means secure. His army was small, his treasury growing daily more and more empty. He knew that if he were to save his crown, he must raise a large army; but he had no money with which to do it.

It was then that a great soldier, Albert of Waldstein, generally known as Wallenstein, came to his aid. Wallenstein was the son of noble, but by no means rich or powerful parents. He, however, very soon showed that he meant to be both rich and powerful. He married a wealthy lady, and when she died and left him all her lands and money, he married another rich heiress. In many other ways he added possession to possession, and lastly he bought huge tracts of land taken from the conquered Bohemians.

He was now immensely wealthy, and he offered to raise an army of 21,000 men at his own expense. But after it was raised the Empire was to pay all salaries, and Wallenstein, as commander-in-chief, was to have the ransom of prisoners, a share of the spoil, and almost kingly power over the conquered.

The Emperor agreed to all that Wallenstein asked, and Wallenstein more than kept his word. For soon he had a far larger army in the field than he had promised. He welcomed all alike to his army, Protestants or Catholics, honest men or scoundrels; all that he asked was that they should fight. And he got what he asked. "God help the land to which these men come," cried a terrified onlooker, as the wild horde marched past him.

Wallenstein himself travelled in princely magnificence. He kept as great state as the Emperor himself. He had a suite of more than two hundred pages, servants, bodyguards, priests, and courtiers about him. A thousand horses were needed for the use of his followers alone. His table was served with the greatest magnificence, with the most splendid foods and wines; and the members of the greatest families, both knights and nobles, were eager to wait upon him.

Wallenstein himself was dark and silent. He spoke little, laughed never. He was tall and thin and very still and mysterious. His small bright eyes seemed to be the only living thing in his dark and gloomy face. In this strange man the Emperor soon learned to put his whole trust. But at the same time he learned to dread him.

In 1627 Wallenstein's army defeated the Protestant army under Count Ernst of Mansfeld at Dessau. Mansfeld was an outlawed noble. He had been a Catholic, and had fought against the Protestants. But having been converted, he now fought on their side. But soon after the defeat at Dessau Mansfeld died. He was a brave and fearless soldier, and he refused to die in his bed. Feeling that he had not long to live, he bade the sorrowing friends who watched around his death-bed to dress him, put on his armour, and gird him with his sword.

"Up, then," he cried; "the end is near. Dear friends, bear me to the open window, so that once again I may feel the morning air upon my face. Death which has ever spared me in the battlefield shall not take me on soft pillows. Standing, I will give back my soul to the God of battles."

So, held erect by two friends, his dim eyes looking full into the wintry dawn, the brave general met his last enemy. "Keep together," he murmured with his latest breath; "make a brave stand."

Another great leader on the Protestant side, Christian of Anhalt, died the same year. Christian IV of Denmark, too, was defeated, and forced to sue for peace. Everywhere the Emperor, with the help of his great general, Wallenstein, seemed victorious.

But at length, before the town of Stralsund, on the shores of the Baltic, Wallenstein's triumphant career was checked. Wallenstein and his hosts lay about the walls, but the people of Stralsund would not yield to him. Week by week they held out, and week by week Wallenstein's determination to take the town grew stronger. "I will have Stralsund," he cried, "even if it were fastened with chains to heaven." And he meant to have it without conditions of any kind, to do with as he would. So when the citizens tried to make terms with him, he treated them with scorn. "Your town shall be as flat as that," he said, as he passed his hand over the table in front of him.

But week after week passed, and Stralsund still held out. At length the great general was forced to eat his proud words, forget his proud threats, and march away.

This siege of Stralsund was a great turning-point in the war. But the Emperor did not know it. In spite of it he believed himself to be completely victorious, and upon Wallenstein's advice he signed the Peace of Lubeck in 1629.

Feeling himself now all powerful, Ferdinand issued what is called the Edict of Restitution. By this Edict he commanded that all bishoprics which had fallen into Protestants' hands should be given back to the Catholics, and that Catholic priests should everywhere replace the Protestant ministers. This Edict burst like a thunderstorm over Protestant Germany. The people were struck helpless with surprise. Everywhere officers and soldiers appeared to see that the Edict was obeyed. Protestant services were stopped, pulpits and bells were carried off, Bibles and hymn-books were seized and burned. The Protestant cause seemed dead.

But now just at this time bitter quarrels began to show themselves on the other side. Many of the nobles had long been jealous of Wallenstein. He was too powerful, too haughty, and they hated him. Now they persuaded the Emperor that he and his army were a danger to the Empire, and begged him to dismiss Wallenstein.

For a long time the Emperor hesitated. He too had grown to fear Wallenstein, but he knew also how much he had done. At length, however, he yielded, and two of Wallenstein's former friends were sent to tell him that the Emperor wanted him no longer.

They were a little afraid to go, for they knew not how Wallenstein might receive them. But the message they brought was no news to Wallenstein, for he had friends at court who had warned him of what was afoot against him. Wallenstein, therefore, had had time to think the matter over. He had decided that it would be best to take the Emperor's dismissal quietly. So he received the messengers very courteously, and entertained them nobly. When at length, with much hesitation, they began to explain their message, he stopped them. "There is no need," he said, "I have already read my destiny in the stars. I do not blame the Emperor, though I am sorry that he has forsaken me so easily. I will, however, yield obedience to him."

So without a murmur the great general retired into private life. Part of his army was disbanded, and part was placed under the leadership of Tilly, his great rival.

CHAPTER 55

# FERDINAND II

BUT at this very time a new and great enemy had landed in Germany. This was Gustavus Adolphus, King of Sweden. He was called the "Lion of the North." And a lion of strength he looked with his mane of tawny hair and great broad shoulders.

Gustavus Adolphus came with only a small army. But he expected that the Protestant nobles would receive him with joy, and hasten to join his standard. The Germans, however, looked upon his coming with suspicion. They could not make up their minds that he came as a friend, and they received him coldly.

At first, too, the Emperor thought lightly of this fresh foe. "We have a new little enemy," he said scornfully.

Magdeburg had resisted the Edict of Restitution, and now Tilly with his army lay around the town. Gustavus Adolphus sent messages of encouragement to the people and promised help. But surrounded as he was with men who were hostile or suspicious, he dared not move quickly. So before he arrived the city was taken.

And when it was taken there followed a slaughter too awful to think about. The victorious soldiers seemed to have lost all human feeling, and to be changed into pitiless demons. No cry for mercy was of any avail. Old men, defenceless women and children, were murdered as mercilessly as the armed soldiers who could fight for their lives.

At length, seized with a kind of desperate courage, the citizens resolved to die by their own hands rather than await the brutality of the soldiers. So they set fire to the town. Then began a new horror. On all sides fires sprang up, and soon the roar of flames and the crash of falling houses were added to the general tumult.

The air quivered with heat, grew dense with smoke. It was impossible to breathe freely, and even the blood-maddened soldiers were at length forced to leave their savage work.

Night came on. It was a night of noise and horror, and leaping flames. The fire roared unceasingly from street to street, until, finding nothing else to feed upon, it at last died down. When morning dawned it showed Magdeburg a heap of blackened ruins. Nothing was saved but the grand

Cathedral and one or two houses round it. In a few hours one of the finest cities of Germany had been laid in ashes.

The cruelty of the conquerors of Magdeburg made many of the wavering Protestant nobles turn to Gustavus, and on September 7, 1631, he defeated Tilly in a great battle at Breitenfeld near Leipzic.

After this the southward march of the Swedish King was a march of triumph. Again he met Tilly in battle, and again Tilly was defeated. It was the old General's last fight, for in it he was so sorely wounded that he died about a fortnight later.

There seemed nothing now left to the Emperor but to recall Wallenstein. He alone, it seemed, would know how to check the triumphant march of the bold young King.

But Wallenstein had been spurned and insulted. He had appeared, indeed, to take his dismissal quietly. But deep in his heart anger burned, not only against the nobles who had brought about his dismissal, but against the Emperor who had allowed it. He wanted to make the Emperor feel what it meant to "insult a cavalier," as he said.

He began in secret to make terms with Gustavus Adolphus, and when now the Emperor implored him to come to his aid, he scornfully refused.

"I shall not stir," he said; "no not if the Lord of heaven came down to ask it of me."

But Wallenstein's plotting with Gustavus Adolphus came to nothing, and in the end he yielded to the Emperor's persuasion, and consented to help him. So once again the magnificent, despotic old General was head of the Imperial army. But he made his own terms—such terms as never before or since has a General made. He took command, not as a mere soldier, but as a ruling Prince. Not even the Emperor was to give him orders.

The Emperor's army was well-nigh shattered. But there was magic in the mere name of Wallenstein, and as soon as it was known that he would once more take the field, thousands flocked to his standard.

And now the great struggle began between the old warrior and the young. Battles were fought and broad lands laid desolate as the two played the deadly game, marching and counter-marching.

At length, at Lutzen, on November 6, 1632, the great battle of the war took place. The day dawned dark and dreary, but both camps were early astir. The Swedes, in battle array, knelt to pray, then, rising, they sang Luther's hymn, "A strong fortress is our Lord."

Then, Gustavus, mounting his horse, spoke to his men.

"Comrades," he cried, "make ready to show yourselves the brave soldiers you are. Stand shoulder to shoulder, and fight for your religion and your King, and I will reward you all. But hold yourselves like cowards, and not one of you will ever cross the Baltic again and see your native land. May God keep you all."

Then, turning to the German army, he bade them too be brave, and follow him. "God, I trust," he cried, "will give you a victory which will be memorable for all time. If not, then farewell to your religion and your liberty."

In Wallenstein's army Mass was said, but their leader made no speech. He had no need. The sight of him, the mere magic of his name, was enough to fill them with courage.

So, one side shouting "Jesus, Maria," the other "God with us," the battle began.

When the fight was at its fiercest a thick fog fell upon the field, and in the darkness the King, charging at the head of his horsemen, dashed into the enemies' lines. Shot after shot was fired upon him, and, mortally wounded, he fell to the ground.

The regiment swept on, and Gustavus was left with only a young page beside him. He tried to raise his master and carry him to a place of safety. But in vain; for the King was of great stature and was too heavy for him.

Then, even as the page tried to bring his master into safety, some of the enemy riding up demanded the name of the wounded noble. The page would not answer.

But Gustavus Adolphus himself replied. "I am the King of Sweden," he murmured.

Right glad were the horsemen when they heard that, and bending from his saddle one of them put his pistol to the King's head and shot him dead. Having stabbed the faithful page, they robbed both him and the King of everything, even of the clothes they wore. Then they rode away.

Meanwhile, the King's great white horse, all flecked with blood and foam, dashed madly among his men. Its empty stirrups and dragging reins carried to them the dreadful news. Seeing his riderless horse, they knew to a certainty that their King must be either dead or mortally wounded. But instead of making them lose courage, that certainty roused them to fury. Eager to avenge their beloved leader's death, they dashed wildly upon the foe.

The Imperial troops began to waver. Through their ranks rode Wallenstein, drawn sword in hand, encouraging them, urging them onward. Shots flew thick and fast around him, his cloak was riddled, but he himself passed through the deadly hail unharmed. It was as if he bore a charmed life.

For seven hours the battle lasted. Then Wallenstein, acknowledging defeat at last, ordered his men to retreat, and the pursuing Swedes drove them in disorder from the field.

The victory remained with the Swedes, but it was all too dearly bought. For among the slain, his fair face trampled and disfigured, his yellow hair clotted and dark with the dust and blood of battle, lay the "Golden King of the North."

The death of Gustavus Adolphus was a terrible blow to the Protestants of Europe. But the war continued, the Swedish Chancellor, Axel Oxenstierna, taking the dead King's place as leader.

Wallenstein now wanted to make peace. He wanted to make a peace which would bring much profit to himself and add another great principality to his already huge possessions. He found, however, that he could not do exactly as he wished, so he began to have secret dealings With Oxenstierna. But Oxenstierna did not trust him.

And now once more the Emperor became eager to be rid of Wallenstein, once more there were plots against him, and many of his soldiers deserted.

Wallenstein had always been very sure of himself and of his power. But at length finding himself deserted by many of his friends, he could no longer shut his eyes to the fact that he was in danger of something worse than merely being dismissed a second time. He determined therefore to flee and join the enemy.

The Emperor longed to be rid of Wallenstein, still he hesitated. "Why this delay?" whispered the Spanish Ambassador. "A pistol or a dagger would soon make an end of him." Still the Emperor seemed to hesitate.

Then without the Emperor's orders, but perhaps not without his knowledge, some of Wallenstein's officers swore together to kill him and four of his chief friends.

The conspirators resolved to begin with the friends, and they asked them to supper in the castle of Eger, to which place Wallenstein had fled. Suspecting nothing, the four accepted the invitation. But as soon as they were within, the gates were shut and guarded, and soldiers were posted in the rooms near that in which supper was served.

*Through their ranks rode Wallenstein, drawn sword in hand.*

The evening passed merrily, in feasting and drinking and so friendly were their hosts that the doomed men suspected nothing. At length dessert was placed upon the table. At the same moment the doors at either end of the hall were thrown open, and armed men rushed in. "Long live the House of Austria!" they cried. "Who among you are good Imperialists?" and awaiting no answer they fell upon their unsuspecting victims.

The four fought desperately for their lives, but the struggle was soon over. They could do little against such odds, and one by one they fell dead.

It was now near midnight, and the conspirators set forth to Wallenstein's house to finish their deadly work. He had but just gone to bed, and as they noisily mounted the stairs, his servant, coming down, begged them to make less noise, as his master was going to sleep.

"But this is a time for noise," shouted their captain, and pushing the man roughly aside, he strode on to Wallenstein's room.

The door was locked, but a few blows soon burst it open, and the soldiers rushed in.

Clad in a long sleeping robe, the old warrior stood by the open window.

The rebel captain did not hesitate a moment; no feeling of pity or respect for the General he had so often followed in battle, touched his heart. "Traitor, you must die," he cried.

Wallenstein answered nothing. His lips moved, but no word came. Standing proudly erect, his arms thrown wide, calmly he awaited the death-stroke. It took him fair in the breast, and without a groan he sank to the ground dead.

Thus ended the life of this strange man. He was not wholly good nor wholly bad. But he was hated by both sides—by the Protestants, of whom he was the open enemy; by the Catholics, who believed him to be a traitor. But traitor or no, he was the one man who could have brought peace to Europe at the time. He died, and the war continued.

The murderers were richly rewarded by the Emperor. He heaped money and lands and honours upon them. And in order to prove that that which they had done was not a murder, but a just execution, he published a letter setting forth all the bad things Wallenstein had done, and all the still worse things he had meant to do.

CHAPTER 56

# FERDINAND III

FERDINAND II died in 1637, and was succeeded by his son, Ferdinand III. He was forced to carry on the war, but now its object was very much changed.

Louis XIV now ruled in France, and France had joined with Sweden against the Emperor. And both were fighting now, not to give religious freedom to the Protestants, but to conquer some part of Germany for themselves.

But at length all parties became weary of the terrible war, and in 1648 peace was signed. This is called the Peace of Westphalia, from Osnabruck and Munster, the two towns in Westphalia where the treaty was signed; the Swedes meeting at Osnabruck, the French at Munster.

The war which was then brought to an end was one of the most terrible ever fought in Europe. Germany was a waste of ruined cities and blackened homesteads. More than half the people were dead; of those who remained many were reduced to the utmost poverty. Trade and manufactures were almost at a standstill, the shipping and commerce for which Germany had been so famous were ruined, and the Great Hansa League almost broken up.

It was with a sigh of relief that the people of Germany received the news that the terrible war which had desolated the land for thirty years was at length at an end. Yet the joy was not unmixed with anger and discontent. Few of the Catholics in Germany were really pleased with the Peace of Westphalia. For, except in Bohemia and Austria, which belonged to the Emperor by inheritance, and where he refused to tolerate Protestantism, the Protestants were given entire freedom. That displeased the Catholics.

The Protestants also were not entirely pleased. They had long ere this begun to fight among themselves, and were divided into Lutherans and Calvinists. They were both given equal freedom, so neither party was pleased.

But, worst of all, Germany had lost much territory, and this was bitter to every German, Catholic and Protestant alike.

To Sweden the whole of Western Pomerania had to be given up, as well as several other towns upon the Baltic and North Seas. France received all Alsace except the city of Strassburg. And both France and Sweden now claimed a right to interfere in the affairs of the Empire. But there was a difference between the parts of the Empire given to Sweden and to France. The part which France received was no longer looked upon as a part of the Empire, but became part of France. And thus the Rhine became the boundary of France, a point for which the French had long fought. The land which Sweden received still remained a part of the Empire, although under the rule of Sweden. And by right of these new possessions the King of Sweden joined the German Diet.

Both Switzerland and the Netherlands had long since ceased to be a part of the Empire. But it was at the Peace of Westphalia that they were for the first time openly acknowledged to be free.

Though, in fact, it was not only Switzerland and the Netherlands which had become independent. Nearly every prince in the whole of Germany did as he liked, and the Empire was now little more than a name. The Emperor's power was a mere shadow, and each prince ruled his own small state as he chose. He made war or peace at will. He made friends with one foreign state or with another, paying but little heed to the desires of his overlord, the Emperor.

CHAPTER 57

# LEOPOLD I

FERDINAND III reigned for twenty years. But, except for the Treaty of Westphalia, nothing of great importance happened in his reign. He died in 1657, and was succeeded by his son Leopold I.

Louis XIV was now reigning in France. The most gorgeous and arrogant ruler of the age, he had a tremendous idea of his own grandeur and importance, and he tried to bribe the Electors into choosing him as Emperor. Some of the Electors, however, refused to be bribed. Weak, good-natured eighteen-year-old Leopold was chosen to succeed to his father, and the wily arrogant Louis was ever after his enemy.

Both openly and in secret Louis was the enemy of the Empire. He fought against Germany himself, and he encouraged others to do so also.

Meanwhile, all the little German princes tried to copy the splendour of Louis's court, laying heavy taxes upon their poor subjects to pay for these new grandeurs. They spoke French, or mixed so many French words with the German that it sounded like a foreign language. They aped Louis in his elaborate etiquette and ceremony, in the smallest matters, and hotly debated whether lesser princes might sit on green velvet chairs like the Electors, or whether they might only be allowed purple velvet. They gravely discussed who might eat off gold plate and who only off silver, and many other like matters of as little importance. "Alas!" writes a German who lived in those days, "it is but too well known that ever since the French demon has possessed us Germans, our way of living, our manners, and our customs have changed sorely. Once we held the French cheap, now everything must needs be French—French speech, French clothes, French food, French furniture, French dances, French diseases, and I fear me following thereon French death."

But there was one German prince who refused to be led away by this foolish French fashion. That was Frederick William, Elector of Brandenburg, who has come to be known as the Great Elector. Save for him the Empire might have fallen to pieces.

Louis XIV was greedy of land, greedy of conquest, and he invaded first the Spanish Netherlands which we now know as Belgium, and then the United Free Provinces, which we now call Holland. For the most part the German states looked coldly on, but some of them even joined with Louis against Holland. The Great Elector alone took the part of the gallant little Republic.

The Dutch fought gallantly, but they were not united amongst themselves, and they could do little against their great and powerful foe. But suddenly in Holland itself there came a revolution. The Dutch found a new and splendid leader in a German Prince, William of Orange. He turned the tide of war, and soon Louis's great generals were defeated again and yet again.

Then at length the Emperor and the King of Spain, Holland's oldest and most bitter enemy, also joined with Holland against France. And the war was carried into Germany, into the Rhine country.

The allies gained some victories, but on the whole the French had the best of it, and at length first Holland and Spain, and then Germany made peace with France. Louis XIV was able to make his own terms at this peace, and he won so much by it that it made him more insolent than ever, and more greedy of land than ever. So suddenly he announced that he was going to take possession of all the lands and cities which had ever at any time belonged to those parts of the Empire which he had conquered. He then set up what were called "Chambers of Reunion" or councils which were to decide what places lawfully belonged to him. After they had gone into the matter, and reported on it, Louis quietly took possession of lands and towns, abbeys and monasteries, to an enormous extent, caring little for the fact that some of them had been separated from the provinces he claimed for more than a thousand years.

The whole people of Germany were enraged at these bold robberies. But their anger ended in words, and while they talked Louis acted. More than any German town he longed to possess Strassburg, for it was a strongly fortified town, and the key to the whole of southern Germany. It was the centre of German trade and industry, and the seat of German learning, and for all these reasons, when the rest of Alsace had been given up at the Peace of Westphalia, it had been retained.

Ever since then the citizens of Strassburg had lived in terror of the French. They had done what they could to make their fortifications stronger, and day and night they kept watch and ward.

But there were traitors within the gates. Louis spread his golden net abroad, and found some only too ready to fall into it.

There is a story told of how Louvois, the great French General, one day called an officer to him. "Go," he said, "set out at once for Basle in Switzerland. It will take you three days to get there. On the fourth, exactly at two in the afternoon, you must stand on the bridge over the Rhine with paper, ink, and pen. You will examine and write down with great care and exactness everything you see during two hours. You will have your horses ready in your carriage, and at four o'clock exactly you will once more set out, and hasten as fast as you can back to me with your note-book. It matters not what time of night or day you arrive, come straight to me."

The young officer was very much astonished at being given such a childish mission to perform. But he set out without question. He arrived at Basle, and on the day and at the hour he had been told, he took his stand, note-book in hand, upon the bridge over the Rhine.

Carefully he noted all who passed. First it was a fruit-seller with his baskets of fruit, then a horseman in a blue coat, a peasant in rags, a porter. Every one the young officer noticed.

The clock struck three, and just at that minute a man in a yellow coat and trousers stopped in the middle of the bridge. He leaned over the side and looked down at the river, then, stepping back a pace, he took his stick and struck three distinct blows upon the parapet.

All this and a great many other things the officer noted very carefully. Horsemen and foot-passengers of all descriptions streamed over the bridge—every one going down in the note-book. At length four o'clock sounded. Quickly the officer left his post, jumped into his waiting carriage, and hurried back to his general.

Two days later, at midnight, he arrived, rather ashamed at having so little to report, but as he had been ordered, he went straight to Louvois's house.

He knocked, and was at once allowed to pass in. Eagerly the General seized upon the note-book, and read it carefully. When he came to the man in the yellow suit he jumped for joy. He ran to the King at once, insisted that he should be wakened, and talked for a quarter of an hour at his bedside. Then messengers were sent off post-haste in all directions.

French gold had done its work, and the three strokes of the stick given by the man in yellow was a signal that some of the magistrates of Strassburg were ready to yield their town to King Louis. And now, French troops slowly closed round the city.

But although there were traitors within the gates, all were not ready to yield, although indeed resistance seemed useless. Without the walls there was a mighty host of thirty-five thousand men, within a mere handful, hardly enough to man the walls. For the traitors had chosen their time well, and most of the men were away at country fairs, where in those days much of the trade was done.

The leaders now gathered to council, and the women and children crowded to the churches to pray.

Louvois sent a message demanding the surrender of the town. "Yield at once," he said, "and you will go free. Resist and you will be treated as rebellious subjects."

But the governor replied, "We owe all duty and obedience to the Emperor, and we cannot dispose of ourselves without breach of faith. If King Louis thinks that by right of the Peace of Westphalia or the Peace of Nimeguen Strassburg belongs to him, let him settle that with the Emperor. Strassburg will obey the Emperor."

This answer made Louvois very angry. "I will not have these evasions," he cried. "I want a clear plain answer. Will Strassburg own King Louis as its sovereign lord, and open its gates? Or will it wait to be made an ash-heap? I give you till to-morrow morning at seven o'clock to decide."

In mingled hope and fear the people of Strassburg awaited the return of their messengers. And when they heard the French General's answer a great cry of despair broke from them. Their last hope was gone, yet some would have fought to the death. With others, however, French gold had done its work, and so the city yielded.

A few days after Strassburg yielded, Louis entered in triumph. At once he set to work to make the town as French as possible. German costume was forbidden, French names were given to the streets, a French garrison took possession of the fortress, and the great French engineer, Vauban, planned the fortifications afresh, and made Strassburg one of the strongest cities in Europe. And no prince in all Europe dared to say a word to Louis, or to call in question his insolent robbery, and for nearly two hundred years Strassburg was a French city.

CHAPTER 58

# LEOPOLD I

BESIDES fighting directly with the Empire, Louis encouraged other rulers to do the same. The Turks, as you know, had long been a danger to the Empire, and Louis, who delighted in the name of Most Christian King, now constantly encouraged the Sultan to make war against Leopold. At length a great Turkish army entered Hungary, and marched towards Vienna.

The host of dark-faced, turbanned warriors rolled through the land like a destroying plague. Terror went before them; they left desolation and misery in their train. The Emperor fled from Vienna, leaving the Count of Starhemberg to defend the city. And gallantly he defended it. For two long months the Turkish host raged around the walls. They laid desolate the country, until for miles it was a desert, strewn with ruins and ashes. Famine and plague stalked through the city. The garrison were utterly worn out, and not only the garrison but all the able-bodied citizens, the students, and working men, who had fought manfully to defend their homes. Ammunition, too, was almost at an end.

For three days more the brave commander knew he could hold out; but for three days only. Then, unless help came, the Turks would be masters of the city.

By day the watchers on the walls strained their eyes in all directions, hoping against hope to catch the flicker of a banner, or the glint of sunshine on burnished steel. By night, from the high tower of St. Stephen's Church, rockets were sent up as signals of distress, in the hope that some friendly on-coming host would see and answer. But the autumn days went past and no one came.

At length, however, one night the rockets were answered. Three cannon shots boomed forth in the silence of the night, and a thrill of joy ran through Vienna. Help at last was at hand. It was John Sobieski, the King of Poland, who came with a great army of Poles and Germans.

The next day a battle took place. From morn till night the battle raged, but at length the Turks fled in utter confusion, leaving a great quantity of rich booty behind them.

The day after John Sobieski rode into the town in triumph. The people thronged the streets, cheering and weeping with joy. They crowded round their deliverer praising and blessing him, happy if they touched his clothing, or kissed his stirrup.

But the Emperor did not share in his people's transports. A few days later, when he returned to his liberated city, he greeted the King of Poland with cold politeness. It hurt his dignity that his capital should have been saved by such a petty King, so he neither raised his hat nor got off his horse to greet him.

This battle did not end the war. But now many of the people of Europe joined in helping Leopold against the Turks. At length they were driven out of Hungary, and in 1699 the war came to an end by the Peace of Carlowitz.

But in the meanwhile war had once more broken out with France, and Louis's soldiers overran the Palatinate, doing deeds of unheard-of cruelty.

All Europe now joined with Leopold against Louis. But still for seven years the struggle lasted. It was a European rather than a German war, and was brought to an end by the Peace of Ryswick. By this Peace Germany had again to give up some of her possessions. As usual France gained some.

But Europe was not long to enjoy peace, and in 1701 another terrible war burst forth. This was the War of the Spanish Succession.

In 1700 Charles II, King of Spain, died, leaving no son to succeed him. A short time before he died he had been persuaded to make a will leaving all his many possessions to Philip of Anjou, the grandson of Louis XIV. Philip was also the grand-nephew of Charles II, for Louis XIV had married his sister Maria. But when he married the Spanish princess, Louis had given up all claims to the Spanish throne.

Now the Emperor Leopold had also married a Spanish princess, the younger sister of Maria, and upon his marriage with her he had not given up any claim to the Spanish throne. He therefore claimed the Spanish crown for his son Charles.

As neither side would give way war began. But it was not a war merely between France and Germany; it was a European war. The Protestant powers, with King William III of Britain at their head, took sides with the Emperor. And although William died before the war was fairly begun, Queen Anne continued it. And the great leaders on the Emperor's side were the Duke of Marlborough and Prince Eugene of Savoy.

Prince Eugene of Savoy was a shabby little man, and Louis XIV called him the little Abbot, because as a child he had been so sickly and small that his parents thought he could not possibly be a soldier, and decided to make him a priest. Eugene, however, did not want to be a priest. He wanted to be a soldier, and when he was nineteen he asked Louis to give him a place in his army.

Louis, however, only laughed at the sickly little man. So Eugene, with wrath in his heart, left France and joined the Austrian army. There he soon gained great fame and became a field-marshal in the Imperial army. Louis was sorry then that he had laughed at the shabby little man, and did all he could to win him back. again. He sent messengers to the Prince offering to make him a marshal of France; but Eugene would not go. "Tell your King," he said to Louis's messengers, "that I am field-marshal to an Emperor, and that is as good a title as any he can offer me."

Now this little man, clad in a big blue coat, a huge wig, and a battered old hat, all of which seemed too large for his thin little body, shared the honours of the war with Marlborough, who was dashing and splendid, the handsomest man of his time.

Eugene's soldiers loved him for his courage and his kindness, and were ready to follow him everywhere. Soon he won victory after victory.

The war was fought in Italy, in Spain, in Bavaria, in the Netherlands, and in Germany. And while it still raged Leopold died. He was sixty-five years old, and had reigned for forty-seven years. He was a kindly enough man but no great ruler. Like all his house he was bigoted, at times obstinate as a mule, at times wavering and undecided. He hated war, yet his whole reign was spent in fighting.

CHAPTER 59

# JOSEPH I AND CHARLES VI

LEOPOLD'S son Joseph had been chosen King of the Romans during his lifetime. Now he quietly succeeded him as Emperor. He was one of the best of the Hapsburg rulers, and had he come to the throne in times of peace, it might have been well for Germany. As it was, his whole short reign was spent in war.

He carried on the war of the Spanish Succession which had been begun under Leopold I, and he also had to fight the Bavarians who rebelled against his rule. He found himself, too, like so many Emperors before him, at war with the Pope.

But he subdued the Bavarians, forced the Pope to yield to him, and before he died found Louis XIV anxious to make peace.

The great victories of Ramillies and Oudenarde had been won by the allies; and Louis XIV at length bowed his pride to sue for peace. But the allies demanded too much. They demanded not only that Louis should give up all claim to the throne of Spain, but that he should actually take up arms against his own grandson, and drive him from the throne. This Louis refused to do.

"If I must fight," he said, "let it be with my enemies, rather than with my own children."

So the war went on, and at Malplaquet the most terrible of all the battles of this terrible war was fought. The loss on either side was enormous. France could bear no more, and once again Louis was ready to make peace. This time he seemed willing to agree to any terms. But the negotiations were long, and before they were at an end the Emperor Joseph suddenly fell ill of smallpox.

In those days smallpox was a most terrible and dreaded disease. The doctors did not know how to treat it, and few people got better. In the fashion of the day the Emperor was wrapped in yards and yards of red cloth, and shut up in a room with all the windows closed tightly, so that not a breath of fresh air could get in. It is little wonder that he quickly died. He was only thirty-two, he left no son to succeed him, so his brother the Archduke Charles was chosen as Emperor.

Now this was the very man whom the British and the other allies had been fighting to place on the throne of Spain. But now that he had become Emperor they no longer wished him to be King of Spain also. They had no wish to see Charles VI as powerful as Charles V had been. They thought it was better to let Philip of Anjou keep the crown of Spain. At this same time, too, Marlborough's party had lost power at home. So he was recalled, and without consulting the Emperor, the Peace of Utrecht was signed. By this, Philip of Anjou, to drive whom from the throne so much blood had been shed, was acknowledged King of Spain.

The German peoples had suffered much. By the great treaties signed at Nimeguen and Ryswick they had lost much land, and they called them Nimweg and Reisweg, which is German for "Take away," and "Tear away." The treaty of Utrecht pleased them as little, and they called it Unrecht, which means "unjust." Charles himself would rather have clung to the hope of the Spanish crown than accept that of the Empire, and it was weeks after his brother's death before he could be persuaded to leave Spain and come to Germany to be crowned.

He therefore now refused to sign the Peace. Declaring that the allies had deceived him, he went on with the war. But the war now went ill with the new Emperor. He lost again and again. At last, weary of fighting, by the treaties of Rastadt and of Baden, he made peace, first as King of Austria, and then as Emperor.

The Empire, however, was not long at peace. The very next year after the signing of the Treaty of Baden, war broke out again. This time it was with the Turks. Once again little Prince Eugene led the army. Once again he led it to victory. The Turks were defeated, and driven out of Belgrade, which was added to Austria.

While the war was going on between Germany and France, our Queen Anne died. And, as had been agreed beforehand, one of the princes of the Empire, George, Elector of Hanover, became King of Great Britain and Ireland.

The following year Louis XIV also died, and for a few years after the Turkish war the Empire had rest. But in 1733 a fresh war broke out with France. This was again a war of succession, and this time it was fought over the throne of Poland. Augustus of Saxony claimed the throne. So also did Stanislaus Lesczinsky. Now Louis XV of France had married the daughter of Stanislaus, and he took his father-in-law's side. The Emperor took the side of Augustus of Saxony.

Prince Eugene was now an old man of seventy-one, yet once again he took the field. But the great General had lost his old dash and vigour, he had against him a far larger army than his own, and he could do little against it. He was right glad when, after two years' fighting, peace was made. Once again the Empire lost. The fair province of Lorraine was given up to Stanislaus instead of the throne of Poland. At his death it went to France.

France and Germany had been such constant enemies that it was natural that the Emperor should fight with Louis. But the Emperor had taken sides with Augustus of Saxony for a reason of his own. Like his brother Joseph, he had no sons, but only a daughter. Now, when Joseph had died, he left all his hereditary estates like Austria to Charles, but he had made him sign a deed saying that if he too should die leaving no son to succeed him, Joseph's daughter should come before his in the succession. This was called the Family Compact.

Now Charles was sorry that he had signed the Family Compact. His one desire was that his daughter Maria Theresa should succeed him as Queen of Austria. So he drew up what is called the Pragmatic Sanction. By this he tried to make not only all the Electors of the Empire, but all the great rulers of Europe, promise that they would not oppose his daughter, but allow her quietly to succeed to all his private possessions. And in order to get these promises, Charles did all he could to please the Electors and the other powerful princes and rulers in Europe. He fought for one, he bribed another, he begged here, and begged there, he made treaties and broke them. He neglected everything for the sake of this one pet scheme, and in 1740 he died, fondly believing that he had gained his end, and that Maria Theresa would succeed without trouble.

Charles VI was the last Emperor in the male line of the Hapsburgs. He was Spanish rather than Austrian—he loved Spain more than the Empire. Barcelona, he said, would be found graven upon his heart when he died. He surrounded himself with the solemn splendour of the Spanish court, and added to it something of the pomp and extravagance of the French court. No one dared to speak to him except on bended knee, and the people were taught to look upon the Emperor with awe and reverence as no common man, but almost half a god. Thousands of servants waited upon him, and the simplest acts of everyday life were performed with gorgeous ceremony.

And while the people slaved and starved, appalling waste went on in the royal palaces. For Charles was too splendid to pay any attention to such a mean matter as money. So it was flung about on all hands by his crowd of idle servants and hangers-on. Two barrels of fine wine were used, it was said, every day to soften bread for the parrots of the Empress, and twelve buckets of it were required for her daily bath. And in all departments of the royal palace, a like waste and extravagance was the order of the day.

CHAPTER 60

# THE RISE OF THE HOUSE OF BRANDENBURG

THE great House of Hapsburg had been slowly dying out. The Empire had become little more than a name—"neither Holy, nor Roman, nor an Empire," as a witty French writer said of it later. But meantime another state in the Empire had been growing greater and greater, another house had arisen to take the Hapsburg place as first among the princes of the Empire.

This state was Prussia, this house was that of the Hohenzollerns.

You remember in the days of Leopold I, the Elector of Brandenburg had been called the Great Elector. He alone of all the princes of his day stood for what was German. He ruled his own lands well and wisely, and was the founder of the greatness of the house of Hohenzollern. He sheltered the poor Huguenots who fled from the tyranny of Louis of France. Many of them found homes in and round Berlin, and presently the shabby little town became a beautiful city, surrounded with gardens.

At length in 1688, the Great Elector died. His son Frederick, a vain and frivolous man, succeeded him. He was sickly and deformed, yet all the same he was very fond of finery and splendour. He loved to dress up his poor body in gorgeous robes, and surround himself with pomp and ceremony. So the title of Elector did not seem grand enough for him. He wanted to be a King, and he tried to persuade the Emperor to allow him to take the title of King. But the Emperor was not willing to allow another King within the borders of the Empire. He, however, wanted the Elector's friendship, and the help of his stalwart soldiers in his wars, so he at last yielded. But he would not allow the Elector to call himself King of Brandenburg, Brandenburg being part of the Empire. The Elector, however, was also Duke of Prussia, and Prussia, lying outside of the Empire, he was allowed to take the title of King in Prussia. Not of King of Prussia, mark you. But what difference "in" instead of "of" could make, is very hard to understand.

The Elector, you may be sure, cared little for these fine distinctions, he had got what he wanted, and on January 18, 1701, there was a prodigious great ceremony at Konigsberg. And with a grandeur and pomp quite out of keeping with the tiny kingdom, the new King crowned himself.

The King of Great Britain might kneel before an archbishop, the Emperor before the Pope, but the mighty King in Prussia would bow to none. So he placed the crown upon his own head, and then crowned his Queen.

Still bishops had always figured at coronations, and some one must do the anointing. But Brandenburg was Protestant and had no bishops. So the Elector made two for the occasion. "I am told that I have no power to make bishops," he wrote later, "and that the English ones are derived from the Apostles. That is very difficult to prove. Besides it does not matter much whether the English bishops recognise mine or not, for in all their days they will never get as far as England, and here they are acknowledged even by the Catholics." And Frederick was quite content with his toy kingdom and toy bishops.

And now that Frederick was secure in the title for which he had longed and schemed, he kept a splendid court and wasted money right and left in imitation of Louis XIV. "This expensive King," Carlyle calls him.

Yet in spite of his extravagance, Frederick I did a great deal for Prussia. He founded a University, an Academy of Sciences, and an Observatory. He encouraged painting, and sculpture, and architecture. He made Berlin splendid, and the beautiful street Unter den Linden was built and planted in his reign.

In 1713 this "expensive King" died. He was succeeded by his son Frederick William I.

The new King was twenty-five when he came to the throne, and in every way very different from his father. He had a will of his own, and a terrible temper. He was honest and simple, and hated all the French frippery of his father's court. "I am no Frenchman," he said. "I do not want to be a Frenchman. German is good enough for me."

He knew what harm the extravagance and the aping of French manners had done his people, and he was determined to have no more of it. He knew the court was full of swindlers and idle hangers-on, and he was determined to be rid of them. So the very second day of his reign he called for the royal household accounts. He looked at the long list of servants, the grooms of the chamber, the grooms of the kitchen, the pages and the esquires. They were no use, they were there only for show. And he sent them all packing.

A thousand horses were in the royal stable. He sold them all except thirty. Coaches and carriages were sold too, and many other things besides, till in one way and another, the royal household was reduced so much that from costing something like £40,000 a year, it cost only £8000, a sum far less than many a gentleman in England spends to-day.

Never has King lived in plainer style than King Frederick William I of Prussia. Gold embroideries, splendid robes, great French wigs, were all forbidden. The King himself set the fashion, and wore a plain blue uniform, and plain little wig.

All this King Frederick William did because he cared nothing for mere show and grandeur. And he wanted the money to spend on something he did care for. He wanted it to spend on soldiers. And he spent it so well, that soon he had a splendid army.

He loved his soldiers better than anything else. They were his "dear blue children." But his special hobby was great big men, and one regiment called the Potsdam Guard was filled with giants only. Many are the stories told of the ways in which he used to persuade or force men into his giant guard. He had recruiting officers in every country in Europe, seeking for suitable men, and when they could not be persuaded or bribed into his service, they were kidnapped.

Yet with all his splendid army Frederick William did hardly any fighting. Only twice during his reign did Prussian troops take part in a war, only once did he himself lead them to battle.

Frederick William was a thorough tyrant. His word was law, and although he did much for the good of his country, he did it like a tyrant. He ruled without any Parliament other than what he called his "Tobacco Parliament."

This Parliament was held in a room over the dining-room of his palace. It was plainly furnished with wooden table and chairs. Here the King and seven or eight of his chief friends met together after dinner. There was no ceremony, the King being treated just like any common man. But every man admitted to this "Tobacco Parliament" was obliged to smoke. Those who could not smoke had to pretend to. So smoking clay pipes, and drinking great quantities of beer out of china mugs, with metal tops, the King and his cronies sat discussing affairs of state. Never in civilised times, perhaps, has there been a quainter Parliament.

Frederick William loved his "blue children," and often drilled them himself. But woe betide the stupid or the slow, for Frederick William had a temper; he always carried a big stick, and he was not slow to lay it about the shoulders of any who displeased him.

Indeed, the idle and the timid were so afraid of him that they would slink away as soon as the stout little figure, in its tight blue uniform, appeared. One day a poor man seeing the little King with his big stick coming, ran away. But the King, seeing him run, ordered him to be brought back. "Why did you run away?" he asked.

"I was afraid, please your Majesty," answered the trembling wretch.

"And how dare you be afraid?" cried Frederick William, raising his cane. "How dare you be afraid? Do you not know, fool, that I am the father of my people, and that I expect to be loved and not feared?" And again and again the big stick came down on the poor man's shoulders.

Even the King's own family did not escape from his temper and stick. The Crown Prince Frederick especially suffered from it. He was wild and mischievous. He was lazy, untidy, and, like many boys, dirty. He hated lessons, he hated getting up early. He had inherited his grandfather's love of fine clothes, and his carelessness of money. The King was just the opposite in everything. He was spick and span, smart and clean, he wore plain clothes, he got up early, and worked hard from morning till night, he was careful and even miserly over his money. He wanted his son to grow up to be a great King and a soldier. And when he saw him so different from himself in every way, he despaired of it. So poor little Fritz was thrashed unmercifully. He was thrashed because he wore gloves, and ate with a silver spoon and fork, for that was dainty and womanish. He was thrashed because he was slovenly and untidy, for that was piggish.

Frederick was no doubt a naughty boy; but the thrashings did not seem to make him better. His life, indeed, became so miserable that at eighteen he resolved to run away. "A Prince, eighteen years old, cannot endure being treated by his father and beaten as I have been," he said.

But the Prince's plans for escape were discovered, and both he and a young lieutenant named Katte were taken prisoner. This Katte was one of the Prince's great friends, and had been his leader in much mischief and wickedness. Now for his share in this last escapade he was condemned to death. The scaffold on which he was to die was put up outside the window of Frederick's prison, and a messenger was sent to tell the Prince of what was about to happen—to tell him that he must see his friend beheaded before his eyes.

"What terrible words are these you speak to me?" he cried. "Lord

Jesus, take rather my own life!" With tears he begged that his friend's life might be spared. But the Prince's prayers were in vain. And when the time for Katte's execution came, two officers led him to the window.

Looking forth, the Prince saw his friend upon the scaffold. He kissed his hand to him and cried out: "Dear Katte, I beg your pardon a thousand times."

"My lord," said Katte gently, as he bowed to the Prince, "do not think of it. I have nothing to forgive." Then he went bravely to his death, and the Prince fell down fainting.

It seemed for a time as if Frederick William in his wrath meant to put his own son to death too. The Prince himself believed that he was soon to follow his unhappy friend. The King, however, allowed his wrath to cool, and instead of beheading his son, he kept him prisoner, and only after many months of wearisome captivity was he set free.

But as years went on, all these early difficulties and quarrels were forgotten. And when at length Frederick William died, he died thanking God for having given him so good and worthy a son to succeed him on the throne.

CHAPTER 61

# CHARLES VII

FREDERICK William died in May 1740, and was succeeded by his son Frederick II, who was then twenty-eight. In October of the same year, the Emperor Charles VI died, happy in the thought that because of the Pragmatic Sanction, his daughter, Maria Theresa, who was now only twenty-three, would be allowed to succeed to all his lands in peace. But the poor Emperor was greatly deceived.

Prussia was one of the states which had promised to support Maria Theresa. But Frederick had quite other plans in his head now. During his father's lifetime he had taken no interest in soldiers, as a boy, indeed, he had hated them, and called the uniform he was forced to wear his shroud. Now all that was changed. He was a King, and he had great ideas in his head. "There is no reason why a little thing like the death of an Emperor should excite me," he said, when he heard that Charles VI was dead. All the same it did. For he now saw the chance to carry out the plans which he had been forming in secret.

He wanted to increase Prussia, and make a great name for himself. So he sent a message to Maria Theresa saying he would stand by her if she would give him part of her land called Silesia. Maria Theresa looked upon Frederick as little better than a robber, and she refused indignantly. So instead of fighting for her, Frederick sent an army to conquer Silesia.

Nearly all the other rulers in Europe followed his example. Besides Prussia, Maria Theresa found against her, France, Spain, Poland, Bavaria, and Saxony. They all wanted some part of her broad lands. Charles, Elector of Bavaria, indeed claimed her throne. For, said he, if women were to inherit, his claim was far better than Maria Theresa's, for he was descended from a daughter of the Emperor Ferdinand I. So clamour and greedy strife surrounded the young Queen, and among all the powers of Europe she found no friend but Britain.

Forsaken by her friends, harassed on all sides by her enemies, Maria Theresa appealed for help to the Hungarians. Clad in mourning robes, with the crown glittering on her fair hair, and a sword girt to her side, she appeared before them, carrying in her arms her baby son. "Forsaken by all," she said, "I turn to you, trusting in your faith and bravery. In this great danger I trust to you not only my person, but my son, my crown, and my kingdom."

As she spoke her voice shook, and tears ran down her beautiful face. The hearts of all who heard her words and saw her beauty and grief were touched. In an instant every sword was drawn from its scabbard, and holding them aloft the nobles cried like one man, "Let us die for our King, Maria Theresa."

A thrill ran through the whole of Hungary, and brave, wild soldiers, men of strange tribes, with names hardly known in Europe, gathered from the farthest corners of the kingdom. Undisciplined they were, and half savage, but all eager to fight for their beautiful Queen.

They swept through Austria, a wild, many-coloured horde, driving the enemy before them. In a wonderfully short time Austria was reconquered for the Queen. Then the wild horde marched into Bavaria and seized the capital, Munich.

But the very day upon which the Hungarians seized Munich, Charles, Elector of Bavaria, was crowned at Frankfort-on-Main as Emperor.

The power of the Emperor, however, was little more than a name, the Emperor himself little more than a puppet in the hands of Maria Theresa's enemies. So the war raged on, now one side winning battles, now the other.

In 1741 Frederick of Prussia had won a great battle at Mollwitz. He himself had fled from the field, thinking the battle was lost. Not till next day did he learn that he had fled from a victory. When he knew it his gladness was only dashed by the memory of his own flight. He held a thanksgiving service, and ordered the preacher to take for his text, "I suffer no woman to teach, nor to usurp authority over the man, but to be in silence."

Again at Chotusitz in 1742 the Prussians gained another victory. Then Maria Theresa made peace, giving up Silesia to Frederick. Thus she was rid for the time of one enemy, although she had lost to him, she bitterly said, "the fairest jewel in her crown."

Still Maria Theresa had all her other enemies to fight. But now her cause was everywhere triumphant. The Emperor was but a hunted fugitive in his own land, harassed and ill, and often in want. Against the French, the British and Austrian armies won a great victory at Dettingen. In this battle George II himself led his troops, and it was the last time that a British sovereign ever took part in a battle.

At length every one was weary of the war, and ready for peace. Every one except Maria Theresa. Flushed by success, she longed for revenge. She wanted to see her enemies utterly crushed. She wanted to see the puppet Emperor thrust from the throne, and her own husband chosen instead.

That made Frederick anxious. He had no wish to see Austria become so powerful, and once more he made war against Maria Theresa. This time he said that he fought in the cause of Charles VII, the Emperor.

But this time Frederick was not so fortunate. Instead of being able to plant his foot on the neck of his enemies as he had sworn to do, he found himself outwitted and out-generalled again and again. His army was wasted with hunger and disease, it was ragged and disheartened, and when in 1745 the Emperor died, worn out with sickness and misfortune, Frederick would gladly have made peace.

But again Maria Theresa refused. She hoped to humble Frederick, and perhaps win back from him her lost province of Silesia. But once again fortune turned. One after the other Frederick gained three great victories, a fourth was gained by one of his generals. Then Maria Theresa gave way, and on Christmas Day 1745, the Peace of Dresden was signed.

The war with France, however, still went on for some years. But at length that too came to an end with the Peace of Aachen in 1748.

CHAPTER 62

# FRANCIS I

UPON the death of Charles VII, Maria Theresa's husband, Francis, Grand-duke of Tuscany, had been chosen as Emperor. By the Peace of Dresden, Frederick II of Prussia had agreed to recognise him as Emperor, and so for eight years there was peace within the Empire.

After her husband became Emperor, Maria Theresa was called the Queen Empress. And, indeed, if there was any power at all in the empty title of Emperor, it was Maria Theresa who used it, and not her insignificant husband.

The Emperor, indeed, was a mere nobody. The two great sovereigns in the Empire were Maria Theresa, Queen of Austria, and Frederick II, King of Prussia. But there was a vast difference between the two. Maria Theresa was the daughter of a great house, a descendant of the Hapsburgs, who for hundreds of years had taken first place among the rulers in the Empire. Frederick was, in comparison, a mere upstart. Men were still alive who could remember the day when his vain grandfather placed the crown upon his own head. They had laughed at his vanity, now they began to be jealous of his grandson's might.

But Frederick II heeded them not. He went his own way. In the years of war he had showed himself a great soldier, and in the years of peace he showed himself as statesman. He encouraged manufactures, improved agriculture, founded schools, brought order into the laws, and in every way did his best for his country.

He worked hard. "The King," he said, "is not absolute master, but only the first servant of his people." All the same he ruled like an absolute master, and his people were obliged to bow to his will, simply because it was his will. His ministers were little more than his servants. But he knew how to choose them, and he chose men who were honest and true, and willing to work for the good of their country. At length Prussia took a great place among the states of Europe, and Frederick earned for himself the title of Frederick the Great.

Meanwhile the other states looked on with jealous anger, and began to fear this upstart kingdom. Frederick too had a sharp tongue, and a wit which was often cruel, and he said bitter things of some of the other rulers. This helped to make them dislike him. Maria Theresa on her part had never ceased to mourn for her lost Silesia. "She forgets that she is a Queen, and sheds tears like a woman, whenever she sees a Silesian," wrote an Englishman, who lived in those days. And at length she entered into an alliance with Russia and with France against Prussia.

Once again the Empire was divided against itself. Once again, as in the war of the Austrian Succession, France aided one great state against the other. But in the war of the Austrian Succession Austria had stood alone against all Europe with only Britain for friend. Now Prussia stood alone, and again Britain took the side of the one against the many. In spite of the fact that George II hated Frederick, the British took sides with Prussia.

The war which now began is called the Seven Years' War. All Europe took part in it, fighting to crush one impertinent little state. But fighting was not confined to Europe alone, for between France and Britain the fight went on upon the sea, in Canada, and in India.

This war, begun to crush out Prussia, had far greater consequences than those who began it ever thought about, for it founded the great Colonial Empire of Britain, and it founded the Empire of Germany as it is to-day.

But meanwhile it was for Prussia a desperate struggle for life. Frederick knew that if he were defeated there was an end to his kingship, and his kingdom. Should he lose Prussia would be torn to pieces, and vanish from among the states of Europe, even more quickly than it had appeared. He made up his mind never to live to see that day. So as he rode over Germany, fighting now one enemy, now another, he carried poison with him, with which he meant to end his life, when all hope was lost.

But Frederick was one of the most splendid generals the world has ever seen; his army was the most perfect in Europe. So he did not need to use his little poison pills. Battle after battle was fought, Frederick sometimes winning brilliant victories, sometimes submitting to crushing defeats. Once after such a defeat he nearly despaired. "The results of the battle will be worse than the battle itself," he wrote to one of his friends. "I have no more resources, and not to hide the truth, I think all is lost. I shall not live after the ruin of my country. Farewell for ever."

For years Frederick had fought against three great powers, Austria, France, and Russia, any one of which alone was far stronger than himself. Now his country was wasted and barren, his treasury was empty, his army outworn and shattered, and still his enemies showed no sign of weakening. It was hardly wonderful that he despaired. Yet in a few days Frederick gathered courage again, was again ready to fight. But now he was like a man with his back against the wall, fighting his last fight. He grew savage. "It is hard for man to bear what I bear," he wrote. "I begin to feel that as the Italians say, revenge is a pleasure of the gods. I am no saint like those we read of in legends, and I own that I would die content if I could first make my enemies suffer some of the misery which I have had to bear."

Frederick now vowed that while there were bread and potatoes to eat, while lead and gunpowder were left, a man to carry a gun, a horse for him to ride, he would fight on. So the war continued, but still victory was uncertain, now one side, now the other winning victories. But, although making a gallant stand, Prussia was being slowly drained of men and money. The end seemed nearer and nearer.

"The Prussians are in the sack," said the Austrians. "We need only pull the string, and the King and his army are caught."

"They are not so far wrong," said Frederick, when he heard the taunt. "But I trust I shall slit their sack."

Then came bad news for him from Britain. Pitt and his party had fallen from power, and the new government voted for peace. Frederick could no longer hope for men or money from that quarter.

The outlook was black indeed, but almost at the same time as he lost his one friend, Frederick was also relieved of one of his greatest enemies. Elizabeth of Russia died in 1762, and her nephew Peter succeeded her. Peter was a coarse, weak man, but he had an unbounded admiration for Frederick, and he at once made friends with him.

Not content with merely making peace, he set free all Prussian prisoners, and sent soldiers to help Frederick. He caused himself to be made colonel of a Prussian regiment, and wore the Prussian order of the Black Eagle, and always carried a portrait of Frederick about with him.

But the reign of Peter III was short and stormy, and before Frederick could reap any great benefit from this new friendship, the news came that the Czar had been deposed and murdered.

His wife Catherine now became Czarina. She kept the peace made by her husband, but she called back the soldiers who had been sent to help Frederick. So again the Prussian King was left to face his enemies alone.

At length, one by one, each country ceased from war, until only

Austria and Prussia were left. Prussia was still unconquered, and Maria Theresa's hate was still unsatisfied. She would gladly have continued the war, but even she saw that it was hopeless to try to conquer alone the plucky little state, which had kept all the great powers of Europe at bay. So she, too, owned herself ready for peace, and on February 15, 1763, the Peace of Hubertsburg was signed.

So far as land was concerned Austria and Prussia were exactly the same at the end as they were at the beginning of the war. Not an inch of land had changed hands, and all the blood had been shed in vain.

Neither side, it seemed, had gained anything; both had suffered terribly. But in reality Prussia had gained much. The plucky little Prussian King had made all Europe stare at his soldiery, and his statesmanship. He had borne defeats bravely, he had won brilliant victories, when his cause seemed hopeless. From being far back in the ranks of kings he had simply shouldered his way to the front. Henceforth Prussia had to be counted among the powers of Europe. Henceforth Prussia was the rival of Austria, for first place among the states of the Empire.

But, although in a manner triumphant, the war left Prussia desolate and exhausted. Great tracts of land, where once busy villages and cheerful farmhouses had flourished, were left barren and deserted. Whole towns were laid in ruins, and the land was filled with misery and beggary.

Frederick now set himself to cure this misery, and bring back plenty to his land, as well as peace. Seed-corn was given to the farmers free, war-horses were sent to draw their ploughs, money was given to the ruined manufacturers, and so by degrees Prussia recovered her lost prosperity.

But to get money for all this Frederick taxed the people, often in a way they did not like. One of the things they disliked most was the royal monopoly of coffee. No one might buy coffee except from the royal stores. They might not even roast or ground it; that must be done at the royal mills. The result was that coffee cost three or four times as much as it was worth, and there was great discontent and much smuggling. But smuggling was difficult, for the smell of roasting coffee cannot be hid, and "coffee smellers" went from house to house, ready to seize and carry off to prison any who disobeyed the law.

It was only the love the people had for their great King which kept them from openly revolting against his fatherly tyranny. They grumbled openly, and Frederick did not mind. "My people and I," he said, "have

*The plucky little Prussian King had made all Europe stare at his soldiery.*

come to an agreement which pleases us both. They are to say what they like, and I am to do as I like."

Once as he was riding through the streets near his palace he saw a great crowd, all struggling and jostling each other to try to see something which was pasted upon a wall. The King too thought he would like to see what all the excitement was about, and when at length he forced a way through, the crowd he found pasted on the wall a caricature of himself. Between his knees was a coffee mill; with one hand he turned the handle, with the other he gathered up any stray coffee beans he could find. Underneath were some uncomplimentary remarks about "Old Fritz, the Coffee-grinder."

At the sight of this caricature Frederick only laughed. "Hang it lower," he said, "so that the people don't need to crane their necks so much to see it." Then suddenly the people recognised the King. The scowling faces began to smile, growls turned to laughter, and with the sound of ringing cheers in his ears, Frederick rode away.

CHAPTER 63

# JOSEPH II

ABOUT two years after the Peace of Hubertsburg Francis I died. His son Joseph was chosen to succeed him as Emperor, but so long as his mother, Maria Theresa, lived, Joseph II had little power. Maria Theresa and Frederick II were still the great rulers, the two great rivals of the Empire.

The first half of Frederick's reign had been spent in almost constant war. In the second half the peace was almost unbroken, but all the same he added in this time of peace a great province to his kingdom.

Part of Poland was called West Prussia, and this part cut Frederick's kingdom right in two. For years the Poles had been an unruly nation, proving over and over again that they were quite unfit to govern themselves.

Seeing this, Russia, Prussia, and Austria, who were all rather afraid of each other, and all rather afraid that one or other would seize upon the whole of Poland, agreed together to divide a great part of it amongst them. This they did, and Poland was in such a state of confusion and revolt that it could make no resistance.

Frederick, indeed, said he only took his part because if he had not Russia would have taken it all. Maria Theresa grieved over the wickedness of it, and tried her best to stop it.

"When my own possessions were attacked," she said, "and I knew not where to lay my head, I trusted to the righteousness of my cause, and to the help of God. But in this business we have not only no right, but neither honesty nor fairness, and I must own, that all my life through I have never felt so shamed and grieved. But I know I am alone. I know I have power no longer. I must, therefore, let things take their course. But it is pain and sorrow to me."

Maria Theresa was growing old, her son was greedy of more land, so no one paid heed to her, and Poland was divided. This is called the First Partition of Poland. Frederick had the smallest share, but it strengthened and united his kingdom, so that from the Oder to the Nieman Prussia extended in unbroken line along the shores of the Baltic. He, however, pretended to think little of his new province. "It is nothing but sand, moorland, and Jews," he said. But that he only said so that people might not be jealous of his good fortune. In reality he was very pleased with it. After this he called himself King of Prussia, instead of King in Prussia.

A few years after this the long peace was broken, and Prussia was once more at war with Austria. Joseph II, as has been said, was greedy of land, and when the Elector of Bavaria died in 1777, he calmly took possession of a large part of his land.

This made Frederick very angry. He had no wish to see Austria grow more powerful, and he gathered his army and marched into Bohemia to fight the Emperor. But no battle was fought. The Emperor gave way, yielding all the land he had seized, except a small part on the Austrian frontier.

This was nicknamed the Potato War, because it was said the soldiers had nothing to do but forage for food, and roast potatoes by their camp fires. But although no battle was fought, many men died from sickness, and the war added nothing to Frederick's fame as a soldier.

Little more than a year after the Potato War had come to an end Maria Theresa died. Joseph now, at the age of forty, really began to rule. He greatly admired the way in which Frederick governed Prussia. He was full of ideas of reform, and although Maria Theresa had done much for her country, her reforms were too slow for Joseph. He was impatient to see all the old wrongs swept away, and now that he had the power he began his reforms with feverish haste.

Austria had always been Catholic, and Protestants had been hardly treated. Now Joseph decreed that every one should be free to worship God as he chose, and he closed more than half the monasteries, and took their land and money to found schools. He also allowed German hymn-books and Bibles to be sold throughout the land.

At first the people were afraid that this Edict of Toleration, as it was called, was a mere trick to entrap them, but when they became sure that the Emperor meant them no evil, whole villages at once confessed themselves Protestant. For years they had been Protestant in secret, but had been afraid to own it.

All these things frightened the Pope very much, and at length he came himself to try to persuade Joseph to stop these reforms. Thousands of people received him with joy, and as he passed through the streets they knelt to receive his blessing. The Emperor, however, treated him very coldly. He refused to discuss matters of state with him, and no one was allowed to visit him without leave; and to prevent any secret visits every door into the Pope's house was walled up except one, which was closely watched.

For a month the Pope stayed in Vienna, but he could do nothing; he received only insults and coldness, so at length he returned home.

Besides reforms in religion Joseph also tried to introduce reforms in the state. Many of the peasants were serfs or slaves. To these he gave freedom. This made the nobles angry. But Joseph did not stop there, he tried in many other ways to curb the pride and power of the nobles, he made them pay taxes, and when they broke the laws he punished them like common men. That a noble should be made to stand in the pillory, or sweep the streets like a common criminal, was a deadly insult, and by such deeds Joseph made for himself many bitter enemies.

Joseph wanted also to bridge over the terrible gulf which separated the rich and the poor, the nobles and the peasants. Among other things which he did he threw open to every one the great park at Vienna called the Prater. Till then this park had been kept for the nobles and court alone, and now they were very indignant at being asked to mix with common people. But Joseph would not listen to their complaints. "Were I to mix only with my equals," he said, "I should be obliged to go down into my family vault and spend my days beside the bones of my forefathers."

Joseph was in too great a hurry. He tried to do in a few years what would have taken a generation to do well. So he failed. He made enemies of the clergy and the nobles, and the poor for whose happiness he laboured did not understand him, and were not grateful.

Meanwhile the old King of Prussia watched the go-ahead Emperor with a jealous eye. Joseph openly admired Frederick, and even before his mother's death he had gone to visit the Prussian King. Frederick returned the visit, and afterwards a portrait of Joseph hung in his room. Some one noticed this and made a remark about it. "Yes," said Frederick grimly, "I am forced to keep that young gentleman under my eye." And to the day of his death he was suspicious of the Emperor's schemes, and fearful lest Austria should rival Prussia in power.

But the great Frederick was now an old man, and at length in 1786 he died. He was seventy-four, and had reigned for forty-six years. He was buried in the garrison church at Potsdam, beside his stern old father. With tears rolling down their weather-beaten faces, the soldiers who had so often followed him to battle now followed his simple coffin. The people thronged the streets to watch it pass in mute reverence, and as it was carried slowly to its last resting-place the silence was only broken by the heavy tramp of the soldiers' feet and the sobs of the sorrowing people. "Alas! the good King," they cried. Never more would they see the little bent figure in its shabby blue uniform, with red facings and waistcoat, all covered with snuff. Never more would they see the stern brown face with the wonderful grey eyes, which seemed to pierce one through and through. "Old Fritz," as they loved to call him, was gone for ever.

But Germany has not forgotten his name and his work. In his lifetime Frederick laboured to make Prussia great, caring little for the Empire; but although he did not know it, he was helping to found modern Germany, and it is as a great German, and not merely as a Prussian, that the Germans remember him.

Yet, strange to say, Frederick in his own day loved things French rather than things German. He spoke and wrote in French. He built for himself a beautiful palace to which he gave a French name, calling it Sans Souci, which means Without Care. One of his great friends was the French writer Voltaire, and he thought nothing at all of the great German poets, chief among them Goethe, who were growing up around him.

Frederick the Great had no son, so he was succeeded by his nephew, Frederick William II. He proved to be weak and easily led by favourites, and under him Prussia seemed little likely to prove dangerous to Austria.

Meanwhile the Emperor went on with his schemes, but in the midst of all his reforms he was persuaded by the Czarina to join in a war against the Turks. She persuaded him that they would be able to divide Turkey as they had divided Poland, and Joseph, with his greed of land, was willing to listen to her. But the campaign was a failure. Turkey was neither conquered nor divided, and the Emperor returned home sick in mind and body.

He returned home to find his own kingdom in a state of ferment and confusion. The Austrian Netherlands revolted, and in 1789, under the name of United Belgium, they declared themselves free. Then the peasants of Hungary, for whom Joseph had tried to do so much, urged on by the nobles, also revolted.

This seemed more than the Emperor could bear. "I must be made of wood," he groaned, "if this does not kill me." Three weeks later, on February 20, 1790 he died, worn out with illness, broken-hearted at the failure of his plans. "Write on my tomb," he said, "here lies a King who meant well, but never carried out a single plan."

CHAPTER 64

# LEOPOLD II

JOSEPH II left no son, so he was succeeded by his brother Leopold II, who was chosen Emperor on September 20, 1790. Within the Empire the rivalry between Prussia and Austria still continued, but under the rule of Frederick William Prussia soon began to sink from the high place Frederick the Great had won for it. Frederick's rule had been stern and severe, the taxes heavy, but he left the country prosperous and free from debt, and his treasury full. Frederick William at once took away many of the taxes, and sent the French tax-collectors and coffee-smellers packing. And at the same time he scattered money, lands, and titles broadcast. The joy over all this was great. The people were so delighted with their new spendthrift King that they called him the Well-beloved, and they believed that a time of peace and contentment had begun.

But their joy did not last long, for Frederick William did not lead a good life; he allowed himself to be ruled by unworthy favourites. He spent far more money than he had, and soon the treasury was empty, and the country in debt.

Meanwhile Leopold II was using all his wisdom to strengthen the position of Austria. But now a great event was taking place in Europe, which was to have far more effect upon the Empire than any struggle for power within its borders. This was the French Revolution.

The French had rebelled against their King. He, with his Queen and family had been made prisoner, and many nobles had fled from the land. The French Queen, Marie Antoinette, was the sister of the Emperors Joseph II and Leopold II, and she naturally expected that her brothers would help her in her distress; but Leopold was cautious. Even although he was the brother of the unhappy Queen, he long hesitated to take any part against France.

In every court in Europe, however, there were French nobles who had fled from the violence of the people. And they constantly implored the rulers to help them and their King. So at length Leopold and Frederick William met together at Pillnitz in Saxony. Here they agreed together to help the French King, declaring that his cause was the cause of every ruler in Europe, and that they were ready to march against France with armed force. For a little time, however, nothing was done, and before war really broke out Leopold died. He had reigned as Emperor for less than two years.

CHAPTER 65

# FRANCIS II

LEOPOLD was succeeded by his son Francis II, and almost at once he was plunged into war, for the French, angry at the interference of other nations with their affairs, declared war with Austria. But the King of Austria was also Emperor of Germany, so Prussia and the other states soon joined with their Emperor against France.

The allies believed that France would be easily crushed. "Gentlemen," said the Duke of Brunswick to his officers, "do not take much baggage, this is a mere military picnic." "Do not buy too many horses," said another, "the whole affair will be over soon."

And indeed at first the war went well with the allies. Town after town fell into their hands, and they marched into France. Then the Duke of Brunswick issued his famous manifesto. In this manifesto he ordered the people of France to return to their obedience to their King, to lay down their arms, and set him free. If they refused he threatened to march on Paris and raze it to the ground.

This manifesto, instead of frightening the French, roused them to wrath. Ragged, hungry, half-trained as they were, they flocked to the army, eager to sweep the foe from their country.

Then fortune changed. At Valmy, after a slight resistance, the Duke of Brunswick, in spite of all his proud words, fell back before the ragged army of the Revolution, and once more recrossed the Rhine into his own country.

Two months later the Austrian army was also defeated at Jemappes in Belgium. Belgium was at this time called the Austrian Netherlands. But since the days of Joseph II they had been in revolt against Austrian rule, and had declared themselves free. Now for a time Belgium was annexed to France.

But although the French had won victories over both Prussians and Austrians, the war still continued.

Battles were fought and towns were taken and retaken. Now one side winning, now the other.

Meanwhile Frederick William once more turned his attention to Poland. It seemed as if the Poles, following the example of France, would rise and cast off the yoke of Russia. This made the Czarina very angry, and she and Frederick William joined in crushing the Poles. Then followed the Second Partition of Poland, both Russia and Prussia taking large provinces for themselves.

Poland was now but a third of the size it had been, and on all sides surrounded by greedy neighbours. And now the Poles made a last stand for liberty. They found a leader in the great General and patriot Kosciuszko. To his banner they flocked in hundreds, armed with sticks and scythes, or any sort of weapon they could lay hands on. For it was the peasants and the country folk who flocked to Kosciuszko, the nobles for the most part standing coldly aloof.

But great general though he was, he could do little, for there were two large armies against him. At the great battle of Maciejowice, October 10, 1794, his army was defeated, and he himself sorely wounded was carried prisoner to Russia.

The struggle was over. Once more Poland was divided, Russia, Prussia, and Austria each having a share of the spoils, and Poland as a separate kingdom was no more.

Already before this last Partition of Poland, the King of Prussia had withdrawn from the war with France and made peace. Austria, however, continued the war, and now it was carried on most fiercely in the north of Italy, which was at that time under Austrian rule. For there the French army was led by the young Corsican soldier Napoleon Bonaparte.

Victory after victory did this brilliant young leader win. At length the Emperor, humbled and beaten, fearing for the safety of his very capital, was fain to make peace, and so in 1797 the Treaty of Campo Formio was signed. In this peace the Emperor made the best bargain he could for himself and his own kingdom, and in order to do this, he gave up to France other parts of the Empire.

But of course the Emperor had, in reality, no power to give up any part of the Empire without the consent of the Electors. So, by an article in the treaty, a congress was called at Rastadt to settle these matters. Here the princes of the Empire gathered, very angry indeed that the Emperor had cared so little for their interests. But there was no unity among them, every petty prince wanting to get the best for himself, and stooping even to bribe the French in order to get it.

But if the Germans were angry, the French on their side were insolent. There seemed no limit to their demands. Soon war burst forth once more. This time Austria, Russia, and Britain joined together against France.

Prussia took no part in it, but Prussia had by this time fallen so low in the opinion of all Europe that it did not seem to matter. At first, things went well for the allies, the Russians especially gaining great victories over the French, but ere long, fortune again changed.

While this new war was beginning, Bonaparte been away in Egypt carrying on his mad expedition against Britain there. That expedition, as you will read in French history, was an utter failure. And now hearing of the defeats which the French army was suffering at home, Bonaparte hastened back to France.

He succeeded in having himself chosen first Consul, then as absolute ruler of France he marched over the Alps, and swooped down upon the Austrian army in Italy.

With the battle of Marengo he won back with one blow all that France had lost in Italy. A few months later, the French General Moreau again beat the Austrians in the battle of Hohenlinden. The road to Vienna lay open. Austria, crushed once more and humbled, yielded to the insolent young conqueror Bonaparte.

The new peace which Austria now signed was called the Peace of Lunéville. It was very much the same as the Treaty of Campo Formio. But this time Bonaparte would have no delay. The princes of the Empire were not consulted, and Francis was obliged to sign, not only in the name of Austria, but in the name of the whole Empire.

By this Treaty, all the German lands west of the Rhine were lost to the Empire, and for a time the Rhine became the boundary of France. Other parts of Germany were divided, taken from one ruler and given to another, all at the imperious bidding of a stranger and an upstart. Never before had the Empire been brought so low. Indeed, the Empire was little more than a name. It was divided into more than three hundred petty kingships and princedoms, each ruler struggling for his own selfish ends, while Austria and Prussia, the two great powers of the Empire, were rivals and, indeed, enemies, and instead of striving for the good of the Empire they were taken up with their private quarrels.

Throughout the whole Empire there was no such thing as unity, no love of country, no patriotism. There was nothing but pride and oppression on the one hand, weakness and slavery on the other. In all the Empire there was no man great enough to rouse it to strength and union. Frederick William II, Prussia's bad and foolish King, was now indeed dead, and his son Frederick William III had succeeded him. But although the new King was a good man, he was weak and timid, and he did not know in the least how to stand against a conqueror like Napoleon. His great desire was to keep out of war with him, and in order to do this, he had to stoop to much meanness, to submit to many insults.

Meanwhile Napoleon had been climbing higher and higher, and the higher he rose the greater his ambition became. At length, in 1804, he caused himself to be crowned Emperor of the French. Then indeed the Emperor Francis II felt that his title was an empty farce. Napoleon had more than usurped his power. It was the Emperor of the French, not the Emperor of the Holy Roman Empire who was the great power in Europe.

The Emperor writhed under this insult. All Austria too was still smarting under the memory of past defeats, and it was not long before war was once more declared, Austria joining with Russia against France. But the preparations of the two Emperors were slow and uncertain, Napoleon's swift and sure. He marched into Austria, and before the Russian and Austrian armies could join, he had shut up the Austrians in the town of Ulm.

The Austrian army was led by Mack, an old soldier, full of plans and vague dreams, and little fitted to struggle against a genius like Napoleon. He now utterly lost heart, and almost without a struggle surrendered with all his army. Upon an autumn morning 25,000 men marched out of Ulm, and in gloomy silence laid down their arms before the conqueror.

A few months later Napoleon again defeated the Austrians and the Russians in the great battle of Austerlitz. This battle was called the Battle of the Three Emperors, for the Emperor of Germany, the Emperor of Russia, and the Emperor of the French were all present.

It was a terrible defeat, yet neither Austria nor Russia were utterly crushed. Francis II, however, had no heart to fight longer, and he made peace with Napoleon. This peace was more humiliating still than any he had yet signed. Napoleon robbed him of much of his land, and also made many changes in other states of the Empire. He made the rulers of Bavaria and Wurtemburg into Kings, and forced the Emperor to acknowledge them as independent of the Empire. He formed other states into what was called the Confederation of the Rhine, this Confederation being under the protection of the Emperor of the French, not under that of the German Emperor.

Now more than ever did the Emperor feel that his title was but an empty one, so he gave it up so far as Germany was concerned, and henceforth called himself Emperor of Austria only, taking the title of Francis I of Austria. Thus at last the great Empire founded by Charlemagne a thousand years before came to an end.

CHAPTER 66

# UNDER THE HEEL OF NAPOLEON

EVER since the Treaty of Basle, Prussia had taken no part in the war which changed the face of Europe. Indeed, in order to keep the peace, King Frederick William had played a very shabby part. He had stooped even to take gifts from Napoleon, and had earned for himself the distrust of every other nation in Europe. Yet he had, to all seeming, a magnificent army. It was large, the uniforms were grand, and it was splendidly drilled according to old-fashioned ideas. Both soldiers and officers were puffed up with pride, remembering the great victories of the Seven Years' War, but neither soldiers nor officers had any real knowledge of fighting. And now, having crushed Austria and Russia as he thought, Napoleon determined to crush Prussia too, so he treated the King with contempt and insult, and at length goaded him to war.

And now having held back too long, Prussia rushed too eagerly to battle. Though indeed there was little choice, for Napoleon, hardly waiting for war to be declared, marched towards Prussia. On October 14, 1806, the double battle of Jena and Auerstadt was fought. The old Duke of Brunswick commanded the one, the Prince of Hohenlohe the other. Both were defeated, and their armies driven before the foe, mingled in mad flight. The Duke of Brunswick, blinded and mortally wounded, was carried from the field, but when he reached his palace at Brunswick he found it empty. Every one belonging to him had fled. In his blindness and misery the Duke appealed to Napoleon for mercy.

But Napoleon had no mercy. "I know of no Duke of Brunswick," he said, "I know only of a Prussian general of that name who, in 1792, issued an infamous manifesto declaring his intention of destroying Paris. He deserves no mercy."

So the blind old soldier was pitilessly driven from his country. He fled to Denmark and there he soon died. In memory of him, his son raised a regiment which he dressed completely in black, with a skull and cross-bones as their badge. They were called the Black Brunswickers, and wherever the French were to be fought, they were to be found.

After the defeat of Jena the panic throughout the country was terrible. Fortress after fortress gave way, only here and there did one hold out. At the town of Graudenz, the general was told that he might as well yield, for all Prussia was in the hands of the French, and that there was no longer a King of Prussia.

"So be it," he answered sternly, "then I will be King of Graudenz," and he still fought on.

Blücher too, who was afterwards to become famous, fought till he could fight no more, and when at length he was forced to yield, he signed his name indeed to the Capitulation, but after it he wrote, "I do this only because I have neither food nor ammunition left."

But a brave resistance here and there was of no avail, when for the most part the army, seized with abject fear, everywhere yielded, and ten days after the battle of Jena, Napoleon marched into Berlin in triumph.

The King, and even the brave patriotic Queen, fled. The Queen was ill, but still she fled, driving through snow and sleet, and bitter winter weather, for she was willing to die, rather than fall into the hands of the Corsican Conqueror. Without a murmur she bore every discomfort, now sharing a one-roomed hut with the King like the poorest peasant, now sleeping in a room with broken windows, so that the snow was blown on to her bed, suffering cold, and hunger, and a hundred hardships besides.

Meanwhile Napoleon's demands were so outrageous that the Prussian King refused to yield to them, and in spite of the shattered condition of his army he determined to continue the war. Alexander I of Russia now also marched to help him, but in spite of this, Napoleon still triumphed. The war was now carried into Poland, and Napoleon, hoping to rouse the Poles to help him, announced that he had come to free Poland, and issued a proclamation in the name of their hero Kosciusko. Napoleon had no right to use Kosciusko's name, but many of the Poles believed that he had, and they greeted Napoleon with joy.

At Preuss Eylau, one of the most deadly battles of modern times was fought. Both Prussians and Russians fought with fury, there was dreadful slaughter, but all to no end, for this horrible massacre decided nothing.

After it both sides were so exhausted that there was a pause in the campaign. But ere long Napoleon was again in the field, to all seeming as vigorous as ever. Fortress after fortress fell before him, and at length, with the battle of Friedland, the war came to an end.

This battle was one of Napoleon's greatest battles. It was fought on June 14, 1807, which was the anniversary of Marengo, another of his great victories.

After this, Napoleon offered to make peace with Alexander, and a meeting between the two Emperors was arranged. The river Nieman formed the boundary between Prussia and Russia. And so that the meeting between the two rulers should take place in neither country, a raft was built and moored amid stream. And here the two Emperors met.

The King of Prussia was not asked to come. Napoleon treated him with contempt; the Czar, who had sworn eternal friendship to him, betrayed him.

For before this war had broken out, Alexander had gone to visit Frederick William and had made a secret treaty with him against France. At dead of night they had gone with Queen Louisa to visit the tomb of Frederick the Great. Beneath the flickering torchlight the Czar stood bare-headed beside the tomb of the great soldier. He bent to kiss the pall. Then taking the hand of the King of Prussia, he swore eternal friendship with him. "Neither of us shall fall alone," he had said at another time. "It shall be both or neither. We stand and fall together."

Now he forgot those words, he forgot his promise. He allowed himself to be flattered and cajoled while his friend was treated with contempt and insult. He sat within the curtained barge while Frederick William rode up and down the river bank in the rain, shut out from the conference.

Napoleon used all his arts to fascinate the young Czar, and win him to his side. He loaded the King of Prussia with insults, and robbed him of half his kingdom. That he took only half, he said, was out of friendship to his ally, the Czar of all the Russias. In reality he only spared a part of Prussia that it might form a buffer state between France and Russia. For although Napoleon flattered and made much of the Czar, he still regarded him as a possible enemy.

Napoleon had humiliated the King of Prussia. He said and wrote all manner of cruel things against the beautiful Queen Louisa, because she loved her country and encouraged her people to fight against the conqueror. Queen Louisa hated Napoleon, more for the wrongs he had done to her country than for those he had done to herself. She looked upon him as a robber, and felt it hard to treat him as an equal.

Yet for love of her country she now came to Tilsit to see the haughty conqueror and try to get better terms. But it was of no use. Untouched by her beauty, or her courage, Napoleon still held to his terms. The town of Magdeburg especially, the Queen grieved to lose, and she tried every argument she could think of to make Napoleon leave it to Prussia.

After dinner one night, Napoleon offered the Queen a rose. At once she saw the chance of making her last appeal to him.

"Is it friendship," she said; "do you give me Magdeburg with it?"

"It is for your Majesty to take what I offer without conditions," said Napoleon shortly.

The Queen's eyes filled with tears. "Your rose has too many thorns for me," she said sadly, as she turned away.

So the treaty was signed, and the King of Prussia lost half his kingdom. Part of it Napoleon named the Kingdom of Westphalia and gave it to his brother Jerome; another part was called the Duchy of Warsaw, and given to the Elector of Saxony, whom Napoleon now made King of Saxony, as a reward for having helped him against Prussia.

Prussia and Austria now seemed utterly crushed. The rest of Germany was under the control of Napoleon. The great Empire was both shattered and humbled. To resist the tyranny of the French Emperor seemed impossible.

But neither Prussia nor Austria was truly crushed, and now once more the Austrians rose against Napoleon. From all sides men flocked to the army; high and low, rich and poor, all were eager to be avenged upon the tyrant.

The Archduke Charles who commanded the army was, however, slow to move. Napoleon, with a skill and quickness never surpassed, marched against him, and in five days he had won five victories, and on May 12, 1809, he once more entered Vienna in triumph.

But the Austrians were not yet beaten. On the 21st and 22nd of May another fierce battle was fought between the towns of Aspern and Essling. This time the Austrians were victorious. They marched to battle singing war songs, and fought with such spirit that the French were defeated. Had they only pursued the enemy at once, they might have turned this victory into a triumph and driven Napoleon from the land. But the Austrians were too exhausted for the time being to do more. So Napoleon was able to gather his forces again, and a month later he was as strong as before, for it must be remembered he had the most of Europe from which to draw his troops.

On July 6, the battle of Wagram, the last great battle of the war, was fought. It was one of the most terrible battles of modern times. The Austrians fought with wonderful courage, and although Napoleon claimed the victory, it was a poor one. Still, it was enough. For the Emperor, terrified at Napoleon's threat to dethrone him, now made peace. And to please Napoleon and make the peace sure, he even sent his daughter to France to be married to his conqueror and enemy.

CHAPTER 67

# UNDER THE HEEL OF NAPOLEON

STILL, even after the battle of Wagram, Austria was not utterly subdued. For among the mountains of Tyrol the people had risen under a peasant innkeeper named Andreas Hofer, and they still fought on.

For centuries the people of Tyrol had owned the Princes of the House of Hapsburg as their overlord. But among their mountains they had lived a free people, choosing their own magistrates and rulers. Great was their dismay then when they learned that by the treaty of Presburg in 1805 they had been given over to the King of Bavaria. This new ruler oppressed them in many ways, and roused their anger by trying to change the name of the country from Tyrol to South Bavaria.

So when Francis II called upon all Germans to join him in fighting the French, the Tyrolese answered his call with joy. Secretly they made a treaty with the Austrians, and agreed to rise in a body at a certain date. So secret were their preparations that the Bavarians, and their allies the French, had no suspicion of what was going on.

Then one day a little red flag was seen floating down the river Inn. It was the signal agreed upon, and as it passed by the villages and towns on the banks, bells were rung, and men from every side flocked to the standards. They were shepherds and peasants, and their leaders were like themselves, but chief among them was Andreas Hofer, the innkeeper. He was tall and strong, with piercing eyes, black hair, and a great black beard which he had vowed not to cut till his country was given back to the Emperor. "For God, Emperor, and Fatherland," was the watchword which he wove upon his banner. "His weapon is prayer, his ally God," wrote Queen Louisa. "He wrestles with folded hands, on bended knee, then fights as if he wielded the fiery sword of the Angel of God."

The Tyrolese were splendid marksmen, but they had no knowledge of modern warfare. They fought for their freedom as the Swiss had fought hundreds of years before. They gathered upon the heights above the valleys through which the enemy had to pass. There they collected great quantities of huge stones and tree-trunks, and these they sent rolling down upon the enemy, as they marched through the valley below. Crushed by the falling stones and trees, thrown into utter confusion, the

French and Bavarians then fell an easy prey to the unseen marksmen who fired upon them from above.

Thus the men, and women also, of Tyrol tried to drive the invader from their land.

At Sterzing Moos the Bavarians had entrenched themselves so strongly that the Tyrolese, try how they might, could not dislodge them. At length Hofer ordered some wagons loaded with hay to be driven forward, and behind this screen the riflemen advanced. The first wagon was driven by a girl named Anna Gamper, a tailor's daughter. As she drove the slow-stepping oxen onward, the shot from the Bavarian rifles whistled and fell around her like hail. But she heeded them not. "On with you, my men," she cried. "Who cares for Bavarian dumplings? We don't eat them quite so hot as the Bavarians send them to us."

Behind the shelter of the hay-carts the Tyrolese now poured such a murderous fire upon the Bavarians, that they were seized with panic, and yielded.

On this same day the town of Hall was taken from the French, and the Tyrolese had so many prisoners that they could not spare men enough to guard them, and they had to send them off to prison in charge of women. This enraged the French very much.

The Tyrolese treated their prisoners very well with one exception. The one who was ill-treated was a Bavarian tax-gatherer, who had once boasted that he would grind down the Tyrolese until they would be glad to eat hay. Now he was made to pay for his boast, and for dinner one day was given a bundle of hay and forced to eat it.

But while in Tyrol the peasants were making a gallant stand for freedom, the battle of Wagram was fought and lost, the treaty of Schonbrunn was signed, and by it the Emperor Francis was forced to withdraw all his troops from Tyrol, and give back the country to Bavaria. Forsaken by their Emperor the Tyrolese became well-nigh hopeless, and almost without opposition the French marched to Innsbruck, the capital, and once more took possession of it. "Austria has made peace with France, and forgotten Tyrol," wrote Hofer sadly to another of the leaders. And heartbroken he went away to his mountains once more.

But the Tyrolese were not yet crushed. Again and yet again they rose, calling upon Hofer to be their leader. And at their call he left his mountain fastness and took command. He succeeded so well that for a time he even became governor of Tyrol. He lived in the palace at Innsbruck, and ruled the land, but he remained ever a simple peasant. He never wore anything but the peasant's costume. In the Council Chamber he would appear dressed like a peasant in black chamois leather knee-breeches, bare knees and white stockings, a red vest with broad green braces, and over all a short green coat.

But now the French poured into the valleys in ever-increasing numbers. The spirit of resistance was broken, and one after another the peasants laid down their arms.

Once more Hofer took refuge in the mountains. But now a price was set upon his head, and the French sought everywhere for him. The few friends who knew of his hiding-place begged him to flee from the country, and seek a safer retreat. But Hofer refused. "I cannot be in a place more safe," he said. "No Tyrolese would betray me." So secure was he in the faith of the people that he would not even shave off his long beard by which he could be easily recognised.

But alas, there was one traitor among the faithful Tyrolese. He had been Hofer's friend, but he was tempted by the offer of gold. He had never dreamed of so much gold that, for the rest of his life, he could live in ease and comfort. He could not resist the temptation. It would make him so rich. So he prowled about the mountains until one day he discovered Hofer's hiding-place. Then he went to the French and told them of his discovery.

The next morning very early, while it was still dark, the tramp of armed men was heard through the lonely mountain passes, and soon sixteen hundred men surrounded the little hut.

Hofer, with his wife and children, who were with him, were peacefully sleeping when they were awakened by the crash of firearms, and the muffled tramp of many soldiers over the snow-covered ground.

"The French have come!" cried someone within the hut, starting out of sleep in terror.

"So be it," said Hofer calmly, and striding to the door he threw it wide open. Rank upon rank the soldiers stood in solid array surrounding the hut.

"Which of you can speak German?" said Hofer. "I can," replied the captain.

"You have come to take me," said Hofer, turning to him. "I am Andreas Hofer. Do with me as you will—I ask mercy only for my wife and children."

But there was little mercy in the hearts of the rough soldiers. They bound Hofer's hands behind his back, they insulted and ill-treated him, pulling out his beard in handfuls. Then they dragged him barefoot, clad only in his night-shirt, over the icy, stony paths to the nearest town.

Hofer was taken to Mantua, and there tried as a rebel and traitor. By Napoleon's orders he was sentenced to be shot. So on February 16, 1810, he was led out to die. As he passed through the streets other Tyrolese prisoners fell on their knees and asked his blessing, weeping bitterly. This Hofer gave them, asking forgiveness for having been the cause of their present sufferings. Calmly he walked on until the appointed place was reached. Here a party of soldiers was drawn up, and he was told to kneel down. He refused.

"I stand before my Creator," he said, "and standing I will restore to Him the spirit He gave." He refused also to be blindfolded.

So the signal was given. The soldiers fired, and a few minutes later the great patriot lay dead.

For the time Tyrol's struggle for freedom was ended. But the Tyrolese did not forget their hero. Some years later, when Napoleon had fallen and Tyrol once more belonged to Austria, they carried his body back over the Alps, and laid it to rest in the Church at Innsbruck, and in memory of his great patriotism his family was made noble.

CHAPTER 68

# UNDER THE HEEL OF NAPOLEON

GERMANY had now reached the very depths of degradation. There seemed to be no unity, no pride of nation, no love of country left. Half the Empire cringed to Napoleon and fawned upon him, the other half, beaten but unsubdued, hated him with a sullen hatred. But already the turning-point had come.

At the head of affairs in Prussia there was now a great statesman and patriot named Baron Stein. He loved his country, and he believed that it was through Prussia that Germany would once more become free, and great among the nations.

But to do this he saw that the Prussians themselves must be roused out of their sloth and degradation. So he did away with serfs; towns were given municipal rights; posts in the army and in the government, which had been kept for nobles only, were thrown open to every one. And with such deeds Stein seemed to awaken the whole people to a new love of their country, and new desire of freedom. He helped to form a secret society called the Tugendbund, or League of Virtue, the aim of which was to drive the French out of the country.

But very soon Napoleon began to hate Stein for the good work he was doing for Prussia. He gave orders to have him arrested, and in order to escape his great enemy Stein gave up his office and fled to Russia.

But there was another patriot left named Scharnhorst. He was not a noble like Stein, but a peasant's son. He was a soldier, and he did in the army just as much good work as Stein had done in the government.

Napoleon had commanded that Prussia should only keep a very small army. But Scharnhorst determined that every Prussian fit to carry arms should be a soldier. So he kept continually changing his men. He took fresh recruits and drilled them into good soldiers. Then he sent them home and drilled another lot of fresh recruits in their place. In this way, although the army seemed to be as small as Napoleon had commanded, the country was really swarming with well-drilled soldiers.

Scharnhorst carried out many reforms in the army also. So very soon Prussia had really a splendid army, not merely splendid to look at, as had been the case at the beginning of the wars with Napoleon.

Besides Stein and Scharnhorst there were other great men who helped the work forward, and quietly the whole people got ready for the great struggle they knew must come. But some years passed before the right time came. At length, however, it did come.

In 1812 Napoleon invaded Russia. Across the Nieman he marched with his grand army 600,000 strong, full of pride, sure of victory. Six months later a ragged hungry rabble of scarce 20,000 men staggered homeward.

Napoleon had been defeated, his army shattered, and his friend the Czar turned into his bitterest enemy. Now or never was the moment to strike a blow for freedom, and Prussia struck that blow.

The King hesitated at first, but the young men rushed to join the army. One day as the King stood at his castle window in Breslau and watched the long procession of volunteers march past, tears filled his eyes. He forgot the shame and defeat of former days, all his doubts faded away. War was declared.

The whole country was filled with wild enthusiasm. The universities were emptied, field and workshop were forsaken, students and workers alike thronging to the barracks. Even poets joined the ranks, while the whole country sang the songs they made.

To get money for the cause women sold everything of value they possessed, their hair, their jewels, even their wedding-rings. In return for them they received an iron ring engraven with the words "I gave gold for iron, 1813." These were looked upon in after years as their greatest treasures. For they were a sign that those who possessed them had helped to free their country from a hated yoke. For a man to remain at home, for a woman to have given nothing, became a disgrace.

"Brandenburg, Prussia, Silesia, Pomerania," wrote King Frederick William, "you know what you have had to suffer the last seven years; you know what will be your sad fate if the war which we now begin does not end honourably for us. Think of past days, think of the great Frederick, think of the glorious example of our mighty ally Russia, think of Spain, of Portugal. . . . It is a last terrible struggle that is now before us, for we fight for our very existence, for our freedom and well-being. God and our own steadfastness will win the victory, for our cause is just. With victory we win a safe and glorious peace, and the return of happier days."

Russia joined with Prussia against Napoleon. Once more the Czar and King met and renewed their old friendship. But King Frederick William was alone, for his beautiful Queen, who had loved Prussia so much, had died. She had died worn out by sorrow for her country. But even though she was dead her work lived after her. It was for love of their noble Queen, and with a desire to avenge her death, that many of the people took up arms.

But now, in spite of their courage and the love of country which now filled them the Prussians did not begin to win at once. Twice they were defeated, at Lützen, where two hundred years before Gustavus Adolphus had been killed, and again at Bautzen. But in both these battles Napoleon's army far outnumbered that of the allies, and although they were defeated, the Prussians did not lose heart.

At length fortune changed, Austria too joined the allies, and at the battle of Leipzig Napoleon was utterly defeated. It was a three days' battle, on October 16 it began; on the 19th Napoleon and his army were fleeing from the field. The victory was greatly due to the rough old soldier Blücher. And the victors were not slow to acknowledge it. "Behold the liberator of your country," said the Czar, leading him to the King after the battle.

Blücher was a rough old soldier, but his men adored him, and they called him Marshal Forwards. He got this name at the battle of the Katzbach. The enemy were crossing the river, but Blücher held his men back until a good many of the enemy had landed. Then he cried out, "Now my men, I have enough of them—forwards." Ever after that he was known as Marshal Forwards.

In less than a month the French were now almost entirely driven out of Germany, and Napoleon's power over Europe was at an end. Italy, Holland, Switzerland, threw off his yoke, the Confederation of the Rhine was broken up. The Kingdom of Westphalia vanished.

But still Napoleon would not own defeat, and the allies marched into France. Napoleon's grand army was shattered. It was filled now with raw recruits, and untrained boys. Still he kept the foe in check. But even his great genius was of no avail against the overwhelming force of the allies. And on March 29 they reached Paris. France was exhausted, the people worn out with long warfare, and next day Paris yielded.

Then the King of Prussia, who had been humbled and insulted in his own country, rode in triumph into his into his enemy's capital.

Two months later the first Peace of Paris was signed. By this treaty all the land taken from Germany since 1792 was given back, Napoleon was banished to Elba, and Louis XVIII set upon the throne of France.

CHAPTER 69

# THE DOWNFALL OF NAPOLEON

PEACE had come to Germany and to Europe. But Napoleon had caused such confusions among all the states of Europe, that to bring them into order again a congress was called at Vienna. It was a great meeting of princes and rulers, for besides the Czar, the Emperor of Austria, and the King of Prussia, there were the rulers, or the representatives of every state in Europe, except Turkey.

But to bring order into Europe again, and to content each ruler, was no easy matter, and so the Congress soon found. Russia wanted the whole of Poland, Prussia the whole of Saxony. To this the other powers would not agree, and so bitter did the quarrel become that it seemed as if there would be war once more.

The suddenly came the news that Napoleon had left Elba, and had landed in Europe. At once the quarrelling ceased, and all the rulers of Europe joined against the common foe.

In vain Napoleon declared that he only wished to rule France in peace, and that he had no wish to conquer any other country. No one believed him. Armies were gathered with all speed, and from every side marched toward France. Britain and Prussia were the first to be ready for war. Wellington commanded the British, Blücher the Prussian army, and they joined forces in Belgium. But it must be remembered that less than half Wellington's army were British. The rest were Dutch and German. Among them was the Duke of Brunswick with his Black Brunswickers.

It was in Belgium, between the British and German forces on the one side and the French on the other, that this long struggle against Napoleon was fought to an end.

On June 16 the French attacked Blücher, and defeated him at Ligny, he himself narrowly escaping with his life. As he rode forward cheering his men on, his horse was killed under him. It fell, pinning him to the ground. There he lay, helpless and in agony, in danger of being pounded to death by the hoofs of the charging horses. But at length he was rescued by his soldiers, who carried him to a safe place.

On the same day another battle was fought at Quatre Bras, between the French on the one side and the allies on the other. In this the French

were defeated. Two days later the last great battle was fought, La Belle Alliance, the Germans call it, we Waterloo.

It was upon the allies under Wellington that the brunt of the fighting fell. Blücher had promised to come to his aid, but his men were weary with fighting, the roads were deep in mud from the heavy rains, and his march was slow and painful. The cannon stuck fast in the mud, the men weary, hungry, and soaked to the skin, stumbled and fell by the way. "We can go no farther," they cried.

But tough old Blücher cheered them on. He was wounded, and in pain himself. Yet he rode his horse. "I would rather be tied on to my horse," he said, "than miss this battle." And when the men grumbled and cried out that they could go no farther, he answered cheerfully, "It is no good saying you can't. You must, my children," he cried. "I have given my word to my brother Wellington. You would not have me break my word." And so the wearied men pressed onward.

At length, late in the afternoon, the Prussian army reached the field where since twelve o'clock a desperate struggle had been carried on.

Napoleon saw them come and thought they were French troops. "It is Grouchy!" he said.

It was not Grouchy but Blücher, and Blücher's coming settled the day. One more effort Napoleon made. It was in vain. His old Guard was shattered, the French fled in confusion, their Emperor with them.

Not till the victory was won did Blücher and Wellington meet. The old General threw his arms round the Duke and kissed him in German fashion, so great was his delight at the victory.

"I shall sleep to-night in Napoleon's last night's quarters," said Wellington, triumphantly.

"And I will drive him out of his present ones," cried Blücher.

And the Prussians, forgetting their weariness, turned to pursue the fleeing foe. Throughout the moonlit night the pursuit and flight lasted. The wearied French sought shelter in the farmhouses and villages on the way. The Prussians, thirsting for revenge, hunted them forth again. So furious was the pursuit that Napoleon himself was nearly captured. He only saved himself by fleeing from his carriage, leaving everything behind him, even his hat and sword. These, with his jewelled star, Blücher sent to the King of Prussia as tokens of his triumph.

Eleven days after the great battle the allies once more stood before Paris. Napoleon had already abdicated and fled, but, unable to escape, he gave himself up to the British, and by order of the combined powers he was sent a prisoner to the island of St. Helena. There, a few years later, he died.

Meanwhile, on November 20, 1815, the Second Peace of Paris was signed. By this peace the German states tried hard to recover Alsace and Lorraine, but the other powers were afraid that Germany would become too powerful, and they refused to agree. Instead, France had to pay a large sum of money, and give back all the works of art which Napoleon had stolen from the countries he had conquered.

At length everything was settled, and Europe was once more at peace.

CHAPTER 70

# DIVIDED GERMANY

ALTHOUGH Europe was now at peace, Prussia and Austria still continued so jealous of each other that the Empire could not be restored. Had either the King of Prussia or the Emperor of Austria been made German Emperor, war would certainly have broken out.

So having no Emperor most of the states of Germany joined themselves into a Confederation. This Confederation had a sort of permanent parliament or Diet, which sat at Frankfort-on-the-Main. To this Diet members from every state came to discuss matters common to all the states. But on the other hand, in things which concerned itself alone, every state did as it chose.

All the members of the Confederation agreed never to make war upon each other, and never to make an alliance with any foreign power which might be dangerous to any German state. But otherwise there was little union. Each of the German princes was an independent ruler, and most of them were autocrats. They did as they liked without consulting people or parliament.

Now most of the people felt that they had done so much to free their country from Napoleon's tyranny that they deserved to have some share in the government of it, and by the Act of Confederation it was agreed that a Constitutional Government should be set up in every state.

But this promise was only made in a time of great stress and danger. With the coming of peace and security again the rulers forgot their promises, and very little political freedom was granted to the people. The Czar, the Emperor of Austria, and King Frederick William, indeed, joined together in what they called the Holy Alliance. By this alliance they bound themselves to treat one another as Christians and brothers, and to govern their people in a Christian manner. But the real object of the alliance was to increase the power of the rulers, and to crush out any movement on the part of the people towards freedom.

Yet among the people the demand for freedom grew daily stronger. With it also grew a desire for real union. For the Confederation was little more than a name. Each state did very much as it liked. Every state had its own customs and regulations, so that goods could not be sent from one part of Germany to another without paying duty, often several times over.

Lewis I of Bavaria saw that this was hurtful to the whole Confederation, and he made a treaty with the King of Wurtemburg permitting free trade between the two countries. This was the beginning, and very soon the idea of a customs union for the whole of the German states was started. State after state joined the Union, until at length, so far as trade was concerned, Germany was united.

But it was Prussia and not Austria which was the centre of this union, and from it Austria stood gloomily aloof.

With this free trade among the German-speaking peoples, the merchant classes became more and more prosperous. And with their prosperity their demands for political freedom became so great that in many states the refusal of the rulers to grant it brought the people to the verge of rebellion. Then, when in 1830 the French had a second revolution and drove Charles X from the throne, there was great excitement throughout the states of Germany.

In Saxony, in Bavaria, in many of the smaller states there were revolts and riots. Everywhere the revolutionists chose red, black and gold for their banners, for these were supposed to have been the colours of the old Holy Roman Empire. Everywhere they demanded a liberal government. But everywhere the rebellion was crushed out, and Germany sank again into seeming quiet.

But it had needed stern measures to repress the outbreak. And the head and front of this repression was Metternich, the Austrian minister. He thought that peace rather than liberty was what Europe needed, and he crushed out every attempt at liberty. For he did not see that by doing so he was endangering the very peace he desired.

For a time, however, Metternich seemed to have succeeded. But Germany only appeared to be quiet. There was no real quiet, and discontent spread rapidly, the desire for free government and the desire for a united Germany growing ever greater.

Both the King and the Emperor who had suffered so much at Napoleon's hands were by this time dead. In 1835 Francis I of Austria had died, and had been succeeded by his son Ferdinand, who proved but a weak ruler. He was, in truth, more or less mad, and the power was really in the hands of Metternich.

In 1840 Frederick William III died, and was succeeded by his son Frederick William IV.

Frederick William IV was a strange mixture. He tried to be a constitutional monarch, yet he was filled with ideas about the divine right of kings. He tried to be a practical man, yet he was a dreamer. His reign, however, seemed to begin well, he made fine speeches, and promised his people many things. But soon they found those promises meant nothing, and discontent grew strong against him.

Then when in 1848 the French people had a third revolution and declared their country a republic, the unrest in Germany became more intense than ever. Indeed, the people became so violent in their demands for political freedom that many of the lesser princes yielded, and in all haste changed the government. Throughout the whole of Germany there was a revolution. But it was in Austria and in Prussia that it was most violent, for there it was most keenly resisted.

As day by day news came to the courts of Vienna and Berlin that the lesser states had yielded, the excitement grew ever greater. Petition after petition was sent to the Emperor of Austria. He was, however, entirely in the hands of Metternich, and Metternich had no mind to yield to the demands of the people.

But the patience of the people was at an end, and, suddenly, one day a wild crowd burst into the parliament hall. Amid loud shouts and threats they forced the members to send a deputation to the Emperor with their demands.

While they waited for his answer the noise and confusion grew intense. Benches and chairs were broken, blows were given and received, and above all the clamour was heard the cry, "Down with Metternich, down with Metternich."

Metternich could not stand against the fury of the people, so he gave up his post. A few days later he fled to England. But the fall of the hated Metternich did not bring peace to Austria, and there followed a time of terrible confusion, Austrians, Hungarians, Bohemians, and Italians all struggled together. The Emperor was far too weak a man to guide the state in those stormy times, so at length he abdicated, and his nephew Francis Joseph came to the throne at the age of eighteen. He at once set himself to crush the revolution in Austria. And then he turned his attention to the rest of the Empire, determined to crush the revolution there. At the same time he determined to crush the attempt of Prussia to become leader of the German states.

CHAPTER 71

# DIVIDED GERMANY

MEANWHILE in Berlin the Revolution bad been even more violent than in Vienna. Riotous meetings were held, and to disperse them troops were called out. Upon this the people took up arms. All Berlin became a battlefield and many people were slain.

In vain the King tried to quell the riot. He ran up a white flag upon his palace with the word "misunderstanding" in huge letters upon it. He issued a proclamation, and at length, as a last resource, he ordered the troops to withdraw.

Then and then only the people were quieted. But their hearts were filled with sullen wrath against the King, and they resolved to punish him for having caused the death of his citizens.

So, decked with laurel wreaths, those who had been killed in the street fighting were carried into the castle courtyard. Loudly the crowd cried put for the King to show himself. And at last, very unwillingly, he appeared on the balcony, with his Queen half-fainting with terror. They were greeted not with loyal cheers but with angry howls.

"Take off your hat," yelled the mob.

The King obeyed, and with bowed head he looked upon the dreadful procession of dead bodies, with all their wounds exposed, as they filed past. The mood of the crowd was dangerous. It was hard to tell what they would do next, to what fresh indignity they would force their King to submit.

Then suddenly some one began to sing a hymn. The crowd joined in the familiar tune, it seemed to soften them, and at length the rioters marched away with their ghastly burdens.

A few days after this a placard appeared upon the walls of the city addressed to the German nation. In this the King announced that, for the salvation of Germany, he put himself at the head of the whole Fatherland, and that that very day he would ride through Berlin wearing the old and honoured colours of the nation.

And so through the streets the King rode in splendid procession, surrounded and followed by his ministers and counsellors, all wearing the revolutionist colours of red, black and gold. At various places the

King stopped and spoke. "I feel myself called," he said, "to save German freedom and unity. I swear to God that I will thrust no prince from his throne, but I will protect German unity and freedom."

"Long live the Emperor of Germany," shouted the people in reply. But the King signed to them to be silent.

"Not that," he cried; "that I will not be."

But in all this the King was not sincere. It was a comedy, he said afterwards, which he had been made to act.

A few days after all these wild doings, a provisional Parliament met at Frankfort to draw up a constitution for all Germany. But this was no easy matter. First of all the question of what the new Empire was to consist of, had to be settled. Was Austria to belong to it—Austria with all her non-German speaking peoples, with her Czecks and Slavs and Italians and what not? it was asked. Over this question, argument grew long and bitter. At length it was decided that only Austria proper might belong to Germany, and that all her other possessions must remain outside the union. This meant that the unity of Austria would be destroyed, and the Emperor would not hear of it. "Austria must remain one," he said, "both for the sake of Germany and of Europe." The Austrian Empire, declared Francis Joseph, would enter the Confederation as a whole or not at all.

When this was known, the Frankfort Parliament made up their minds, that if this was Austria's last word, then Austria must remain outside the Empire. And they decided to ask the King of Prussia to take the title of German Emperor, and become head of the new Empire.

With great anxiety the whole of Germany waited for his answer. If he accepted it would mean a united Germany at last, but it might also mean war with Austria.

King Frederick William refused the title. He must have, he said, the free consent of all the German Princes before he accepted the honour. Frederick William IV was a dreamer, his head was full of vague fancies and dreams of splendour. Yet he was not dreamer enough to imagine that the title which the Frankfort Parliament offered him would be anything but an empty honour. So he refused it.

With tears in their eyes the messengers from the Parliament went away. Their dreams of a united Germany had been shattered.

In spite of this disappointment, however, the Parliament tried to persuade the chief German Princes to give their peoples a constitution. A few of the lesser rulers did, but all the more powerful ones either gave a vague answer or refused to have anything to do with the matter. The Emperor of Austria, angry that the King of Prussia should have been asked to become Emperor, recalled all the Austrian members from the Parliament. Prussia and other great states did the same, and soon the Parliament was so small that it was of no importance.

It was moved to Stuttgart first, and then finally dissolved altogether.

The failure of this Parliament was a great grief to many Germans, for they had thought it would be a power for good, and that better days for Germany were about to begin.

Yet in spite of every reverse, the desire for freedom and the desire for unity still continued strong, so too did the rivalry between Prussia and Austria. But it would be impossible to follow the course of the struggle and tell of all the useless Parliaments, of all the rebellions and wars.

At first Austria was thoroughly successful in the struggle for power, and Prussia was thoroughly crushed. But now there rose to power in Prussia a young man named Otto von Bismarck. He was rude and rough, and his hectoring ways were for ever leading him into fighting duels. He wore shabby clothes, and lived in shabby lodgings, but he was clever and he rose to great power. He was cool and calm, too, to a wonderful degree. It was said that if he had been asked to command a ship, or perform a difficult operation, he would have said, "I have never done it before, but I will be quite pleased to try."

The staid old politicians were, however, afraid of this hectoring young man. "He may be clever," they said, "but he goes too fast. He will come to an evil end."

Bismarck, however, had made up his mind that Prussia should be great, and he set himself to show Austria that Prussia did not mean to be crushed.

Meanwhile King Frederick William became so ill that he could no longer rule, and in 1858 his brother William was made Regent. In 1861 King Frederick William died, and the Regent came to the throne as King William I. He was already sixty-three, but he was strong and vigorous, and a great soldier, and he chose Bismarck as his Prime Minister.

CHAPTER 72

# THE STRUGGLE BETWEEN AUSTRIA AND PRUSSIA

AS time went on the state of affairs between Prussia and Austria grew no better. The Emperor called together a Congress of German Princes, and Prussia would have nothing to do with it. The King of Prussia, on his side, proposed to call together an assembly, and Austria would have nothing to do with that. But Bismarck, who was fast becoming the greatest statesman in Germany, had no faith in any peaceful means. "It is not by talk that the great questions of the day must be decided," he said, "but by blood and iron." And so he became known as the Man of Blood and Iron. And he made up his mind to force a quarrel between the two great powers.

Austria and Prussia had joined in fighting Denmark for possession of Schleswig-Holstein and Lauenburg. And having defeated Denmark and won these duchies, they at once began to quarrel about what was to be done with them. Austria wanted one thing, Prussia another, and soon it became plain that the quarrel would end in war, and both sides began to prepare for it.

Many people looked upon this as little less than civil war, and they did their best to stop it. But nothing could stop it. It had to come. And although the quarrel over Schleswig-Holstein was given as the reason, it was not the real reason but only the excuse.

Ever since the days of Frederick the Great, jealousy had been going on between Prussia and Austria, and the question which was to be leader in the affairs of Germany had to be settled. Talk had been tried to no purpose; now, as Bismarck said, it was to be settled by blood and iron. Bismarck hurried Prussia into war. But he had little doubt how it would end. For Prussia was ready, her King was a soldier, and he had Von Moltke, one of the greatest generals the world has ever known, by his side.

Yet although Bismarck at this time hurried his country into war, he was not always for war. Later on he did his best to prevent a war. When he was asked why he had done so, he answered, "We thought of the terrible losses, and of the sorrow and misery it would bring to thousands of homes. You stare at me! Do you think that I have no heart? Believe me, I have one which beats just like your own. War will always be war. There will always be the horror of desolated lands, the cries of the widow and the orphan. It is so terrible that I for one would never turn to it but as a last necessity."

This "brothers' war" began in June, and on July 3 the great battle of Königgratz, or Sadowa, as it is someimes called, was fought. Here the greatest hosts that had ever faced each other on any modern battlefield were met together. The Prussian army was commanded by Prince Frederick Charles, the King's brother, but the King himself was there also. At seven o'clock the fight began, and for hours it raged fiercely, neither side gaining any advantage.

But the loss was terrible. Anxiously the Prince looked and listened for sight or sound of the second army under the Crown Prince Frederick which was marching to his aid. He waited and watched even as fifty-one years before Wellington had waited and watched for Blücher. Would he come in time? the Prince wondered. At last Frederick came, and with his coming the doubtful battle was turned into a victory.

The Austrians fled, the Prussians in hot pursuit. The King himself led the cavalry, and as he rode along he was greeted with thunderous shouts of applause. Officers pressed round him to kiss his hands while cannon roared, and muskets cracked and crashed about them. But the King seemed to have a charmed life, and he rode along, thanking and cheering his men, heedless of danger.

After the battle of Königgratz the Prussians were everywhere successful, and soon Austria asked for peace. On August 23 the Peace of Prague was signed, and the Seven Weeks' War was at an end. Never has so short a war had such great results, for by the Peace of Prague, Austria was parted from Germany for ever, and Prussia became the undisputed head of the German Confederation.

Now at length a united Germany was not far off. The South German states, indeed, still remained independent, but the northern states all joined together into the North German Confederation acknowledging Prussia as their head. A few months later the first Parliament of the North German Confederation met at Berlin, and began to form a constitution.

The friends of union rejoiced greatly, but they were not yet satisfied. They could not be satisfied until all South Germany had joined the Confederation, and they worked hard to bring this about.

CHAPTER 73

# WILLIAM I—UNITED GERMANY

BUT now, having settled its national quarrels, Germany was soon plunged into another war.

In 1869 the Spaniards offered the throne of Spain to Prince Leopold of Hohenzollern, a distant relative of King William of Prussia. Now the French had long been jealous of Prussia's growing power, and when they heard of this offer they became very much alarmed. They cried out that the days of Charles V would come again, and that Spain and the German Empire would be united under one crown. They declared that this they would never allow, and indeed they created such a storm that Prince Leopold at length promised not to accept the crown offered to him.

But this did not satisfy the French. They demanded a promise from the King of Prussia that he would never at any time allow a Hohenzollern prince to accept the throne of Spain. They even suggested that King William should apologise to the French for ever allowing the Prince to think of accepting the crown.

At this King William was very angry. In Paris too excitement rose to white heat. The French, from the Empress Eugenie downwards, clamoured for war. "Your throne has fallen into the mud," cried the Empress when the Emperor hesitated. So war with Prussia was declared amid frantic excitement.

There was frantic excitement in France, but over Germany there swept a great wave of patriotic enthusiasm. The Germans rose to a man, and flocked to the standards, not only in Prussia but all over Germany. The South Germans too forgot their differences with the North Germans, and threw in their lot with their brethren.

Prussia was absolutely ready for war. Long ago Von Moltke had planned it all out. He had played with little tin soldiers, and settled exactly what should be done in case of war with France. And now everything was carried out just as he had planned it. There was no hurry, no confusion. Each man knew what he had to do, and did it.

Far other was it with the French. They had boasted that they were ready for war "down to the last button." But in reality they were not ready at all. From first to last all was confusion, and the lives of thousands of brave men were thrown away for want of forethought and order. "I have confidence in the success of our arms," said Napoleon III proudly, "because I know that France is behind me, and France is in God's care."

But while the French Emperor talked thus bravely, the minister of war was wringing his hands in despair over the complaints which poured in upon him. "You send me maps that are no use to us," said one, "and we have not a single map of the French frontiers." "There is no money in the corps treasury," says another. A general in wild despair telegraphs, "Can't find my brigade, can't find my division. What am I to do? Don't know where my regiments are."

And this was the army which was "ready twice over," which "could fight for a year without feeling it." Little wonder, then, that from the very beginning things went well for the Germans. They won victory after victory, and the war, begun on German soil, was carried into France. Here, too, the Germans were victorious, and at length, on September 1, the great battle of the campaign was fought at Sedan. The French were stationed in the valley, the Prussians were on the heights above, and so had their enemies at their mercy. The French were caught like mice in a trap, and bravely though they fought, there was no escape for them. With dawn the fight began, and all day it lasted. Closer and closer the Germans pressed upon the French, hemming them in on every side.

As the day went on, the Germans wondered much if the Emperor Napoleon was with his troops. "No fear," said some one, "the old fox has long ago run to earth." But he was mistaken. The Emperor was with his troops.

At length, in the late afternoon, a breathless messenger came to King William.

"Sedan will capitulate," he cried. And there sure enough a white flag was seen floating over the town.

The King turned to a general, "Let the firing cease," he said.

A few minutes later the terrible crash and roar of the cannon died away in silence, and a deep and solemn stillness succeeded to the frightful noise of battle.

Then in the silence a second messenger approached.

"Your Majesty," he said, as he saluted, "Sedan surrenders with the Emperor and the whole army."

For a moment those who heard held their breath. In the group around the King there was a tense stillness, then followed an outburst of joy. Tears dimmed their eyes as, with voices choked with sobs, they congratulated each other and pressed round the King to wish him joy.

Again a messenger came. This time he bore in his hand a letter from the Emperor.

"Sir, my brother," it ran, "not having been able to die in the midst of my troops, nothing remains to me but to place my sword in the hands of your Majesty."

King William accepted the Emperor's surrender. He treated Napoleon with great courtesy, but sent him to the castle of Wilhelmshöhe, where he remained a prisoner until the war was over.

When the news of the defeat of the army and surrender of the Emperor reached France, there was a terrible outburst of rage and anger. The people declared the French Empire at an end, and once more proclaimed a republic. They would now gladly have made peace. But when it became known that the Germans would demand Alsace and Lorraine as the price of peace, the French refused. "Not an inch of land, not a stone of our fortresses will we yield," they said.

But the Germans were determined to have back the land they had lost. "With whom are you fighting?" asked a Frenchman of a German.

"With Louis XIV," quickly replied the German. For it was Louis XIV who had taken Alsace and Lorraine from Germany.

Now, as the French refused to accept their terms, the Germans marched towards Paris, and in little more than a fortnight after Sedan the splendid city was ringed round by a fence of steel.

The siege of Paris is one of the most tremendous undertakings in all modern war. Von Moltke did not want to bombard the town, and ruin the splendid buildings. He hoped, in a few weeks, to starve the people into surrender. But the French were far more brave and enduring than he had expected, and the months went by, one by one, and still Paris would not yield.

Bismarck and others grew impatient. They did not care whether the fair city was ruined or not. They wanted to bring the war to a quick and victorious end. "The people of Paris have too much to eat," they said, "and not enough to digest. Iron pills are what they want, and too few of them have been used."

So at length opposition was broken down, and the bombardment of the city began.

Meantime, while the people of Paris were suffering untold misery,

"Long live his Imperial Majesty Emperor William I."

the King of Prussia had taken up his abode in the splendid palace of Versailles. All Germany had been thrilled with the events of the war, and now all Germany, south as well as north, desired unity at any price. They desired it so eagerly that they would not even wait for peace, but while they were still in the throes of the terrible struggle with France, both northern and southern Germany asked the King of Prussia to take the title of Emperor. And to this King William consented.

So on January 18 a brilliant company met together in the Hall of Mirrors at Versailles. It was the anniversary of the day upon which the first King of Prussia, Frederick I, had crowned himself, and now, with solemn ceremony, King William was proclaimed German Emperor.

Deeply moved, William spoke to the gathered princes and nobles. "May God grant," he said, "that both we and our followers upon the throne may ever be Emperors of the German Empire, not through warlike conquests, but through works of peace, and so lead the nation to happiness, freedom, and prosperity."

As he ceased speaking, a great shout went up: "Long live his Imperial and kingly Majesty, Emperor William I." Again and again the hall rang with the joyous shouts. The Crown Prince knelt to kiss the Emperor's hand, but his father quickly raised him, and throwing his arms about him, kissed him again and again. After the Crown Prince the nobles thronged round the new-made Emperor to pay their homage.

Thus was the German Empire born again. "And God be with us," says one who was present, "and may it all redound to the rich blessing and true weal of the German people and land."

The latter part of the Franco-Prussian war became little more than a series of sieges. The chief of these sieges were Strassburg, Metz, and Paris. But already, on September 27, Strassburg, after a brave defence, had yielded. A month later Metz followed suit, and now, ten days after the German Emperor was proclaimed, Paris too gave way. The Germans marched in triumph into the city, and at length peace was signed.

Alsace and Lorraine were given back to Germany, and France had also to pay the enormous sum of £200,000,000 (six billions in francs).

CHAPTER 74

# FREDERICK THE NOBLE AND WILLIAM II

WILLIAM I was seventy-four when he became German Emperor. And having reconstituted the German Empire and united all the scattered states under his rule, it might seem as if his work was done. But he was a hale old man, and he ruled for seventeen years longer. He indeed left much to this great chancellor, Bismarck, but he was no mere figurehead. He died on March 9, 1888, greatly to the sorrow of his people.

The Emperor William I was succeeded by his son Frederick. He is known to us as Frederick the Noble, but it is more for what he was as a man than for what he did as an Emperor that he earned the name. For his reign was one of the shortest on record, lasting little more than three months.

Already, during his father's lifetime, Prince Frederick had become ill, and he had gone to spend the winter in Italy in the hope of finding relief there from his suffering.

There one day a telegram was brought to him. He looked at the address and read, "To His Majesty, the German Emperor." Without opening the envelope he turned away in tears, for he knew that his dearly-loved father was dead.

The new Emperor was so ill that it seemed doubtful if he were strong enough to take the long journey to Berlin. But he would hear of no delay, and early on the morning after he received the news of his father's death, he set out for his own land.

All his life, Frederick had been making himself ready for the time when he should be a ruler. He had meant to do great things for his people, and be indeed a father to them. Now he came to the throne only to die. All his short reign was full of suffering, but he bore it nobly. "His courage was indeed something heroic," said Bismarck. "To his last breath he was an Emperor every inch." At length, on June 15, 1888, he died, and on the anniversary of Waterloo he was laid to rest.

"He was a frank, honest man, of pure mind and warm feeling," says one who knew him well, "with a heart full of kindliness, and able to rejoice over everything good or great." He stands out as one of the finest figures in German history, a great soldier, a true patriot, and a good man. When he died there was grief throughout all Germany.

There was grief, too, in Great Britain, for Frederick had married Victoria, the daughter of our Queen. And for his wife's sake, Frederick had a kindly liking for the British people. Indeed, because of it, the Germans sometimes call him not Frederick der Dritte (the Third), but der Britte. And the British people returned that liking, and many a British heart mourned with the widowed Empress.

Frederick III was succeeded by his son William II. He was twenty-nine when he came to the throne, and he still rules over his vast Empire. Under him, Germany has continued to be prosperous and united, and at peace with all Europe.

In this time of peace and unity Germany has grown great. In commerce and manufactures it is now among the foremost countries in the world. In learning and science it has no equal. Peace has done for Germany far more than all the wars and conquests of the Holy Roman Emperors, and the Germans who love their country well know the value of that peace, and pray that it may long continue.

www.ingramcontent.com/pod-product-compliance
Lightning Source LLC
LaVergne TN
LVHW092008090526
838202LV00002B/54